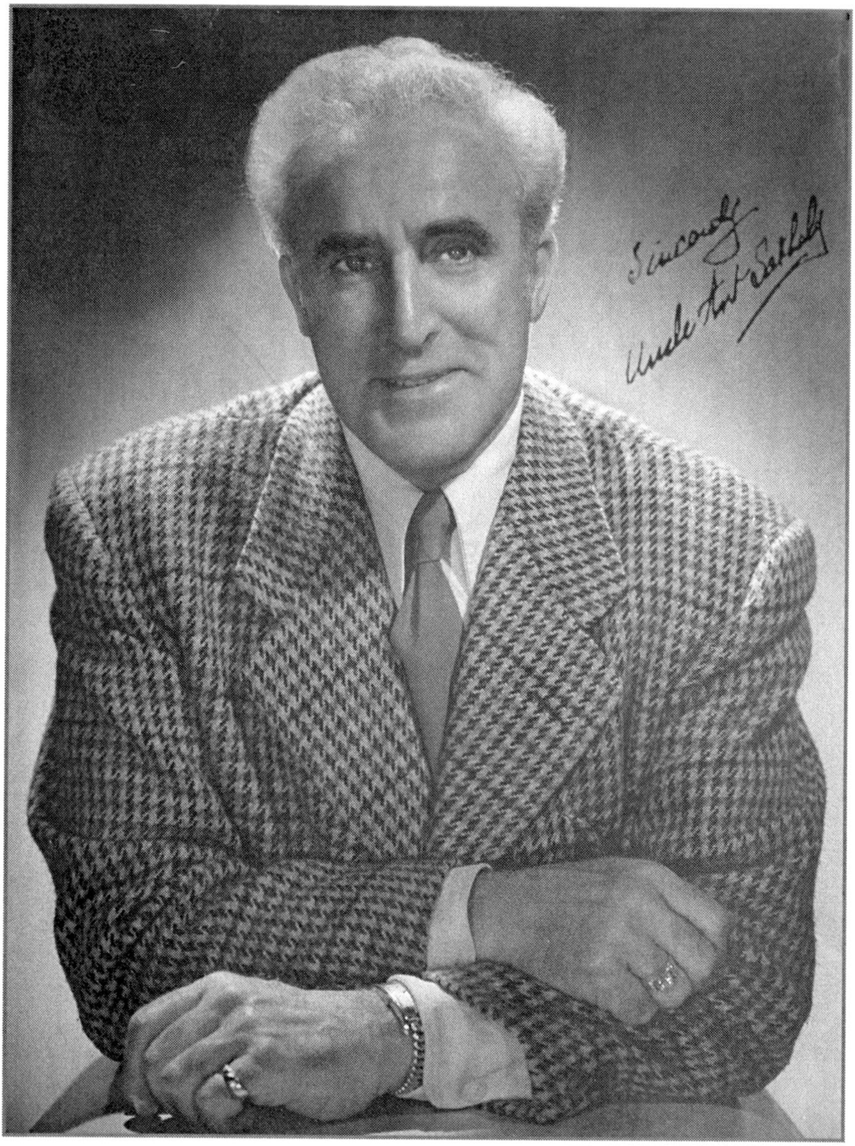
Sincerely

UNCLE ART

ALAN JOHN BRITTON

To LEE

All the best

Alan John Britton JULY 2011

authorHOUSE®

AuthorHouse™ UK Ltd.
500 Avebury Boulevard
Central Milton Keynes, MK9 2BE
www.authorhouse.co.uk
Phone: 08001974150

First published by AuthorHouse 12/2/2010

ISBN: 978-1-4520-8388-9 (dj)
ISBN: 978-1-4520-8389-6 (sc)

This book is printed on acid-free paper.

STUDIO LOG
(ACKNOWLEDGEMENTS)

"I must be quite difficult to live with sometimes when the music won't flow as I'd like."

That's a line from a song I wrote a while back. Now, insert "words" instead of "music", and I think I might be getting close to describing how it's been for my long-suffering family during the research and writing of *Uncle Art*.

My wife, Shirley, who has had to listen to my ramblings like "You'll never guess who was responsible for… " To which Shirley would say "Don't tell me; let me guess; it was… " And the kids, Lara, Elizabeth, Victoria, and Alex, had to hear it as well. Thanks for hearing me out. Oh, and Shirley took some of the photographs.

Etta D. Jackson – Etta, thank you for recognizing the potential in the story and helping to assemble the first treatment back then. And, you are now a best-selling author yourself. Go girl! What a journey!

Pete Willington, a Thornburyite, lived in Nashville writing songs and playing bass, and when he wasn't doing that, he was a guide at the Country Music Hall of Fame, or he was flipping burgers in Brown's Diner. I didn't know Pete then but eventually made his acquaintance because he was an old mate of two of guys in the sixties band that I play in. Anyway, we got chatting, and I said I want to write a song about the life of Uncle Art, so we did, and darn good it is, too. I was going on about having to go to Nashville to do research, and to my grateful surprise, he funded the trip. Thanks, Pete. Priceless.

Judy Keigley is Art's granddaughter. Your input was priceless as well. You were able to join dots about home life. Thank you for flying down to Nashville to meet me with the photos and letters, for supporting the project, and for telling me about Jo Walker-Meador, Art's friend.

Jo Walker-Meador – Thank you so much, Jo, for your gracious help, meeting me at the Country Music Hall of Fame Museum, and all the subsequent e-mails, which were invaluable.

Ray Price – Thanks for sharing your first-hand memories of Art and Don Law.

Ricky Skaggs – Thanks for the photo of you and Art and for sharing your knowledge of the music.

A posthumous "thank you" to Chet Atkins, who shared some of his memories with me, and because of that, I've been able to share them here, as the story of the country music recording industry is revealed with Art's story.

John Rumble, senior historian, Country Music Hall of Fame and Museum and Michael Gray, museum editor at the Hall of Fame – for making everything available to me. You must have spotted that I was a rookie at this book-writing game. Thanks for making me feel at home.

Doreen Stapleford, Art's niece – I'm glad you kept all those pictures, Deen, and the memories of life in Fraser Street as a girl that you passed on to me.

The Satherley Family in England. You are a large family, and thanks to all of you that were able to help with the book. And thanks to Colin Momber for the photo of the Royal George.

The late Kelvin Henderson for all he did to get Art recognized in his home city and the UK music scene.

Roger Cook – Thanks, Mate. Perhaps we can get this story recognized in "The Capital of the West Country", the City of Bristol. Or, should that be "Bristle"? (Yer, theese nowse what I means.)

Thanks to my proofreaders, Sue and Wendy, for sorting through my dyslexic, Bristolian wonderings and pointing out the error of my ways (when I was a kid we hadn't heard of dyslexia; they just said "yume fick").

UNCLE ART
(THE SONG)

Alan Britton/Pete Willington
Britton Music Publishing 2007

1.

HE LEFT THE CITY OF BRISTOL 'ROUND 1910
DID'NT KNOW IF HE'D COME BACK AGAIN
LOVED THE TALES OF THE OLD WILD WEST
COWBOYS INDIANS AND ALL THE REST
TOOK A BOAT TO MONTREAL IN CANADA AS I RECALL
TRAVELLED DOWN TO WISCONSON WORKED WITH THOMAS EDISON

2.

IN THE GRAMAPHONE FACTORY
SAW THE POSSIBILITY
HE KNEW HE HAD TO FIND AWAY
TO CAPTURE THE MUSIC THAT THEY PLAYED
THE HILLBILLY TUNES HE HEARD AS HE ROAMED SAID IT REMINDS ME OF SONGS FROM
HOME
NO PLACE THAT HE WOULDN'T GO CUTTIN SONGS FOR THE RADIO

CHORUS

UNCLE ART FOUND THE SINGERS, UNCLE ART FOUND THE SONGS
TURNED THEM INTO COUNTRY MUSIC GOLD
UNCLE ART GOT HIS NAME IN THE COUNTRY HALL OF FAME
YOU'RE A LEGEND AND THE STORY MUST BE TOLD
UNCLE ART GOD BLESS YOUR COUNTRY SOUL
HE LOOKED FOR THE SONGS OF AMERICA IN THE BACKWOODS AND THE HILLS
COWBOY BALLADS AND WESTERN SWING COUNTRY JIGS AND REELS

3.

MOVED TO NASHVILLE, TENESSEE
HEART OF THE MUSIC INDUSTRY
COLUMBIA AND RCA
ART SHOWED THEM ALL THE WAY
AS TIME WENT ON HE MADE SOME FLICKS: ROY ROGERS, GENE AUTRY, AND OLE TOM MIX
WENT TO CALIFORN-I-A MARRIED MISS AMERICA ALONG THE WAY

CHORUS

UNCLE ART FOUND THE SINGERS UNCLE ART FOUND THE SONGS
TURNED THEM INTO COUNTRY MUSIC GOLD
UNCLE ART GOT HIS NAME IN THE COUNTRY HALL OF FAME
YOU'RE A LEGEND AND THE STORY MUST BE TOLD
UNCLE ART GOD BLESS YOUR COUNTRY SOUL

HE LOOKED FOR THE SONGS OF AMERICA IN THE BACKWOODS AND THE HILLS
COWBOY BALLADS AND WESTERN SWING COUNTRY JIGS AND REELS

INSTRUMENTAL BREAK

FROM THE WEST COUNTRY TO AMERICA A PIONEERING MAN
FROM WINDMILL HILL TO THE BEVERLY HILLS AND ALL ACROSS THE LAND

UNCLE ART FOUND THE SINGERS UNCLE ART FOUND THE SONGS
TURNED THEM INTO COUNTRY MUSIC GOLD
UNCLE ART GOT HIS NAME IN THE COUNTRY HALL OF FAME
YOU'RE A LEGEND AND THE STORY MUST BE TOLD
UNCLE ART GOD BLESS YOUR COUNTRY SOUL
UNCLE ART GOD BLESS YOUR COUNTRY SOUL

INTRO

Where to start? At the beginning of course. Sounds easy enough, but it was never my intention to be the writer of *Uncle Art.* I intended to be someone to spread the word on this historical journey of music with a feeling of " We should know about this," particularly in my home city of Bristol, England, and then the rest of the British Isles, once someone else had written it that is. The best laid plans etc, etc. I have written it as if it was a song (it's what I do), so chapters become verses and so on, giving a musical feel.

There had been several attempts in the past by different people to write a book on this pioneering man, but for various reasons they had not progressed.

Uncle Art Satherley (who was also from Bristol, England) first came to my attention in 1994. Little did I know the impact he would have on my life twelve years later, when I decided it was about time the story was told.

I have written it, as my proofreaders said, "conversationally", or was that "confrontationally"? No, I think it was conversationally – as if I was telling it over a beer, or a coffee, or a cup of tea and a cake (tea made the English way, hot tea with cold milk, of course!). Anyway, I took it as a compliment. I didn't want the story to come over as stiff or scientific; there are technical parts as I interweave the history of the recording industry and the part that Art played. The discography is minimal; there are plenty of good works already out there.

There are little bits of light-heartedness, humour, even the odd joke (some might say very odd). To find the right balance and keep it interesting, for whoever in the world will read it, was my plan. Most of all, I wanted to portray what made Uncle Art Satherley tick. From an ordinary family living in Windmill Hill, Bedminster, Bristol, to the Beverly Hills Hollywood lifestyle, it's a fascinating story of human endeavour. There are parts of his private life that he did not wish to speak of, (except for tantalizing snippets in interviews, that is). It's all here.

It's because of Dolly Parton! Yes, Dolly Parton, and an out-of-the-blue phone call, to request help to book her for a concert in Bristol.

That was the starting point of a chain of events that would lead to this journey.

Dolly won't be aware of this, of course, but then, with her interest in history, the settlers, and their music, who knows? She may become aware.

There was the gig in Bristol with Chet Atkins, a one-off event that turned out to be a major key change, to use a musical analogy.

The introduction is Forrest White's, written for his book on Art. Being close friends with Art, Forrest was ideally placed to write it, but sadly he died suddenly with only that part written. It is with respect for their friendship that I include it unabridged.

Verse One is called "My Story"; it's autobiographical, including some history of the port of Bristol and the West Country, giving the reader an understanding of the background of the young Arthur, who grew up in Bristol at the turn of the twentieth century.

And, then, it maps out the life of the man Arthur Edward Satherley, who went on to become country music's Founding Father – something he did with great dignity and often with acts of philanthropy.

It could be seen that my interest and passion for the subject, discovering codes and shapes in the ancient music, was shaping my life leading to this point. I learned guitar, recognized a certain something in country music, wrote and performed songs, became qualified in electronics, and found out how sound works. I realized that music and electronics were preparing to leap forward together. Then, I took an interest in the history of it all. So here it is, from one Bristolian about another Bristolian. Bringing it all back home.

* * * * *

There are times when things conspire, even though you're not aware of them, to lead you toward a goal. Here is what I consider proof of "synchronicity", when the human spirit's energy connects with a universal lattice to make a timeless now.

It was September 2007 when my wife Shirley was asked to go to Turkey as an envoy for a charity called Seven Springs. It has opened places for children who have disabilities to go and play, and parents can get respite and counselling. Shirley is a wheelchair user and had become official photographer for Hop Skip and Jump, the play/care centres.

Turkey had copied the format for these centres and was putting on a photographic exhibition; half the exhibition was by Turkish photographers and half were Shirley's photographs. I went along as Shirley's caregiver. Seven Springs, the Rotary Clubs of Great Britain and Turkey, and the Soroptimist International Turkey made the whole trip possible.

Two days after our return home, I took a call from *The Bristol Evening Post* newspaper.

The journalist Hugo Berger said, "Your number has been given to me by a colleague, who said you are always doing interesting things, and I'm looking for features for the paper."

I told him about Hop Skip and Jump and Turkey.

He said "Sounds just the kind of story I can use. I'll arrange a photographer and we'll be round. Any thing else?"

So, I told him about the Uncle Art story.

"Let's do the Turkey story first and then have a look at the other one."

* * * * *

The following week, there was a good feature in the *Evening Post* about the trip. The same reporter then did a page on the Art Satherley story, which followed the week after. I had a very good response to the article from members of the Satherley family and people glad the story was going to be told, and then out of the blue I had an e-mail from Richard Melrose living in Southern California, reprinted here with his permission.

> Hi, Alan
>
> My wife and I have become somewhat friends with someone who works at a Home Improvement store in So. California and just today, he was telling me that his grandfather was Art Satherley and that Art was hired at one point by Thomas Edison in some way related to Edison's invention of the phonograph.
>
> I thought that was pretty cool, so I decided to Google Art Satherley and came across an article that mentions

you, entitled, "ART PUT WEST IN COUNTRY AND WESTERN" << http://www.thisisbristol.co.uk. At the end of the article, it said that if anyone had any information regarding Art that you'd be interested.

I'm writing you, not because I have any information for you, but because -- if you'd like (and if you respond to my e-mail) -- I'd be happy to ask Art's grandson if he would mind contacting you. He's a very nice guy, so I think he'd be okay with contacting you.

It's apparent that he's extremely proud of his grandfather, and he even pulled his grandfather's old membership card out of his wallet (It was for "Country & Western [something] organization"), and Art's membership number was #0001: for whatever the organization was. Art was it's very first member.

I don't really know how much he knows about his grandfather more than what you could probably find out by searching the Internet, but he might have some interesting family knowledge that would not be readily found. For instance, he mentioned that his grandfather was the person who invented the formula for the first colored vinyl record disks, which were red. Let me know if you're interested, and I'll ask him.

Richard

This, of course, can only happen now because of the Internet. Ten years previously, it probably wouldn't or couldn't have happened. Still, I think that the chance of this particular event happening is quite rare: first the phone call from the journalist, then the feature in the paper, the "This Is Bristol" entry on the Internet, and then the conversation in Southern California (5,000 miles away) leading to the Googling and subsequent e-mail from Richard Melrose.

The date of the newspaper article was 27 September 2007, and Richard Melrose's e-mail came on 23 October 2007 – all this in twenty-six days. This led me to the contact with Art's grandchildren, who have been incredibly helpful, and was the main reason for my knuckling down and starting the full-time research. It was a definite "the time is now" feeling if ever there was one.

Also, there was the great act of kindness by a friend by funding a trip to the Country Music Hall of Fame and Museum in Nashville to get closer to archival material.

There are references in Forrest's introduction to taped interviews, and I have had the privilege of listening to every one of them, so the claim of word-for-word that Forrest refers to still holds, and there's more.

If there is anything that can be added to the story that has been missed or needs correcting, please feel free to contact me by e-mail: alanjohnbritton@aol.com

Alan

FORREST WHITE'S INTRODUCTION

Forrest White was preparing to write a biography of Uncle Art when he died unexpectedly on 22 November 1994. Used with permission of Forrest White's son, Curtis.

"In the beginning" were the first three words of the greatest book ever written – they mean simply, "this is how and when it all started."

Are you a country music fan or ever wondered how country music became popular?

Do you like to hear country music records, and have you wondered how the phonograph record discs originated and how they were transformed into an enjoyable finished product? If your answer[s] to these questions are in the affirmative then I will consider it to be a privilege, and certainly my pleasure, to tell you, "how and when it all started." Because – in the beginning of the record industry and the early year[s of] recording of country music – there was Uncle Art Satherley, [a] man who was born in England but [who] came to America where he hoped to find, of all things, cowboys and Indians.

In a relatively short period of time he began working for Thomas Edison, the man who invented the phonograph. He learned to mix the material formulas for making the record discs, and he supervised the presses that were used to manufacture the completed product. He later travelled the highways and the byways to find country-music talent and then he signed them to a recording contract for his company. He supervised the preservation of the early-year approved talent sound in the grooves of the wax matrix that was centred on a crude hand cranked operated recording machine. But that is only part of the story.

It required his dogged determination and perseverance to eventually pry open the doors of recording studios in those early years to make possible the recording of his discovered country-music talent who so many of the recording executives ridiculed and held in utter contempt. Their idea of acceptable music was confined to the talent of the singers and musicians found in the big bands, Broadway musicals, and the classics.

I first met Uncle Art Satherley in October 1971, the year he was inducted into the Country Music Hall of Fame, in Nashville, Tennessee. At that time, he was eighty-two years of age and he seemed to be in good health and exceptionally good spirit[s]. The next time I saw him was at the memorial service for a dear deceased friend Johnny Bond. He had reached the age of eighty nine. I noticed that Uncle Art seemed to be very quiet at the time, however I assumed it was because of the loss of his very close friend, Johnny.

Soon after that, on September 12, 1978, I visited with Uncle Art at his home and was disturbed at what I found. I was right about my feeling that he seemed unusually quiet at our last meeting.

I was now convinced that Uncle Art was close to becoming a recluse; however, this was by no means his choice. This was because he believed that the majority of those he had helped on the "road to success and stardom" had forgotten him. Here is what he told me during my visit. I quote, "I get letters for my autograph and interest in my days with Thomas Edison. But, from the boys and girls that I actually worked with, it's a very sad affair. Maybe they think that they are too busy, but I never hear from them. I know they all think a lot of me, I know that, because I've heard it many, many times. But, one would think, you know, that you would be remembered with a Christmas card, or something like that once in a while. But, never the less, I must say I'm thankful to my Lord."

Friend, please rest assured that absolutely all quotes used in this book were taken word for word from recorded voice tapes I made of Uncle Art and my many friends in the music industry through the years. The recordings were made with the knowledge and permission of all those persons recorded.

There is absolutely no such thing as a self-made man. We all have to have help from many along the way. It is too bad that human nature does not allow us to show a feeling of gratitude as much as our zeal for seeking help.

I believe many of us can remember those persons who were extremely friendly with us when we were in a position to help them materially or by way of influence. Then the time came when they no longer needed help or we were not in what they considered to be an influential position. Remember how quickly their interest and alleged friendship seemed to cool or disappear completely? I can tell you for sure – it happened to me, and I will explain.

I had the privilege of meeting and establishing long-lasting friendship with Uncle Art Satherley and the majority of those mentioned in this book through my association with Mr. Leo Fender as the vice president and general manager of the Fender Electric Instrument Co. during the early years prior to the acquisition of the company by CBS.

We had been working with a very well-known country artist and his band members for a long period of time. They were partial to our line of Fender guitars and amplifiers. One day the artist's manager called me and told me that there was a singer/musician/song writer that he knew who I should get to use Fender equipment because he was sure the guy was going to become a country-music star. I asked what his name was and, when told, informed the manager that I had never heard of the name but send him on down and I would be glad to talk to him. So, the guy shows up at my office with his girl friend and you would never expect to be treated any nicer than I was. I was completely showered with courtesy and compliments that were dripping with the milk of human kindness. Well, I admit, I was impressed. I hadn't realized I was so important. To make a long story short, I gave the guy some Fender musical equipment so he could start on his first personal-appearance road tour. The manger's prediction came true. The guy became a big country-music star. And he still is. I took Uncle Art to a country-music concert in Long Beach where he was performing. He shook hands with Uncle Art and then looked at me like I was so much excess baggage. After all he was a big star and didn't need my help anymore.

So, I know, to some extent, how Uncle Art must have felt because of the many stars who no longer needed help and, sadly enough for Uncle Art, they knew he was in no position to offer any help now even if they needed it. It was then that I decided to do all I could to help him. I took care of all of Uncle Art's music-industry affairs, at his request, from September 25, 1978, until his passing February 10, 1986. I informed the media of his demise and condolences were received from his friends nation wide.

Uncle Art knew potential recording talent when he heard it as well as he knew the complete manufacturing process of the records. There were forty-three members elected to the Country Music Hall of Fame, in Nashville, Tennessee, between the year 1961 (the first) and 1986 (the year of Uncle Art's death). He had signed and recorded fifteen of those members as of the year 1986.

He was going to sign Jimmie Rodgers the next day before Jimmie's death. Jimmie was the first artist to be elected into the Hall of Fame in1961. Uncle Art was inducted into the Hall of Fame in 1971.

Uncle Art recorded some of the Hall of Fame members who were honoured with titles depicting their status, or contribution, to country music: Gene Autry, "the Singing Cowboy," and "Idol of All America;" Roy Acuff, "King of Country Music;" Bill Monroe, "King of Bluegrass;" Roy Rogers, "King of the Cowboys;" Bob Wills, " King of Western Swing." By the time you finish reading this book, I believe you will agree with me that Uncle Art Satherley deserves the title of "Mr. Country Music."

I made four promises to friends during my active years associated with the music business:

1. I promised Leo Fender that I would write a book telling what really happened during the early years at Fender. I kept that promise. The book is called, *Fender – The INSIDE STORY.* Publisher, G.P.I. Books, Millar Freeman Inc.

2. I promised Leo Fender I would show the early years (VCR converted) movie film that I took at the Fender Electric Instrument Co. Factory in the years 1954 and 1955. The video also shows footage of Fender and a few other musical instrument companies at the national music show in Chicago, musicians, Leo Fender and his friend on his boat, etc., during those early years. It's titled, *FENDER and the MEMORABLE YESTERYEARS.* The video is available through my book publisher, G.P.I. Books, Millar Freeman Inc. Leo and I both agreed that many would be interested in how it happened in those wonderful years.

3. I promised Uncle Art Satherley that that I would help produce a memorable album made for him. This was done. He introduced many of his all-time hits on the album with famous artists who recorded them. I was one of the executive producers of *Uncle Art Satherley, Country Music's*

Founding Father, Columbia Record's American Originals, CK 46237 and PCT 46237.

4. I promised Uncle Art that I would write this book to let country-music fans around the world know how much he contributed to their enjoyment.

Uncle Art Satherley was truly a legend in his time. When you read this book I doubt if you will be able to think of a person who has done more for the music he loved and who is more deserving of his place in the Hall of Fame.

Forrest White

VERSE ONE

MY STORY

"This is the great 208 station of the stars, Radio Luxembourg". The radio crackled, and faded in and out as it warmed up. It was the fifties. My parents would switch the radio on most evenings to listen to Radio Luxembourg. I was ten years old in 1957; they allowed me to listen for a while before bed. The reception was poor at times, the signal on 208 medium wave was travelling a long way, even though the pirate station had the highest output transmitters in Europe for the night-time service to the British Isles, and the shortwave frequency covered most of the world. This was my introduction to the popular music of the day, not only the British scene but American charts as well. There were a lot of GIs still posted in Europe, and for these guys it was a chance to touch base with home, along with the American Forces Network.

Mixed in with the hits was a kind of music I didn't hear anywhere else, in particular the guitars and the kind of special sound they made. Just one year later, I was given a guitar for my eleventh birthday. After the initial pain barrier and broken skin on the fingertips, I went on the search for the guitar players I heard on 208 – one in particular: Chet Atkins, plus many others. I had no idea that I was listening to a Kentucky thumb-pick style used by these players or that it was country music. I have the feeling that if reincarnation is real, I must have made a wrong turn on the way in and instead of Nashville, USA, I was attracted to Eastville, Southville, Northville (all districts of Bristol), and Acton Turville, a village in the countryside just east of Bristol England! Well it did have a "Ville" in it and it was in the country.

What happened to me, listening to the music back then, I'm not sure. It touched somewhere deep, real deep. A soul experience? A memory? Remembering? I don't know, but the effect of it was life changing for me. I had recognized something. I could pick out the shape of a country song no matter how it was hidden.

It could have been on the very straight-laced BBC radio or TV (there was only the BBC on air back then), but without fail I would hear it, so much so that by the time I was sixteen I just had to have a guitar like Chet: a Gretsch 6120. I remember going into Bristol Musical, a guitar shop in Old Market, in 1962 and asking the man if he could order a Gretsch for me. It was as if I had punched him; he reeled back in shock.

"What?"

I repeated the question.

" Well ...ha – ha – have a big deposit ready" he stuttered, obviously thinking, "*This kid is taking the Mick,*" but I wasn't.

I had borrowed £250 from a well-off aunty and uncle, which I would pay back when I could. It was a lot of money back then!

I pointed to a picture in a catalogue by Arbiter.

"That one," (an orange Gretsch, Chet Atkins, double-cutaway guitar with Filter'Tron pickups). "How much deposit? "I asked.

Still looking stunned, he said "It'll take ages to get. The deposit will be £125. It'll probably have to be ordered in from the States. I'll let you know when it's in."

Months passed. No guitar; I rang; still no guitar.

My mother was on a bus going shopping in town, and the route passed Bristol Musical.

When she returned home, she said, "Was that guitar you ordered orange, because there was an orange one in the window of that music shop?"

When I rang the shop, Chris (I had got to know him quite well by then) said "Oh, I thought we'd let you know. So, I put it in the window until you collected it. When you collect it, bring something to wrap it in. It doesn't have a case."

As it was the first Gretsch in Bristol he had decided to put it on display, and let me know – eventually. I collected my Gretsch, wrapped it in a blanket, and took it home on the bus, It's been with me ever since. It now has Chet's signature on it in permanent marker.

Alan with new Gretsch 1964

During the week before the gig at the harbour, Chet walked past it in my studio and asked, "Does that ole thing still play?".

Thinking Chet was going to play it, I said "yes."

He said, "Pick me something."

So there I was, playing my old Gretsch in the presence of my guitar idol. My fingers felt like they had just turned into pork sausages. I played a part of a tune I had written. Chet asked, "Are ya gonna play that on the gig?" "No," I said sheepishly. "Good" said Chet. I think he was just being kind.

Chet signed Gretsch 1994

* * * * *

With a title *Uncle Art*, this could be a story about one of my relatives or a friend of the family, but it's not. This is the story of a pioneering man that you might expect to be about the Gold Rush, the Wild West, or a great inventor or scientist and such.

Instead, it is a true story of a man who had a massive influence on music and changed the direction of the people he would meet, the ordinary people of America – a man who forged a path in the newly unfolding music industry.

Chet in Alan's studio

I first heard about of this story in

1994 after being contacted by Bristol City Council regarding country music. I had been involved with country music as a songwriter and guitar player for many years when the Council called me and said, "We understand you are something to do with country music."

"Yes, how can I help?"

"Can you help us book Dolly Parton?"

I swallowed hard and with tongue in cheek I answered "Yes," thinking, *This should be interesting.*

After many phone calls, I finally talked with Dolly's manager, who told me that Dolly was not touring at that time, being busy in Hollywood.

The Council wanted to book an artiste connected with country music because of past connections with early settlers and trade to the Americas, so I suggested the legendry guitar player Chet Atkins. Dolly was a very close friend of Chet's so I thought that maybe this could be good for the future.

The gig was on 29 July 1994 at the Lloyds Amphitheatre, Bristol Docks, which was the weekend of the harbour Regatta (now called Harbour Festival). You know how some things are meant to be.

I had rung Chet, who answered the phone himself, and I said, "I didn't expect you to answer personally."

"It rang as I passed the damn thing!" he said.

I held myself together just long enough to blurt out why I was calling. I could hear pages turn.

To my surprise he said, "Yep, I might be free. Ring my booker Bobby Cudd. Here's his number."

And so, I got to play a gig with my guitar inspiration and present the Gibson Guitars' Living Legend award to Mr Guitar, Chet Atkins, cgp (certified guitar player). I wasn't the one originally intended to present the award. We thought we had a coup. Chet had spoken to Mark Knopfler, who agreed to guest with Chet, and maybe play a duet they had recorded called "Poor Boy Blues." So, we contacted Mark, who agreed to present the award. We felt very pleased with ourselves at pulling this off. However, on the day before the show, Mark rang Chet to apologize: he could not be released from a studio appointment to record a new album. We were devastated.

At the sound check of the show, a guy from Gibson showed up with the award. We told him what had happened, and suggested he might present it.

"Me? Oh no, you won't get me In front of four thousand people," he said loudly" Well, who is going to do it?" exclaimed the compère of the show, local radio broadcaster Trevor Fry. We were stood in a little huddle: me, the Gibson guy, Trevor Fry, and George Lunn (Chet's road manager). All eyes turned my way, and almost in unison they said, "It'll have to be you." "But – " I squeaked. "It's got to be you," they said.

So, I opened the show with my band, Country FM: piano Andy Christy, drums Charles Hart, bass Barry Cook, rhythm guitar Pete Tucker, fiddle John Hinchliffe, and special guest vocalist Kaz. When time came for Chet and his band, "inspirational" is the word that springs to mind.

In the week leading up to the concert, Chet was asked to do some promotional appearances, local radio interviews, and the like. Because of the release of his album *Read My Licks*, Chet was asked to do a solo set in the Virgin Megastore in the Galleries (now the Mall) Bristol, and he agreed.

After I set up my PA equipment in the store, Chet passed me his guitar, and said, "Can you make sure it's working, Al?"

I played a couple of bars of "Windy and Warm" on his Gibson natural-top, nylon-strung electric, passed it back, and said "Everything's good."

I introduced him, and then it was forty-five minutes of pure Chet – all those licks and phrases that I had heard and tried to learn as a kid, a guitar player's heaven. The record store was packed to the doors with guitar players who never thought they'd see the day with Chet Atkins, Mr Guitar, standing just in front of them in a record store in Bristol playing live. There wasn't a dry eye to be seen. There is a picture of Chet in the store taken through the people over the top of display stands.

Chet ticket

Chet playing Virgin Megastore

The following night, I stood in the wings of the stage as Chet and his band played. I was reviewing everything that had happened that week and drifting away as the music wafted around me.

Coming back to the present, I asked George Lunn "When shall I present the award?"

"As he introduces his last tune," he said, "Just walk out and interrupt him. He never does an encore."

"Just interrupt him"? I said.

George replied "Yep."

The moment had arrived. Over and over in my head I was thinking what to say and hoping not to sound like a babbling fool. This is how it went.

"Chet I have to interrupt you; it's for something really special. Do you remember your first guitar inspiration?"

Chet looked at me and said, "It was my brother, Jim. He was a fine guitar player, and, of course, Merle Travis."

"Do you remember how it felt when you first met Merle?" was my next question.

"I sure do," Chet said with a laugh.

"Well, that's how all these people feel here tonight, and it's with all those feelings I present, on behalf of Gibson guitars, this Living Legend Award."

Alan presents the Gibson living legend award to Chet Atkins 29th July 1994

He took it, looked at for a while, and said, "Will you look at that? They spoiled a perfectly good guitar to make this."

The award was the headstock of a guitar mounted on a block of wood and inscribed "Chet Atkins – Living Legend Award – Gibson Guitars."

The audience responded with thunderous applause. Chet put down the award and carried on with the last tune of the show, and then, an encore!

At that point. George Lunn threw his arms in the air saying, "What's he doing? He hates travelling; hates flying; and now he's doing an encore? What are we doing here?"

I think I said, "Calm down, George. It was obviously meant to be."

As the people cleared, I went to meet my wife and our children, Lara, Elizabeth, and Victoria, who had helped so much to make it all happen. My son Alex was running about all over the place. The girls were crying, overcome with the emotion of it all, and Alex, who was eight years old, had insisted earlier during the day that Chet sign his half-size Strat at the gig. Chet duly signed this little guitar, and Alex ran onto the middle of the stage and posed like a rock star.

Having had to hold it all together for the show, the time had come for a communal cry. Amazed that we were able to pull off this very special event, I'm sure that evening is etched in a time library somewhere on another level.

* * * * *

I was researching the history of country music at this time and came across the name Uncle Art in the Country Music Hall of Fame, listed as the founding father of country music and born in Bristol England. I found it unbelievable that this fascinating story of music history is relatively unknown in his home city, and the rest of the UK for that matter.

In talking to some local musicians who play country music, I found one or two that had heard vague snippets of the story. Steel guitar player Bob Dixon suggested I speak to local singer Kelvin Henderson. Kelvin also presented a country-music programme once a week on BBC Radio Bristol. He knew of the story and featured it on his show from time to time. I had produced a track for Kelvin called "Whiskey Eyes" written by Sonny Curtis, of "Buddy Holly and The Crickets" fame. We did a music video of the track that we eventually got played on Country Music Television (CMT) , which was on Sky satellite in the UK at that time.

Kelvin had interviewed Art on the telephone for his show. The story had hooked Kelvin, but because of his touring schedule he couldn't spend the time on it. There is a picture of Art holding one of Kelvin's albums, with Harriet (his partner of 40 years), taken by Colin Momber from Bristol on a visit to Art's home in California. The picture is reproduced courtesy of Colin and passed to me by a relative of Art: Mike Satherley. Colin also is the editor of a magazine called *B Westerns*, hence his interest in the story.

* * * * *

Arthur Edward Satherley was born in Bedminster, (Bedminster was in Somerset until boundary changes in 1897) Bristol, England on 19 October 1889. In a true pioneering fashion, he was going to be responsible for making music history.

Arthur's father Levi Satherley (Courtesy Doreen Stapleford)

Arthur was born into a religious family. His father, Levi, was a lay preacher at a chapel in the street where the Satherley family moved to when Arthur was in his teens. Art's father Levi had been married before, to Ellen Willey. They had four children: Amelia Ellen born 1875, Sarah born1877, Emily Ann born 1879, and George born1881. Ellen died at the age of thirty three. Levi married again in 1888 to Alice Ann Hooper, whose first husband had also died. Popular local belief has it that the family lived at Number 35 Fraser Street, Windmill Hill, Bedminster, Bristol. In a narrow street of terraced houses on both sides, the chapel known as The Mission Rooms was opposite Number 35.

In later life, Arthur referred to Fraser Street as his birthplace, but his birth certificate shows that in fact he was born in Number 2, Anchor Cottages, Bartley Street, just around the corner from Fraser Street. The cottages are no longer there, having been replaced with a small industrial estate. From Bartley Street the family moved to Number 1 Quantock Road, Windmill Hill, barely a mile away. The deeds for Number 1, Quantock road are dated 4 February 1898 and show that Number 1 became Number 13 when more houses were built. Unusually, on the deeds it shows joint ownership between Levi and Alice. (Normally, it was only the head of the house in those days). The 1901 census listed at Quantock Road Levi age forty six; Alice age thirty nine;

Arthurs younger sister and brother Millicent and Henry 1905 picture courtesy Doreen Stapleford

Amelia age twenty five; Arthur Age eleven; Edgar age ten; Ernest age nine; and Millicent age one,. (Another son, Henry, was yet to be born.)

On a conveyance dated 1 August 1919, an amendment was made to the deeds. A line had been put through Alice Ann Satherley's name with this explanation "and whereas the said Alice Ann Satherley died on the first day of March one thousand nine hundred and eighteen". The property was being sold, so only Levi could sign the documents. The document also said "of 35 Fraser Street Windmill Hill", that shows that they had moved into Fraser Street after 1901 and before 1910. A directory of Bristol for 1910 had Alice listed as a dressmaker at 35 Fraser Street. This information came to me after I had contacted the Windmill Hill community association where secretary Christine Higgott was happy to help. In no time at all, Christine came back to tell me the present owners Simon and Christine Hayward of 13 Quantock Road had the deeds with relevant information and gave permission for me to use their information. My many thanks to everyone at the residents association.

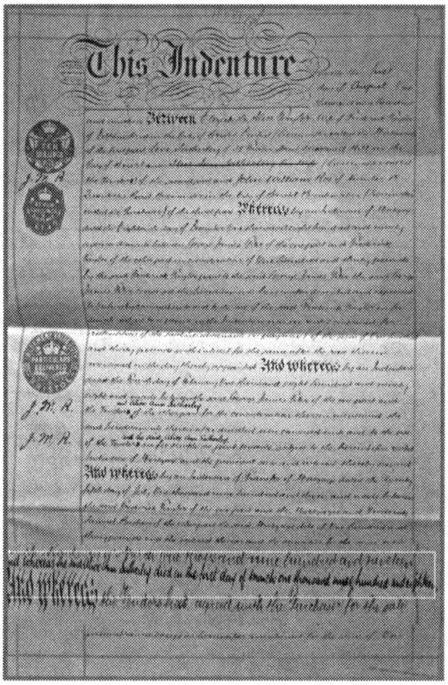

This Indenture

As well as the quote about Fraser Street, Arthur also said his father was a minister. In the children's eyes perhaps he was, and it made a better story in years to come. In reality, Levi was a tanner at a Bedminster tanning factory situated on the banks of the river Avon. In an interview, Doreen Stapleford, Art's niece, who was born in 1920 and raised in 35 Fraser Street (her mother was Art's stepsister, Emily) recalls her grandfather Levi taking her on a Sunday as a small child across the road to the chapel, sitting her in the front row, and saying. "Now be a good little girl," whilst he preached to the congregation.

Doreen also recalls the stepchildren talking of being cruelly treated by stepmother Alice, who would wrap their hair around her hand and bang their heads against the wall to make them behave. Doreen, known as Deen to the family, gave me photographs still in her possession of those early days.

It was good to talk with Doreen with her first-hand memories. Doreen also recalled her granddad being strict but fair. There was perhaps some embellishment in Arthur's story in several areas and some things left out to make a more romantic story. Art was reluctant to talk about some aspects of his early life in Bristol. As the story unfolds, maybe we'll see the reason,

Doreen and her mother Emily about 1923.

* * * * *

Arthur went to school in Victoria Park Infants School in Windmill Hill, but Art talked only of going to Queen Elizabeth Hospital and living in Clifton. It seems quite a few people thought it was Arthur romanticizing, but in fact around the age of ten, (1899-1905) Levi put him forward for a place at the Queen Elizabeth Hospital School for Boys, Clifton, Bristol (known as QEH). I was under the impression that the QEH was a fee-paying private school, so I rang the development office at QEH for some background and spoke to a very helpful lady called Charlotte.

She gave me some history on QEH. She told me that fee-paying students did not start until 1920 and that the school was set up in 1590 by a local soap maker and merchant whose name was John Carr. He had a factory in Baldwin Street, Bristol, and in Stratford- by- Bow, London. A hospital called Christ's

Hospital in Newgate London was the inspiration for QEH, a school set up to deal with the very acute social problems of the area, particularly orphaned and very poor boys.

John Carr lived at Congresbury Manor just outside Bristol, and he drafted a will with very precise instructions:

> You are to erect and found by due form of law in the city of Bristol and in some convenient house and place which the Mayor and Aldermen for the time being shall appoint and prepare ... an hospital or place for the bringing up of poor children or orphans, being men children, such as shall be born in the city of Bristol or in any part of my manor lands or tenements in Congresbury, and whose parents are deceased or dead or fallen into decay, and not able to relieve them; and for those chiefly to provide in such order, manner, ordinance, laws and government as the Hospital of Christchurch nigh Saint Bartholomew's in London is founded, ordered and governed in every respect. The Mayor and community of Bristol to be patrons and guides and governors of the same Hospital to be founded for ever."

Extract from 'WHILE WE HAVE TIME...' 1590-1990 (QEH 1990) by J.R. Avery. (This was to celebrate 400 years of Royal Charter)

On the death of John Carr just three months later, the mayor and corporation acted promptly and enthusiastically to transform John Carr's aims into practice and applied to Queen Elizabeth I for a charter. On her visit to Bristol in1574, she was impressed with the city and recognized the plight of the poor, and the charter was granted on 21 March 1590.

At the top of the charter is written, "Dum tempus habemus, operemur bonum" (While we have time let us do good).

In 1660, a revised set of rules were introduced and were in place, or some very similar, until 1920 when the school started taking fees. The rules were:

1. No boy be admitted that hath any loathsome or infectious disease or any deformity or imperfection that may prevent his being placed out as an apprentice.
2. No boy be admitted unless his petition be signed by the Mayor, four Aldermen, and the treasurers.
3. He must have a certificate that he is ten years old and not under.

4. His father must be a free burgess of Bristol (an inhabitant of a borough with full rights, a citizen) or he must be a poor boy of Congresbury.
5. No boy is to be continued past the age of sixteen.
6. The master is not to teach or entertain any tablers (i.e.private pupils) without leave of the Mayor
7. Boys to be instructed in reading, writing and casting accounts, and rendered capable of being apprenticed out.
8. The boy on admission with payment of 20 shillings to be furnished with one suit of apparel, two shirts, two bands, two pairs of stockings, and shoes.

Levi Satherley would have been aware of the criteria for entry to QEH as a preacher, albeit part-time. To get a better education for young Arthur and at least one of his brothers, Levi was listed on some documents as a tanner or tanner's labourer on poor wages.

Charlotte told me that the Bristol record office held the registers of the school before 1920, and would you believe it, after trawling through record after record, the years I needed were missing! But in the 1903 register was Arthur's younger brother, Edgar.

I spoke again with Charlotte at QEH, and she said that, if the family had been accepted, it would be certain that Arthur would have had a place for five years at the school until he was fifteen, and he would have lived in the school as it was boarders only (they were known as foundation boys). According to Doreen, Edgar, (Art's younger brother), became mayor of Pembroke Dock, South Wales in later life.

Charlotte asked what the interest was in one of their old boys, so I explained, ending by saying Art was vice president of Columbia Records USA until his retirement in 1952.

Charlotte paused for a while and then said, "You are not going to believe this. Another one of our old boys was in here the other day, and he is currently the managing director of Columbia Records UK."

Here's some more history of QEH's uniform. It was quite striking, and Art would have been required to wear it:

> Britain has a number of 'bluecoat schools', the name deriving from the quaint costume formerly worn by the pupils. Nowadays most of these establishments are bluecoat schools in name only, having long ago abandoned the cassock-like bluecoats, knee breeches and stockings in favour of a more up to date mode of dress. However, a number of schools still retain the bluecoat uniform for special occasions and pupils at the most famous bluecoat school of all, Christ's Hospital, wear the antique dress at all times – keeping alive a tradition that dates back to the mid-16th century. (www. Flickr. com/photos/anvilessex/ 152505093)

The subjects that Art took at QEH were grammar, geography, and bookkeeping. In addition to reading and writing, the schooling had moulded his dress sense, the way to present oneself, and watered down the strong Bristol accent. But it still was there – the dialect obvious to anyone from the area. And the art of buying and selling was to turn Art toward being a salesman.

Now I feel I should try and explain the Bristol accent, Bristoleze as it's known. So, are we ready? Here we go. First a lyric, then the explanation. Wott ,ave I tak,n on ,ere? Oops! slipped into it already!

The Wurzels are a famous band from round 'ere, one of their songs is used to welcome Bristol City football team onto the pitch at home games. Art had said in an interview he was a City fan. The Wurzels describe their music as Scrumpy and western. Scrumpy being rough, cloudy, potent, apple cider that Somerset farmers would take with them to the fields with bread and cheese, for refreshment.

Here are some lines from a song by Adge Cutler and the Wurzels:

"Theese got'n where theese cas'nt back'n ass'nt, theese never gonna get'n out'a there"

Translation: "You have got it where you cannot back it out of haven't you, you are never going to get it out of there."

OK, still with me?

And we will use as a greeting, "Awwright then, my babby?" or "Awwright then my luvver?" meaning: "All right my friend," and "Oww biss?" (How are you?*)* "Woss fink of ee then?" ("What do you think of that then?") "Gert lush" ("Very nice.")

Winmill 'ill, Beminster, Bristol (pronounced "Windmill Hill, Bedminster, Bristle or Brizzle) is where broad Bristolian would have been spoken in Uncle Art's day (and still is). The dialect varies between districts, just to complicate things. There is a tendency to add an "l" to the end of words that end in a vowel e.g. Americal = America .

We have a famous songwriter from Fishponds, Bristol, Roger Cook, now living in Nashville, who mixes up southern states dialect with his Bristoleze when he greets people with "Awwright then, y'all?'

When I visited the Smokey Mountains in East Tennessee I was surprised to hear a dialect that was not too dissimilar to the West Country accent I am used to. It was slowed down.

There was even some West Country dialect in one of the hit tracks that Art produced with Little Jimmy Dickens called "Take an Old Cold 'Tater (and Wait)." "Tater" – short for potato – is still a term used today.

The West Country accent has become quite fashionable. For instance, *The Lord of the Rings* movie trilogy cast the hobbits with a West Country accent. So, too, with Hagrid in the Harry Potter movie series. J. K. Rowling, the writer of Harry Potter, grew up in the Yate and Winterbourne districts on the outskirts of Bristol. In the comedy series, *Little Britain,* Vicky Pollard with her catch phrase, "yeah but no but" depicts a girl from Bristol speaking a way that the writers David Walliams and Matt Lucas picked up on while attending Bristol University. In fact, there is now a company called Beast Clothing that specializes in selling T-shirts worldwide with Bristle sayings.

* * * * *

So, getting back to Art, from 1906 at the age of sixteen (the time line of events is not clear) it seems he spent a lot of time working on a relative's farm. The Satherley family came from East Lambrook, a village near Martock in Somerset, which is very rural. There was no shortage of farms to work at during the school holidays or when he finally left school. Bedminster is now an inner city district, but at that time it would have been close to countryside and, being on the southside of the very tidal river Avon, it would have been considered separate from the inner city.

QEH however, would have groomed Art for better things, such as an apprenticeship. Here's what Art had to say about that in an interview on 29 March 1974 with Douglas B. Green for the Country Music Foundation:

> Now, I'll tell you something about my apprenticeship days in Great Britain. I'm working for five shillings a week at a place called F.C. Tuckett and Company, 108 Stokes Croft, Bristol, England. Tucketts was a grocery and provision store until 1920; it's still known today as Tuckett buildings.] I was working as a young lad as a cashier at the cash desk. They had (hard) money in those days. The only paper money they had was a five-pound note made of parchment; outside of that it was gold: sovereigns, half sovereigns, and silver. I would like to mention a few of these coins, because they had a coin in gold called a guinea, I'll tell you, if we had a thousand of them we could probably sell them for $250,000 because they are that scarce. They were yellow gold; beautiful coins. They had a five-shilling piece that was like our American dollar. They had a half crown, a two shilling piece, commonly known as a florin, they had a shilling a sixpence –

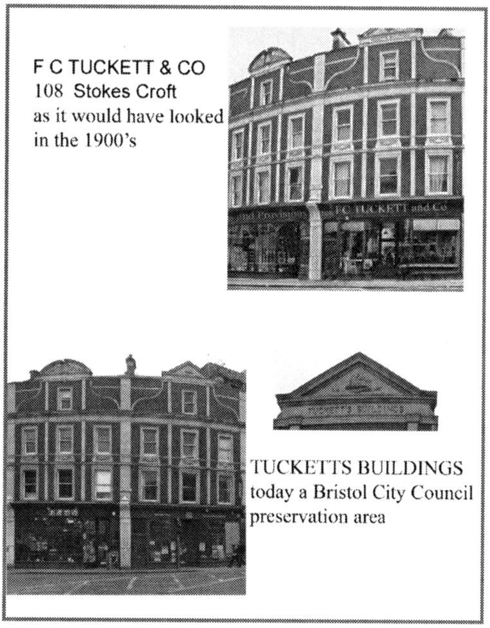
F C TUCKETT & CO
108 Stokes Croft
as it would have looked
in the 1900's
TUCKETTS BUILDINGS
today a Bristol City Council
preservation area

At this point there's an interruption. He would have continued to say there was a silver three-penny piece or bit pronounced "threppnee", a penny, a halfpenny, and a farthing (quarter penny).

So, we know that Art was an apprentice, probably a placement by the QEH, and worked on relative's farms, and then joined the army. It was not compulsory to sign up until the draft of 1916. Was the reason for joining the North Somerset Yeomanry to get a military career or just travel? In the photograph (courtesy Judith Keigley) dated 1911 of three soldiers, Art is the one sitting on a bucket on the right. He was invalided out of the army after a fall from a horse. During his time in the army, he caught typhoid fever, a contagious disease that affected his hearing. One ear hardly worked, but the other was three times as sensitive. It's fortunate that stereo wasn't to be invented for many years!

* * * * *

Here's more background on the city of Bristol, which has been a trading port for a thousand years, and a university city since 1876. "Shipshape and Bristol fashion" is a well-known nautical saying. Samuel Plimsoll (another Bristolian) gave his name to shipping with the Plimsoll line to show the maximum loading limit on ships and boats. The city of Bristol's wealth was built on the wool trade, the brass/zinc works, sugar, shipbuilding, and the tobacco trade. Bristol's Blue Glass is famous world wide today.

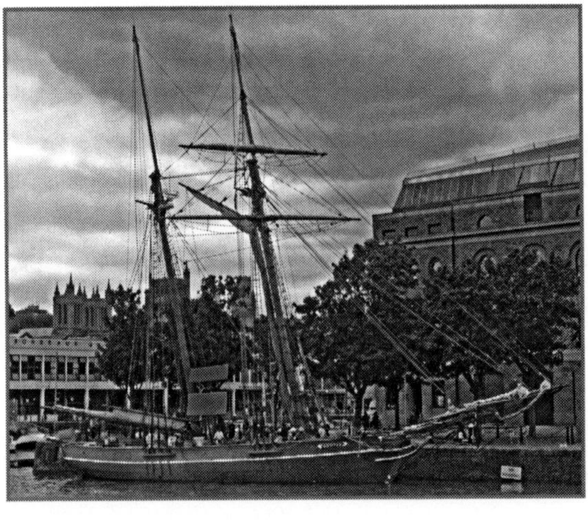

It was also a main port in the slave trade, all because of the very busy docks right in the centre of the city. It was big business, and the rich merchants were made much richer from the trade. In 2007, there was a visit by the sailing ship *La Amistad,* the ship featured in Steven Spielberg's film of the same name to coincide with the exhibition in Bristol called "Breaking the Chains," a £1 million Heritage Lottery Funded exhibition created to mark the 200-year anniversary of the 1807 Act that abolished the British transatlantic slave trade. *Amistad* is about an 1839 mutiny aboard a slave ship that is travelling towards the northeast coast of America. Much of the story involves a courtroom drama about the freeman who led the revolt.

In earlier times, Bristol was a haven for pirates, with lots of hiding places and crew quarters in the Avon gorge.

"Ah ahrr now then, me 'earties shiver me timbers!" (West Country accent again.) The notorious pirate Blackbeard – real name Edward Teach, or Thatch, born Edward Drummond in 1680 in Staple Hill, Bristol – would tie lit gun fuses in his hair to scare his victims. Why is it that the mere mention of pirates turns us into a member of the crew?

Anyway, this would spawn many a story; for example, a pub in King Street on the waterfront called "The Llandogger Trow" (named after a type of ship) was a meeting place for all kinds of sailors. It was in this pub the castaway Alexander Selkirk, who had been marooned on Juan Fernandez Island for five years and rescued by Captain Woodes Rogers, met the author Daniel Defoe. Selkirk became the inspiration for the character Robinson Crusoe. Robert Louis Stevenson was also inspired by Selkirk's story and the character Benn Gunn in *Treasure Island* is said to be based on him, as well as the story *Gulliver's Travels*.

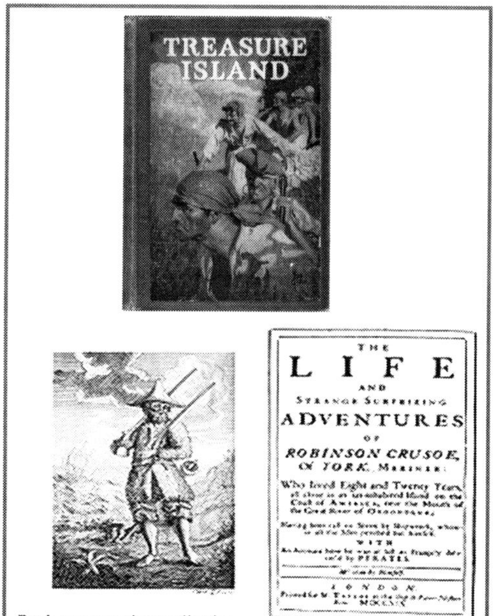

Book covers authors collection

A lot of early settlers left the West Country for the Americas through Bristol, taking with them the folk music and instruments of the British Isles. Apparently, one of the first townships in America was named after Bristol.

Earlier, John Cabot in 1497 had set sail on the *Mathew* from Bristol and discovered Newfoundland. John Cabot (originally Giovanni Caboto, a Venetian seaman) had become a well-known mariner in England, and he came to Bristol in 1495 looking for investment in a new project. On March 5, 1496, Cabot received a letter of authority from King Henry VII to make a voyage of discovery and claim lands on behalf of the monarch. Interestingly, the Caboto family came from the same area as Christopher Columbus (real name Chrisobal Colon). He apparently already had information about the new land.

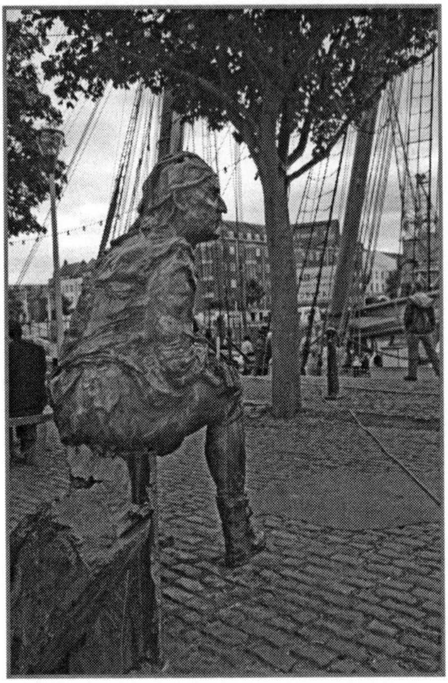

John Cabot statue (Picture Shirley Britton)

A working replica of the *Mathew* was built in1997 and does many trips from Bristol docks where she is moored. Isambard Kingdom Brunel's *SS Great Britain*, the first iron steamship, has also been restored and rests in a dry dock where she was originally built. It is open to the public as a museum and received Museum of the Year award 2007 (as well as fourteen previous awards), and from that very position, Brunel's Clifton suspension bridge can be viewed. Brunel was made city engineer in 1831.

Brunels Clifton Suspension Bridge, the Avon Gorge Bristol. Picture Shirley Britton FDPS ARPS

Some historians say that a rich merchant and politician of Bristol, Richard Amerike (also spelt Ameryk), gave his name to America and not **Amerigo Vespucci, the** fifteenth-century Florentine merchant, and that Amerike helped to fund John Cabot's voyage. (In Bristleze, "Oh aa this is bound fer that John Amerikel's place.") Historians still disagree how America was named.

Bristol featured as an important hub throughout history, with many well-known facts and some not so well-known:

The blue plaque on the wall where the Pricess Theatre stood + statue Bristol

(Authors collection)

Barroud showing his painting

  - The dog on the HMV record label, "Nipper", was from Bristol.
  - Film legend Cary Grant (real name Archibald Alexander Leach) was born in Horfield, Bristol in 1904
  - Russ Conway, a piano player who had quite a few hits with sing-a-long music
  - Author Dick King-Smith, who lives in Bitton, a village between Bristol and Bath has had some of his books, *Babe the Sheep Pig*, *Babe in the City*, and *The Water Horse*, made into Hollywood movies.

- Songwriter Roger Cook, now living in Franklin, Tennessee, just outside Nashville, is currently the only Brit in the Nashville songwriters' Hall of Fame, and, at the time of writing, inducted to the world songwriters' Hall of Fame with song-writing partner Roger Greenaway, both from Bristol.
- John Wesley preached his first sermon to a crowd of poor, uneducated people in 1739 on Hanham Mount, four miles east of the city centre. This event is commemorated with a beacon light that can be seen for many miles.

  It was the preacher connection that was responsible for naming many a town or settlement in the New World. There are twenty-seven Bristols (there were forty before name changes) in the USA. Bristol was where John Wesley ordained his first preachers to go to America, and from that action the American Methodist Church came into being.

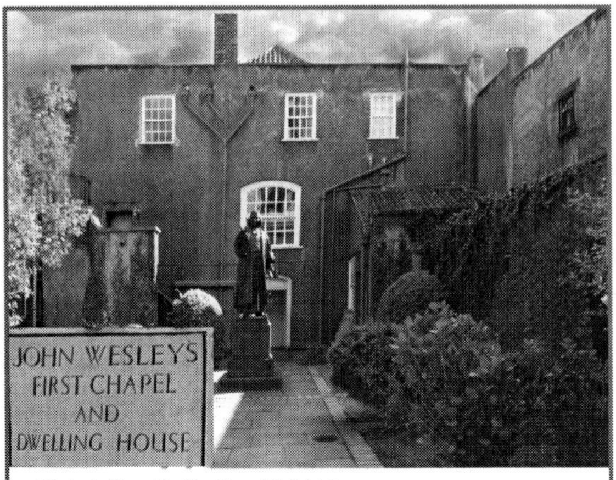

Wesley's Chapel in The Horsefair Bristol

- Let's not forget the world famous BBC's Natural History Unit is based in the city, as is Aardman Animations, (Wallace and Grommet)
- Bristol born comedians, Lee Evans, Justin Lee Collins
- Script co-writer of hit shows *The Office* and *Extras,* Stephen Merchant
- And a new phenomenon, graffiti artist, Banksy
- In 1913, a song was published by Fred E. Weatherly a Lawyer from Portishead near Bristol called "Danny Boy" He added his lyric to an old Irish Air that his sister-in-law had heard commonly known as "Londonderry Air". The song was adopted by Irish people everywhere as an anthem, forgetting that Fred was from Portishead. Fred was a prolific songwriter; his lyric "Roses of Picardy" was a big hit during the First World War

Being a major commercial player whose captains used the trade winds to the West Indies and America, Bristol supplied goods both ways, one being hats. Christy's hat factory was situated in a village called Frampton Cotterell about seven miles outside of the city, and it did a lot of trade through the port of Bristol. In 1820, Christy's built the factory employing over a 120 people in Park Lane, nicknamed Penny Lane because locals would be paid a penny for a bucket of urine used in the leather process. I bet you wanted to know that!

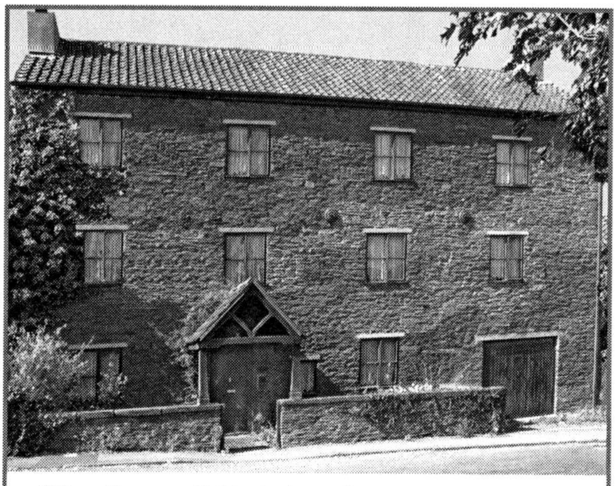

This residence was Christys hat factory Frampton Cotterell in the 1800's authors collection 2009

Frampton Cotterell was chosen because of the plentiful supply of materials. Mercury was used to stiffen the fur; the factory windows were kept closed to eliminate any movement in the fine materials, leaving no ventilation for the toxic mercury fumes. Enter the "Mad Hatter" stories because of the inhalation of fumes by the workers.

The story goes that Christy's made a broad-brimmed, high-domed hat for the sugar cane workers in the West Indies. Mr J. B. Stetson saw this hat and allegedly copied it. As a result of a court case he had to pay Christy's a royalty. It seems, however, the companies wanted to keep the story as quiet as possible with very little written about it at the time; however, correspondence apparently does exist.

The Royal Canadian Mounted Police and the Boy Scout movement also took up the hat. The Stetson ten-gallon cowboy hat was to play a considerable role in Arthur Satherley's future.

* * * * *

Young Arthur would have been used to seeing a very busy port, and the comings and goings of world goods that must have widened his horizons. He dreamed of travelling, especially in light of his very strict family life.

Art got a job as a salesman the newly invented pneumatic tyres and aeroplane fabrics for the Continental Tyre and Rubber Company Great Britain of Hanover, Germany. He carried a sample case with pieces of tyre to help sell the idea that it was not a solid tyre. He travelled the length and breadth of the British Isles, including Ireland, at first on a bicycle, then on a Triumph motorcycle.

A 1912 Triumph Motorcycle. (Authors collection)

Having taken geography at school and learned about Native Americans, he was keen to explore, and there was, of course, the new entertainment of the picture house. The first cinemas opened near where young Arthur lived in Bedminster, Bristol, starting in 1909 with the Town Hall Cannon Street; then in 1911, the Picturedrome East Street opened. Travelling shows would have been hiring halls or putting up tents to show silent "flicks" (they were called "flicks" because of the flickering images on screen) before then. In fact, cinemas were opening in every suburb of Bristol from 1909 onwards, so it would have been easy to go to the pictures for one penny. Such picture houses were nicknamed "penny gaffs".

These establishments would have provided plenty of opportunities for young Art to see silent westerns, despite being a boarder at QEH. Some of those films would have been the short westerns made by Edison's company to show off his new equipment.

Art loved cowboy & Indian stories the visit of this show in Bristol when he was a boy inspired him

By then, Arthur had got hooked on stories of the Wild West,

The visit to Britain of Colonel William F. Cody and his Buffalo Bill Wild West show caused a great stir. The show visited every big city in the British Isles and was a complete sell-out wherever it appeared. The show played Bristol in1891 on Horfield Common in a field that became known as Buffalo Bill's Field. The real Annie Oakley, Sitting Bull, and Frank Butler were just some of the performers in the show, and the re-enactment of Custer's Last Stand must have been quite spectacular.

The Clifton Rugby Club played on the field for a few seasons, and during World War I, it was dug up and used for allotments. After the war, it was reopened as the Memorial Ground. The Bristol Rugby football club and the Bristol Rovers (soccer) football club (nicknamed the Pirates) own the Memorial Ground now. The song that is identified with Bristol Rovers is "Good Night Irene," and Arthur would be the man responsible for recording the song sung by Huddie Leadbetter (Leadbelly). The Wild West Show visited again in 1902 – that time on the Downs.

It was during Arthur's teenage years that Mr Edison's phonograph was making an appearance around the world. It was at one such event, in 1904 at Trafalgar Square, London, where a demonstration of an Edison phonograph – a hand-cranked box on a stick – that Art heard hit song of 1900 "Only a Bird in a Gilded Cage". Art recalled: "I had to listen through a doctor's stethoscope to hear it."This, along with the cowboy stories and films, captivated Arthur.

* * * * *

I spoke again with Art's niece, Doreen Stapleford, and although she didn't know Arthur because he had already left for America before she was born, she remembers how life was in Fraser Street and the stories of how strict Alice and Levi were with the children, making them recite and learn chapter and verse from the Bible before they were allowed to eat. Doreen dug deep into an old box to show me pictures of the time, some of which are reproduced in this book. The house must have been pretty full, what with Alice's father and five children, but according to Doreen, although the house looked small outside, it was big and roomy on the inside, with chickens outside at the bottom of a fairly large garden. To the side of the front door of Number 35 was a brass plaque that is visible in the picture Doreen gave permission to use, which reads "Alice Satherley Dressmaker".

The chapel was built as part of the Windmill Hill development in 1888 and was labelled as "The Mission Rooms" on the plans. There was no specific denomination; it was more of a community place to worship. In some interviews later in America, Art's father was referred to as an Episcopal minister, but this does not hold up because he would have received a stipend (salary) or bursary and been responsible to hierarchy such as a bishop. There aren't any records substantiating this. The Mission Rooms are still there, having been returned to two houses in the late fifties as can be seen in the photographs I took in research.

The confused family rumour mill speaks of Arthur's marriage around twenty years of age. Doreen showed me a picture of Arthur with a girl she thought was called Gladys; she assumed this was his wife. Research into the marriage records of the time revealed no marriage certificate. Of course, if this turned out to be true, it could be one of the reasons why Arthur chose not to talk about this part of his life and made no mention of divorce. It seems no one in the family would speak about the reason Art left, so it died with them.

It's clear that something was brewing in Arthur's life in his early twenties – something that led him to decide on a life-changing experience. Maybe the falling-out with the family was brought about by the young Arthur's going against his parents' wish for him to become a minister and choosing instead to be a travelling salesman.

By 1913, at the age of twenty-four, he took the decision to book a single, third-class passage (steerage) for the sum of twenty pounds on the steamer *Royal George* of the Royal Shipping line, sailing from the Royal Edward Dock, Avonmouth, Bristol, to Montreal, Quebec, Canada. The date was 15 July 1913. Ten days later, Arthur was in America. (The image of the "Royal George" is reproduced courtesy of Colin Momber, historian of Bristol Docks.) Art spoke of the conditions on board the steamer, particularly in steerage class.

The Royal George coming into Avonmouth docks Bristol. Tugboat the Bristolian This is the steamship Arthur sailed on 15th july 1913 picture courtesy Colin Momber

He found the smell of the oil and engines particularly bad. He had taken food provisions with him in order to avoid seasickness.

It was another year before the start of World War I, but since Arthur had been invalided out of the army, it was unlikely that it played a part in his decision to emigrate. I can't imagine what it must have been like travelling alone on an ocean-going steamship to the New World. It was just one year after the *Titanic* had gone down on a similar crossing in 1912.

* * * * *

Montreal in the province of Quebec, Canada, was the destination. Arthur spoke of the beautiful scenery as he travelled along the Saint Lawrence River, seeing log rafts hundreds of feet long, tethered together to make the trip to the mills, and the beautiful houses along the riverbank (he thought they looked like dolls' houses), and the wonderful forested hillsides – sights that he had never seen before.

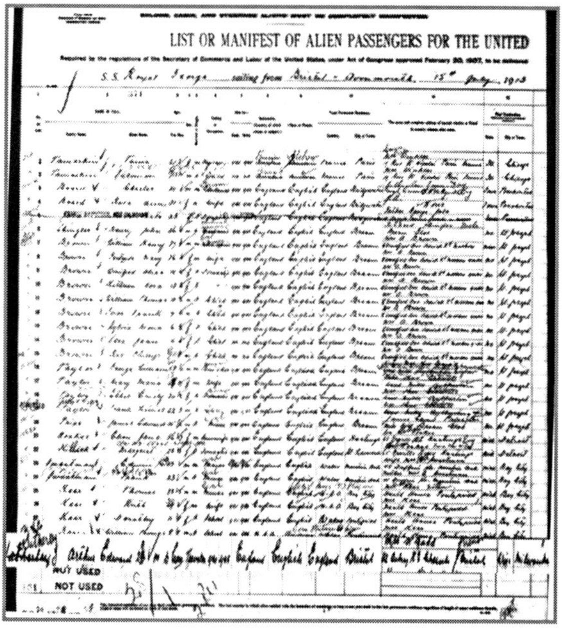

LIST OR MANIFEST OF ALIEN PASSENGERS FOR THE UNITED

NOT USED

NOT USED

He travelled from

Quebec down to Wisconsin in the USA by train. The border crossing card dated 20 July 1913 shows clearly his destination was an address in Milwaukee. To add to the intrigue of Art's personal life, his answer to the question on the border crossing card about next of kin did not contain any family members at all, Bearing in mind that the Satherley family was quite large, this goes to show how big the rift had become. There is just one name on form: Miss S. W. Hudd, "friend" at 112 Aubrey Road, Chessels, Bedminster, a short distance away from the family home in Fraser Street adding more speculation about a family split.

Whatever the reason, the split must have played a large part in the decision to emigrate. Not speaking about the reason for the rumours, as Art never did, leaves room for wide speculation. Was there a marriage or a girl left in "trouble"? The family back home certainly thought so. Art was a travelling salesman and must have had company when he stayed over in so many towns and cities and in the army before that, or was his upbringing in a strict religious family the reason for a clean-living puritanical approach to life? Again, this is all speculation.

* * * * *

In the interview for the Country Music Foundation on 27 June 1974, Art said that he had studied geography at QEH and when he arrived in 1913 he was going to draw maps showing different dialects in America as the settlers migrated across the States, in particular the settlers originating from the West Country in the British Isles. He brought his case of tyre samples with him so he could get work, and then there was his interest in cowboys and Indians.

In the same interview, Art recalled how his personal suitcase was ruined on the voyage but his sample case was intact, and that he almost got arrested within minutes of arriving in Milwaukee for jaywalking. A police officer with an Irish accent let him off, only because he had just arrived. The policeman escorted

Art to the Pfister Hotel, the address he had written to for accommodation and booked before he left England.

Taking his samples, he went to the Cudahy Federal Tyre Company where, "I was hired straight away for $15 a week."

Whilst familiarizing himself with Milwaukee, Art came across a sign for Underwood typewriters. He had become interested in Underwood typewriters in England, so he went in for a chat. The lady in charge realized he had recently come over from England and offered to train him free of charge on using the machine. She told Art that she knew someone who was looking for a well-educated young man. He had something to do with a large local company, his name was Dr Barrett, and she could arrange a meeting, Art agreed – nothing ventured, nothing gained.

At the meeting, Dr Barrett told Art that the company was the Wisconsin Chair Company and later introduced Art to Fred A. Dennett at his home in Sheboygan. The Wisconsin Chair Company had been incorporated in 1888 in Port Washington, Wisconsin, by Dennett. Dennett offered Art to have a look around, and if Art liked what he saw, he could sign on for the next fifteen years at more money than the tyre company could pay.

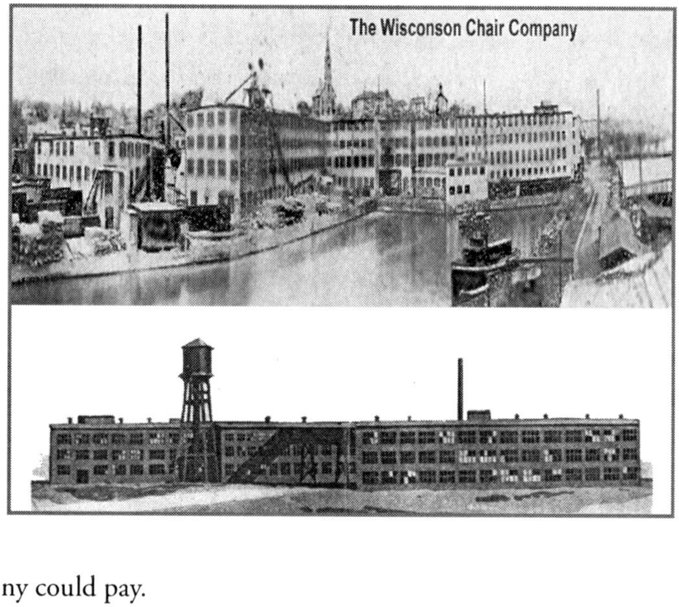

Arthur joined the WCC after his meeting with Dr Barrett and Fred Dennett. His first jobs were at the Port Washington factory and the Grafton, Wisconsin, factory and then at the New London factory, which was called the Wisconsin Cabinet and Panel Company.

In 1917, Thomas Edison was about to purchase the Wisconsin Cabinet and Panel Company to produce wooden cabinets for his C-250 phonographs, and Art was told that Mr Edison had asked for him as assistant and secretary. The company was renamed Edison Wood Products, Inc. In 1927, the company began producing infant furniture (Edison Little Folks Furniture) and today, still in New London, it's known as Simmons Juvenile Products Co. Edison Wood Products Inc. also produced musical cylinders for coin-slot phonographs, which some of the subsidiary companies had started to use. These were forerunners of the jukebox – "juke" being a derivative of an African word "jook", meaning dance. So, jukebox = dancebox.

Art's long association with the Wisconsin Chair Company had begun. They trained him as a lumber grader and as a salesman selling chairs on the road. Art was requested by Mr Edison himself to be a secretary/bookkeeper for the great inventor. As Art said, "I could handle the office work and double-entry bookkeeping. I was trained to do it at school. Just think, there's Mr Edison's signature with Arthur Satherley's signature on many a document, but I didn't care much for just sitting in an office, what we called back home a 'sabs'." (Office clerks would be nicknamed "sabs" short for "shiny ass brigade" because the seat of their trousers would shine through sitting all day!).

For those who are not that familiar with Thomas Edison, he was responsible for inventing the phonograph (Emile Berliner invented the flat disc and the term gramophone), modifying and promoting recorded material, speech, and music, and many other well-known inventions, a total of 1,093. Edison said, "*Of all my inventions, I liked the phonograph best....*"

Art would say that Mr Edison was somewhat of an erratic, eccentric man, and he told the story of a visit to the shop floor by Mr E., who was smoking a large cigar. The waxes, polishes, and varnish would make the atmosphere very volatile, so Mr E had had No Smoking signs installed, but when they were pointed out to the great inventor, he said in a rage, "Take them down 'til I've gone."

* * * * *

I decided to contact Columbia Records in Nashville to get more on Uncle Art. I spoke with Jack Lameier, a record producer, who said, "We still have his picture on the wall, but you should speak to Forrest White."

I rang Forrest and told him that Jack Lameier suggested I talk to him in connection with Art Satherley.

"Well, I was Art's best friend" he said, I told Forrest I was researching the history of country music and that I came from the same city as Art in England.

"Excuse me, Forrest," I said, "but I don't know who you are."

"Oh, of course. Have you heard of Mr Leo Fender?" he asked.

Well, as a guitar player I most certainly had, and I thought, who hadn't? Forrest continued, "Well, I worked with Leo as general manager and right-hand man and friend and designed the Music Man bass with Leo, and I wrote the book Fender, The Inside Story. Art gave me the power of attorney over his business affairs in 1978." Insert Art/Forrest letter

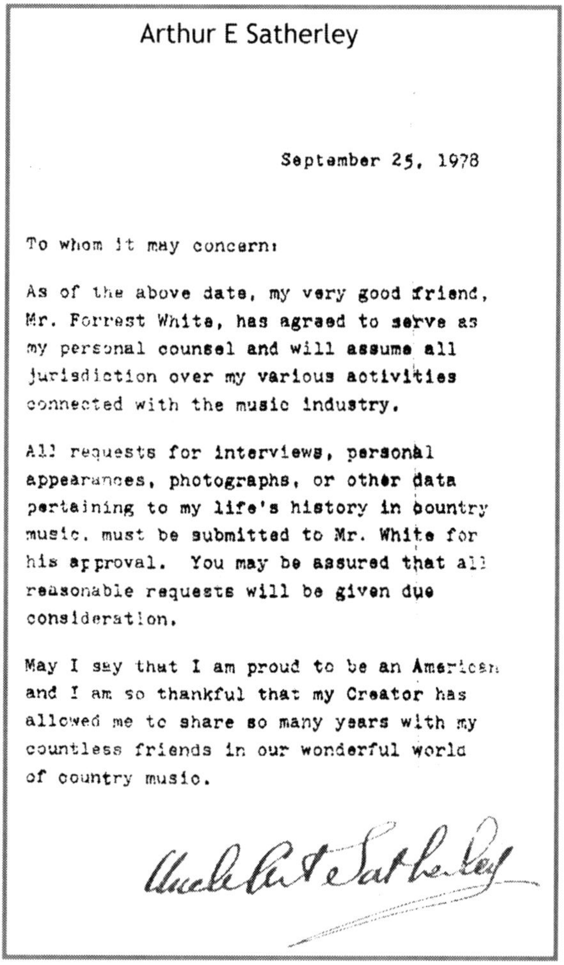

Arthur E Satherley

September 25, 1978

To whom it may concern:

As of the above date, my very good friend, Mr. Forrest White, has agreed to serve as my personal counsel and will assume all jurisdiction over my various activities connected with the music industry.

All requests for interviews, personal appearances, photographs, or other data pertaining to my life's history in country music, must be submitted to Mr. White for his approval. You may be assured that all reasonable requests will be given due consideration.

May I say that I am proud to be an American and I am so thankful that my Creator has allowed me to share so many years with my countless friends in our wonderful world of country music.

Uncle Art Satherley

He continued, "I am about to write a book about Art's life. Seeing that you live in Bristol, perhaps you could contribute something about those early days."

Of course I could, so off I went to do just that. Forrest had been keen and gushing about Art's achievements, and he mentioned Fraser Street so that's where I started. There were more conversations and faxes, and then, out of the blue, a fax came from Forrest quoting his attorney and warning me off collecting information about Art!

This is the fax warning me off

February 1, 1994.

Alan Britton,
Riviera Records,
The Powder Keg,
Chesley Hill,
Wick,
Bristol.
BS15 5NR

Ref: FAX: 0272 374594

Dear Alan:

For your information, Arthur E. 'Uncle Art' Satherley was a very dear friend of mine. He told me that I seemed like a son to him because he had not had children of his own. You will note, by the separate FAX sheet, that he asked me to assume power of attorney for him and to take care of all his personal business relating to the music industry. He asked that his request not be rescinded at his death and, therefore, I am still taking care of any business that is related to his career in all fields of the music industry.

My attorney has advised that I do not divulge any information regarding Uncle Art until I know exactly how it is going to be used. He said it would be best for us to receive direct communication from Bristol City Council as they can inform us of their interest in the life of Uncle Art, and how it relates to them. They should tell us what information they would like to have and how it is to be used. My attorney said that our information should then be forwarded direct to the City Council so that the information could not be used for personal reasons such as a book, video etc., by someone other than a Council member. I hope you understand.

To answer your question in the first FAX. I do not know who is doing the research on the life of Uncle Art. Most everyone connected with music industry in the United States is aware that I am the only one who Uncle Art authorised to make his life story known... Which I am doing in my book.

Yours truly,

Forrest White

I wrote back to point out that I didn't take kindly to his fax and that my interest was ensuring music history was in it's rightful place and that I was waiting for *his* book to be finished so I could get the story told here in Bristol and the whole of the British Isles! I also knew that any one can write a biography on anyone, so I decided to let contact cool down and wait for the book.

I wonder if Forrest, although well intentioned, had warned off others interested in writing a book on Art? We'll never know.

* * * * *

Bristol was almost sistered (same as twinning) with Nashville at that time;

I say almost. Shall I say that if it were a school report it would have read, "The Council could have done better". In the spring of 1994, the Bristol City Council organized a trip to Nashville to finalize the Chet Atkins concert. My assistant John Stokes and I were invited to join a Council official from the Council Leisure Services on the trip. We had VIP treatment as soon as we arrived; accommodation was in the Hermitage Hotel, with many meetings arranged, such as, a meeting with Kelly Brooks, Garth's brother and road manager for a possible gig in Bristol using Ashton Court. It could hold up to a hundred thousand as an open-air event – it would have been where Dolly would have appeared if things had worked out.

We met with a sistering committee. They were looking for a city in Europe to sister with Nashville, and they were really hot on Bristol. John Stokes and I had worked very hard before the trip, and things looked good. This kind of thing could only be dealt with by the City Councils of course, and there's where the sticking points were. It was out of our hands.

Can you imagine what it would have meant to music in our city? Not just country, but all genres of music and trade if it had happened, but it didn't. I don't know why exactly, only to say that I spoke to a spokesperson in the Nashville Chamber of Commerce who said, "They [the Bristol Council] pooh poohed the idea. We weren't good enough." I feel embarrassed to write that. I guess that's why I'm not a politician. Nashville was sistered with Belfast, Ulster, Northern Ireland, later that same year, 1994.

During all this, we paid a visit to Opryland, first with CEO of Gaylord, the company that owned the Grand Old Opry, Mr E. W. (Bud) Wendell. I had first met Mr. Wendell at a gathering at the American Embassy in London to celebrate the inaugural flights of American Airlines' direct flights to Nashville from Gatwick London. Mr Wendell came over to my wife and myself, introduced himself as Bud Wendell, and asked us what we did. We had no idea who he was, but we engaged in conversation saying, "We have been invited because we are putting together a proposal to open a country-music radio station in England."

With this, he handed us a card, adding, "Give me a call, I might be able to help."

That was what led to a meeting in his office at what had been Roy Acuff's old home at Opryland. I was thinking he would be able to help with funding, but what he meant was he could sell us syndicated programmes. The radio station idea was pursued, but it turned out you could get a licence for a station that sounded like all the other stations, but not if it was different.

The evening spent as guests at the Grand Old Opry was a wonderful glimpse into the history of the show. Centre stage was an inlaid round of old stage from the Ryman Auditorium with the main mike. Before the show started, I stood on that spot imagining the people that had stood there looking out at the audience. Because we were invited quests, we were allowed to sit at the back of the stage with the performers in the old tradition, looking out through the musicians. The announcer, who also read the adverts, stood at his WSM Radio lectern and looked out at the 4,000 people watching the show – an unforgettable experience.

The Dollywood resort invited us to visit Pigeon Forge in East Tennessee in the foothills of the Great Smoky Mountains. Again, we were treated as VIPs. We had a great day at that wonderful theme park.

Then, there was the reason we were in Tennessee: to meet Chet at his office in Music Row back in Nashville. It was a rather surreal occasion; his office was quaintly old fashioned. His publicist Clarissa greeted us; her desk looked like it was in a Hollywood office of least thirty years ago.

The telephone was in bits, and Clarissa said, "Chet's repairing it. He says just 'cause it's old it don't mean to say it won't work."

Chet came down the stairs, saying, "I was a child of the Depression; I can't throw nothing away. C'mon up."

We followed him up into his office/rehearsal room. His manager and road manager was already there, and we shook hands and sat down. There followed an awkward silence, during which my eyes wandered around. I felt disbelief at where I was sitting. Then, my eyes fixed on two guitars: a classical guitar and, on a stand, a walnut-brown Gretsch twelve-string Country Gent. It had a note on it that said "to Chet from George Harrison." No-one spoke.

I thought that the Council representative might kick things off, but he didn't, so I said embarrassingly, "Hi guys it's good to be here," probably with a silly grin.

Chet was next in with, "What do you want me to do on the gig?"

I thought, *what an odd question*.

Trying to be humorous, I replied, "Perhaps play guitar a bit."

Everyone had a little smile – or perhaps smirk better described it. Stupidity added itself to my embarrassment but at least it got things going.

Chet came back with, "I don't play things like I do on records all the time."

"I'm sure people in the audience will appreciate whatever you choose to play," I said, thinking, *Here is a legendary guitar player worrying about his performance, wow!*

The rest of the meeting went well, and as we were leaving, Chet stopped me and said, "Are you anywhere near the stones?"

There was an atlas open nearby open to the page of Salisbury Plain.

"You mean Stonehenge? It's about an hour away. I'll take you there when you're over, if there's time" I said.

Chet said, *"OK"* and shook my hand.

* * * * *

Months passed. The wonderful Chet Atkins concert came and went and so did the fiascos. It's a minor miracle the concert took place at all!

Fiasco One. The Council had asked me to help further after the act for the Saturday concert at the harbour had pulled out. I got a panic phone call asking me if I could talk with Nashville for help to fill the night. My team did just that, and to our amazement Carl Perkins, who wrote "Blue Suede Shoes", and Scotty Moore, Elvis's guitar player plus band, would do it! Wow, what a coup! Time went on, and the Council had not signed the contract. After many phone calls, I was told that the sponsors, Lloyds Bank, didn't know who they were, so they vetoed it. That left me in a very difficult position. Only lots of negotiations avoided an international law suit, but it did damage relationships for some considerable time.

Fiasco Two: Just one week before the concert, Columbia Records UK (Chet's label) rang to check that the work permits had been organized. We thought we'd better check with the City Council, because they were handling all contractual matters.

A spokesperson said, "He doesn't need one."

We asked, "Are you sure?"

"Yes," was the reply.

We all looked at one another and said almost in unison "Better check."

A call to the UK Immigration Department clarified the situation: work permits *were* required for Chet and his band. Without them, they couldn't play! And it took six weeks to process work permits – *SIX WEEKS* – we told the Council. PANIC!... the tickets had already been released six weeks late!

Just to explain, our team consisted of me, my wife Shirley, her personal assistant Gill Coleman, and my personal assistant Jon Stokes. Shirley was the founder and chief executive of a large franchise at that time, but she helped us out when we needed it, which was often. Jon said he was going to speak to Immigration again. After a period of time, I can't remember how long, Jon appeared with a smug grin and informed me that it was all sorted.

"What? How did you – ?"

Jon explained, "The guy in Immigration just happens to be a Chet Atkins fan; he will pull out all the stops and will get the permits to Gatwick Airport to hand over to everyone concerned as they come through Passport Control."

And that's what happened. Phew!

While writing this account, I asked Gill what she remembered of it all. Here's what she wrote:

> I don't how to put into words, adequately, what it was like at the time of the Chet concert and the days leading up to it. It was almost like working in a parallel existence to the rest of life. There was nothing tangible you could say. It was more of an atmosphere or aura that transformed the working day into something magic. I would be speaking to Chet's management, Sony Music, or other people in America during the day and then go home to the girls and doing the chores. I remember thinking that, if I had told my neighbours what was happening, they would have thought I was making it up. My father and his sister thought I had got the name wrong when I told them what my bosses were trying to arrange. There were a couple of uncomfortable moments when it looked like all the planning would come to nothing due to duff information, but these problems were resolved by Alan and his PA, and thus the concert took place.

At the concert, I was selling tickets on the gate. The concert was held in the open so my bosses thought that there would be a lot of last-minute ticket sales if the weather was good, and they were right. The things I remember most were the comments of the people (obviously great fans) who almost seemed unable to believe that the great Chet Atkins was performing live in Bristol. On a couple of occasions, I was asked," Why Bristol? Why now?" What had persuaded the greatest guitar picker in the world to just turn up at Lloyd's Amphitheatre? The preconcert advertising had not been good, and therefore it was pretty much luck that anyone knew about it. Thus, the feeling that it was an impromptu gig. When he was on stage, he owned it totally, and it was enthralling,

Another lasting memory was that he looked just like anybody's granddad, and I think that at the time of his visit he had his seventieth birthday. I was charged with ordering the birthday cake (guitar shaped), and it just seemed so surreal. His granddad -next-door looks totally belied his unique talents, his involvement in so many hit songs and with so many singers, and his importance in the world of country music of which I was a big fan. To actually meet and shake hands with the man who helped Dolly Parton on her way for me was a biggy.

It is a time of my life that I will never forget, and whilst I find it hard describe, the feeling of the time will always remain vividly with me. I felt privileged to have been involved.

* * * * *

Jon Stokes's recollections:

A few months earlier, I had hardly known anything about Chet Atkins. Having grown up listening to the Beatles, Stones, Pink Floyd, and Led Zeppelin, my knowledge of country music was fairly limited. Over the next few months, I began to appreciate why Chet was a legend.

Discovering that he had produced and played on Elvis Presley records grabbed my attention. That he had discovered Dolly Parton and the Everly Brothers impressed, but it was the fact that he had influenced so many of my guitar heroes that made me realize just how important this man was. When he asked that we invite a few friends for the show he listed Paul McCartney, George Harrison, Mark Knopfler, and the Edge. Wow.

Meeting him was sheer pleasure, and I have memories that have stayed with me forever, but more so the fact that he was such a nice person, especially if you didn't try to impress him with either your own or a family member's talent with the guitar.

Chet came across as a dapper, old granddad who was totally at comfort with life and his place in it. He displayed no attitude, unless you bored him (which luckily I didn't) and there was still a bit of devilment behind those glasses, not to mention an eye for a pretty lady.

There were a number of highlights of my weekend escorting Chet around the Bristol Area:

- On the golf course at Clevedon where, due to my inability to swing a club, we played a round with a young couple who were mesmerized as Chet recounted tales of his time with Elvis and Dolly Parton without a hint of boastfulness.
- Then after a tribute show in his honour asking me, "Jon, do you walk?" as he explained that he always liked to walk as much as possible everyday. To my amazement he then led me off at a brisk pace up the very steep Park Street for a very tiring walk. Seventy years old and still leading the way.
- Finally, the most enduring memory. After he had conducted a series of interviews with the UK's leading music magazines and noticeably tired and bored from the repetitive questions and worshipping attitudes, he curtly ended the interviews, and as soon as we were alone turned to me and said "Jon I like you. Do you know why? Because you don't play guitar."

Honest, humble, immensely talented, and totally inspirational, that was Chet.

* * * * *

Enough time had elapsed so I gave Forrest a call about the book. Joan, his wife, answered only to tell me that Forrest had died and the book not started. I offered my condolences and put down the phone shocked. *Someone will surely pick up the pieces and run with them*, I thought.

Over the past sixteen years, there has been no sign of a book or television programme (something else Forrest planned to do). A lot of people started with the intention of doing something but can't quite be bothered. Or was it that Forrest had actively stopped others formulating a book, as he tried to do to me? I went with a film producer from Hollywood in 1998 to Joan White's house in Banner, California, near Palm Springs to look at Forrest's office and its contents. Joan had left it just as Forrest used it before his death. She told us we could look at anything but not take it away.

It was a treasure trove of information: early Fender bits and pieces, an early Fender amp, and Music Man drawings. Forrest designed the Music Man bass, a three-quarter size acoustic Fender guitar that Leo had made for Forrest's son

Curtis – a one-off never played except by Forrest, Curtis, and me! Joan asked if I would like to play it. Would I!

She added, "Do you think it's worth anything?"

I suggested she talk to her insurers, as she might be a little surprised at its value. I put it back in its case; there was all the Uncle Art material to look at. We sat and sifted through studio logs, recording contracts of now legends, letters to and from Art, and quite a few cassette tapes of interviews with Art. Wow! What a gold mine: fifty years of information in boxes and folders.

After spending an afternoon and early evening enthralled in Forrest's office, it was time to leave. Joan was waiting for a positive move forward before letting any of the material go. Two weeks passed, and I had word that there was not the financing to move forward with a movie on Uncle Art. Back to the drawing board....

Forrest's son, Curtis, has since donated the material that I had looked through in Forrest's office to the Country Music Hall of Fame and Museum. With the help of Judith Keigley, Art's granddaughter, and John Rumble, senior historian at the Hall of Fame and Museum, I was given full access to all of the material for use in this book.

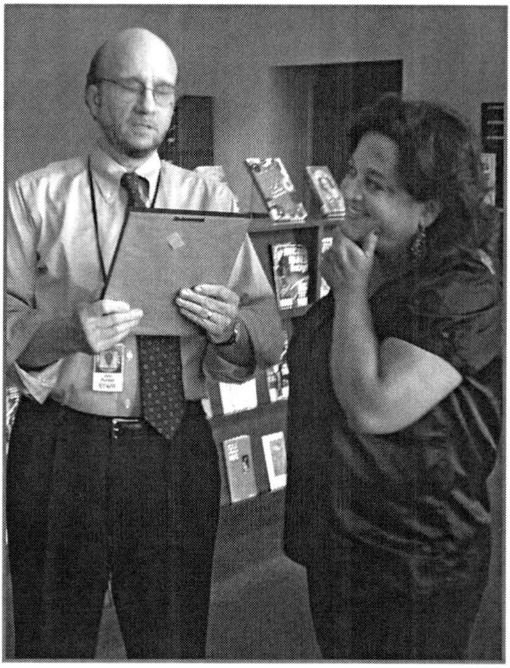

VERSE TWO

AMERICA AND WORLD WAR 1

The year after Art's arrival in the US saw the start of World War I in Europe. America's position was to remain neutral and for three years did just that, but in January 1917, Germany employed unrestricted submarine warfare, meaning that German U-boats would attack any ship that wasn't theirs. So, in April 1917, America declared war on Germany, joining the Allies.

In 1917 and 1918, approximately 24 million men registered for the draft in the United States. These included men born between 11 September 1872 and 12 September 1900. This was every adult male, US citizen or otherwise. Not everyone who registered, however, actually served in the military during World War I. Art's draft registration card, dated 5 June 1917, was filled in

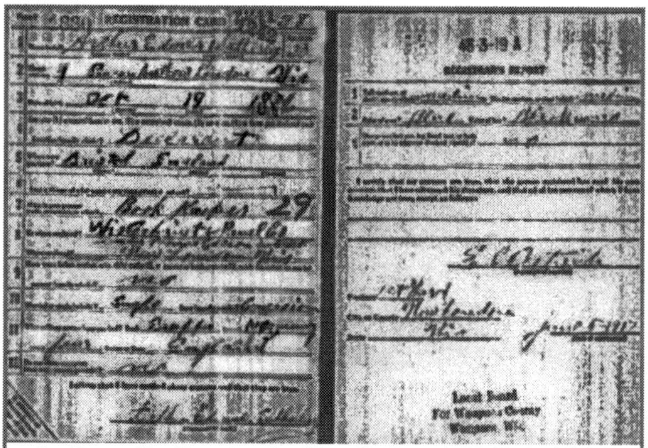

Arthur Satherley's Draft Card U.S.A 1917

with his date of birth as 1886 not 1889. It stated that he was single, worked as a bookkeeper for the Wisconsin Cabinet and Panel Company, and lived in New London, Waupaca County.

I wonder if Art filled in his birth year as 1886 because he had lied about his age when he joined the Somerset Yeomanry. Boys would often adjust their age so they could enlist; however, he was not called up to serve in the U S forces.

* * * * *

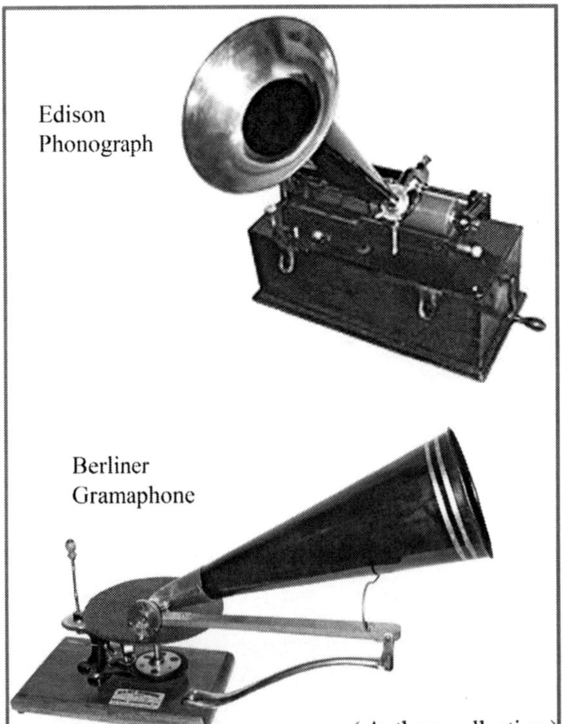

(Authors collection)

The very first record label was established in1888 when Columbia Records was originally set up as a distribution company for Edison's phonographs and the phonograph cylinders. They also sold the product directly to the public, mostly in the Washington, DC, area – thus, the name Columbia derived from the District of the same name where the company headquarters was based. Columbia was the first company to produce pre-recorded cylinders. By 1891, the company had a large catalogue of musical records, and in 1893, cut its ties with Edison and the North American Phonographic Company in order to sell only its own records and phonographs. By 1901, Columbia introduced disc records and these were sold alongside cylinders. Columbia, the Victor Talking Machine Company, and the Edison Phonograph Company were the three main record companies at that time.

Although Art had fallen out with his family back in England, there was

some communication as evidenced by the photographs he sent back home of himself with Gladys Dennick who he was to marry by 1920. In Art's own words, "I was proud to become an American citizen in 1918." There were no plans to return to England, even though his mother Alice died in March of that year. There was no mention in any interviews about his private life.

The Wisconsin Chair Company (WCC) established the New York Recording Laboratories (NYRL) in 1917. Its officers were President J.B. Bostwick; Vice President J.R. Dennett; Treasurer E.J. Barrett; Secretary O.E. Moeser; General Manager M.A. Supper; and Recording Manager A.E. Satherley.

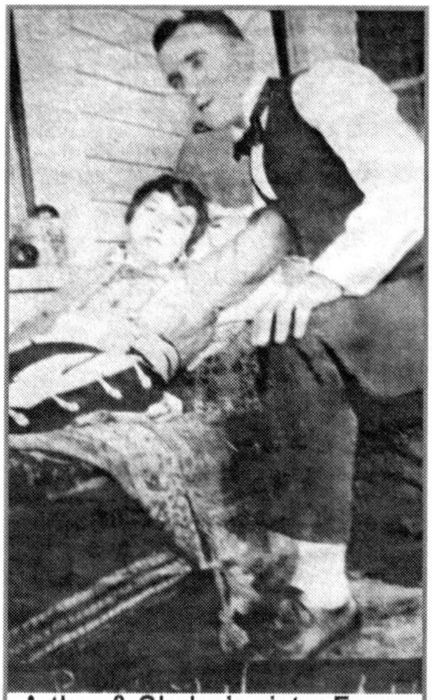

Arthur & Gladys's sister Emma

All of the officers except Art were already board members of the WCC. The United Phonograph Corporation (UPC) was a subsidiary of the WCC and held the trademark of the Paramount record label, which was later passed to the NYRL. The UPC was set up to sell phonographs, playing needles, and anything to do with phonographs.

As recording manager, Art's job was to find the right compounds to make the masters for pressings and the subsequent "mothers", as they called them, to mass produce the records. The quality of sound suffered from surface noise that was not from the recording studio but from the materials used to make the records.

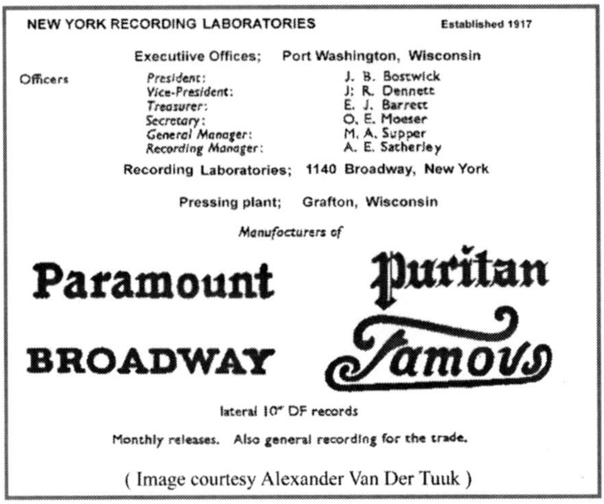
NEW YORK RECORDING LABORATORIES
Established 1917
Executiive Offices; Port Washington, Wisconsin
Officers
President: J. B. Bostwick
Vice-President: J. R. Dennett
Treasurer: E. J. Barrett
Secretary: O. E. Moeser
General Manager: M. A. Supper
Recording Manager: A. E. Satherley
Recording Laboratories; 1140 Broadway, New York
Pressing plant; Grafton, Wisconsin
Manufacturers of
Paramount
Puritan
BROADWAY
Famous
lateral 10" DF records
Monthly releases. Also general recording for the trade.
(Image courtesy Alexander Van Der Tuuk)

Otto Moeser of the Wisconsin Chair Company's board of directors asked Art to come back to Port Washington, just about the time that Art was getting itchy feet. He was ready for the new challenge to help set up the recording business from scratch. (Needles, scratch, excuse the pun!) Edison was involved with the initial set up at the NYRL in some kind of contra back-scratching deal. Before 1925, recording techniques were basic to say the least. There was a horn with stylus attached to a diaphragm that sat straight on the wax cylinder. As the cylinder revolved, a wiggly impression was made in the wax by the sound travelling down the horn, which then in turn exited the stylus. After the "cut" there would be a pile of discarded wax, so the louder the instrument, the better the cut. A band going flat out caused maximum wiggle. Now, as you can imagine, a vocalist had to have lungs of leather and a larynx of steel to rise above the backing, with the drummer being asked to move further and further away from the sound collecting horn.

Just as a side thought, writing about recording techniques reminds me of Stan Freberg's 1955 skit of the "Banana Boat Song (Day o day ay ay o)", during which the bongo player finds the singers on the track far too loud and eventually sends the vocalist outside behind a door where he can hardly be heard and with the door locked. The bongo player says "Yeah, cool man." If you have never heard that track, have a listen – it's hilarious. I bet if you were a fly on the wall back in those early studios you could tell some tales. Anyway, I digress.

Duplication was interesting: there was none. So, the song would have to be performed over and over, sometimes with a bank of recorders. Eventually, a way to duplicate and mass-produce the recordings was found. The lateral cutting system meant metal masters could be made, then mother copies from that master and stampers for duplication.

* * * * *

Here is a firsthand account of recording by bandleader Paul Whiteman. – Excerpt from *Memories in Wax: Records for the Millions* (New York: Hermitage Press, Inc., 1948)

> *The acoustics were far from perfect in the studios of those days.* In the middle of the room stood a tower, made up of four ladder-like supports tapering to a narrow point. This pylon was about eight feet high. Four recording horns, which looked like megaphones, were attached to the pylon in the form of a four-leaf clover. Four or five of us gathered around each horn so that we'd be close enough for the stylus (recording needle) to pick up the sounds we made.
>
> My boys had to be athletes. When a solo passage was to be

Recording session recording horn straight to wax

Recording session multiple horns to wax

played, the musician would move up close to the horn and play directly into it. Then he had to back out in a hurry, dodging out of the way of the next man who was hurrying toward the pylon.

We had to start from the beginning to learn the best methods for successful disk-making. We discovered that ordinary drums could not be made to record properly. The tympani and snare drum were all right, but the bass drum created a fuzzed-up effect when other music was going. We found that the banjo, which until then had been kept in the background and had been heard hardly at all, was effective as a tune drum.

The string section used "Stroh" violins, which were strange-looking affairs totally unlike the string instruments you know. The Strohs were little more than fingering boards, with a horn and tone box attached to the metal bridge. These instruments made raspy noises, like the sounds you used to get from one of the old-time phonographs with the "ear-trumpet" amplifiers, but they were more effective than ordinary violins in vibrating the stylus.

Columbia had started producing flat discs alongside cylinders by 1901. They had started full mass production of the double-sided flat disc with a tune on each side. A logo showing a pair of sixteenth value notes (the famous "magic notes") was used internationally used, and it is still in use today. Nineteen twelve saw the end of new cylinder recordings at Columbia, although back-catalogue cylinders were available for a few years after that; the 78s were now the preferred medium.

A metal master (mother)

The 78 got its name because it spun at seventy-eight revolutions per minute. It was made of a brittle shellac resin

– shellac was a sticky residue secreted by an insect and imported from India. Records made this way were around well into the 1950s. At first, the rpm speed was not at all standard and could be anything between sixty-five and one-hundred rpm, and depending on the record player could sound a bit like Mickey Mouse or someone on helium (too fast and high) or a long, drawn-out, low sound like a hippo on Prozac (I couldn't think of any other simile). The speed was chosen as a compromise among playing time, groove size, needle size, needle wear, and fidelity. There were no electric motors yet, so the recorders and players were propelled by a wound-up spring, and the speed was governed by weights. Seventy-eight rpm was an average.

Now here's a technical bit: when sound was being added to moving pictures, a way of synchronising the two had to be found. By this stage, electric motors were driving the spools of film over the lamp of the projector. Mains electricity has a fixed frequency of alternating current, known as "a/c". Nicola Tesla was the inventor of a/c electricity and adamant as to the frequency. He explained that the planet has a frequency (now called the Schumann cavity resonance) and the a/c mains should be a derivative or a harmonic of that frequency, which he fixed at sixty cycles per second for North America. So, with a synchronous motor an exact speed could be worked out – for instance, with the rpm of 3600, a ratio reduction 46:1 = 78.26rpm.

In England, the boffins chose to ignore Tesla and fixed the a/c current at 50cps (by the way cps is now called Hertz or Hz for short). The calculation for the speed using the same reduction ratio of 46:1 from 50hz at 3600rpm = 77.92rpm; so 78 was set as the standard. Similar calculations can be used to get 33.33rpm for later vinyl LPs and 45rpm for singles.

You can now unglaze your eyes, take a deep breath, and relax, but only briefly. Why? Well, here's another slightly digressing tale of an inventor from Winterbourne (you guessed it), Bristol. Harry Grindell-Mathews, born in1880 invented the talkies, and he demonstrated his invention in the ballroom of the New Passage Hotel, Severn Beach, Pilning, Bristol in 1921. Sadly the hotel is no longer there – I say sadly because I played that venue many, many times as a young singer/guitar player (shortened to git/voc on bill boards).

Anyway, it is purported that he invented everything! Telephones, wireless, a death ray, and a sky projector to project images in the sky. Intrigued? He's worth a Google, and he did work for Warner Brothers later on as a consultant on movie sound. The full story can be found in a book by Jonathon Foster called *The Death Ray: The Secret life of Harry Grindell Mathews.*

* * * * *

The New York Recording Lab was based in Grafton, Wisconsin, not in New York as the name suggested. The Lab was installed in a barn-type building already owned by the WCC and fitted with ten presses to mass produce records.

1st record Grafton June 29. 1917. Courtesy Alexander Van Der Tuuk

At the height of its success, thirty to forty presses were in operation producing 2,100 to 2,800 records a day.

Arthur Satherley was responsible for the pressings; the first pressing was completed just before the official opening in July 1917. From the handout it can be seen that the NYRL had four labels: Paramount, Broadway, Puritan, and Famous;

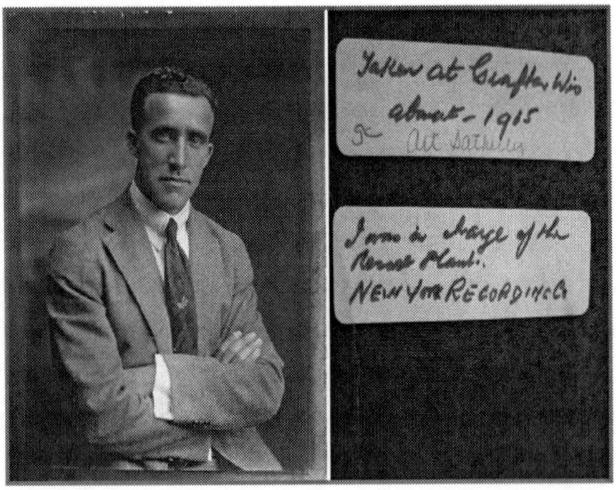

They also pressed for the Black Swan label. The Grafton plant did not have recording facilities unil later but used a studio in Flatbush, Brooklyn, New York that was suggested by Art. Maybe that's where the name came from.

It took Art two

years of trial and error to perfect the compounds to make the records. The compounds consisted of clay, which came from Cornwall, England; cotton flock; gum Arabic; shellac and mineral black or lamp black. By leaving out black and adding other colours, Art was able to create different coloured discs, even a marble effect, but it put the cost up so they were only used as samples. Art held on to the secret mix for twenty years. He even tried to patent the coloured discs, but found you can't patent a colour.

Uncle Art created coloured 78 discs whilst at the Grafton pressing plant here is a multi-coloured example

"original record is the property of John Tefteller and Blues Images. www.bluesimages.com Used with permission."

NYRL imported masters from Europe, because the Grafton area was originally colonized by German, Polish, Swedish, and Flemish immigrants, so the European music would have a market. In fact, Grafton was earlier called Hamburg, then Grafton, then changed to Manchester, then back to Grafton, and is still a relatively small town. Art even brought in masters from London.

By 1920, Art had married local girl Gladys Dennick, who he called his "rosebud" and was living with her and his in-laws in Ozoukee County. Art was thirty-three years old, and Gladys was twenty-four. In interviews over the years, Art never made a reference to his first wife, except for a passing comment in a interview that Douglas B. Green did for the Country Music Hall of Fame 27 June 1974. When asked "Were you ever based in Chicago for a time?" Art replied, "I based myself anywhere! I didn't care." [And here is a rare passing reference to his wife and what may have happened].) " My home – I can imagine I'd have been a very poor married man; I was never home. I was on the road all the time. In fact, I was on the road in England! I'm a born travelling man, and I'd do it all again tomorrow. But I was a very tired man when I gave up Columbia. Very tired, Very tired, anyway I'm glad I did it."

* * * * *

The phonograph produced by WCC had not been as successful as hoped, even when the company gave away records with each sale, as can be seen in a newspaper ad from 1917.

In 1920, a record by Mamie Smith called "Crazy Blues" on Okeh was the first blues hit with a black jazz backing band. This caused a frenzy of recording the blues. Paramount could not afford to pay the artists much money, and they could not break in with the dealers already franchised to Columbia or Victor records. So, Art went on the road as a salesman, with his office in New York, to find a way of marketing this category of music, which was called "race music".

Nineteen twenty one was the year that Paramount started pressing records for Black Swan records. Alberta Hunter and Ethel Waters sang blues songs written by other songwriters that were categorized as "city blues". To sell more records, Art visited county fair show grounds in an attempt to get the records directly to the people. He had no trouble selling them; in fact, in his own words, "The demand was so great that the records were 'eaten up.' "

There was a great cultural change taking place: African-Americans were migrating from the southern states northwards, and Chicago was seeing a huge influx, which of course was reflected in music. The city became second only to New York for new studios and music publishers. The *Chicago Defender*, a newspaper primarily aimed at Afro-Americans, actively encouraged them to locate in the area. Paramount's main catalogue by then consisted almost totally of race music, and by 1923 Art was using Marsh Laboratories studio in South Chicago, Chicago was by then the centre for the blues and attracting more and more musicians songwriters and singers. Alberta Hunters

Paramount's hit "Down Hearted Blues" was advertised as "the most popular record ever released" and she was the first Blues artist ever to appear in Port Washington. This happened because the WCC headquarters were based there.

Marsh laboratories South Chicago. (Authors collection)

Art met with Moeser and Supper back at NYRL headquarters with a suggestion how to improve sales. The *Chicago Defender* was already selling furniture by mail order. Art's idea was to sell directly to the public though agents hired by advertisements. There were no restrictions on who could be an agent,. They could just take ten records, and pay the post office $4.50. The records would be sent from NYRL with a twenty-four hour delivery promise. The newspaper advertising campaign got underway, costing a $1,000 for a full-page; it was decided to place ads in the *Defender*, *The Baltimore Afro-American*, *The Pittsburgh Courier* and *The Norfolk Journal and Guide*. The scheme took off, agents were earning good money, and Paramount extended its advertising to find dealers. They were already the market leaders in race music. In just one year, between 1922 and 1923, Paramount had a thousand agents and dealers and were able to challenge Columbia and Victor.

Ad published in Talking Machine World. November 1919

Art's office was in New York. According to the 1930 census, Gladys and he were living on W.140th Street New York. Art would visit Philadelphia once a week but the territory he covered was from Nova Scotia to Florida. In his travels he would always be on the look out for songs.

As Art travelled more into the South looking for more people and businesses to become agents and dealers. He would seek out and attend country fairs, dances, and religious gatherings, even funerals – anywhere people were making music. He found that "slipping a $10 bill onto the collection plate or straight to the pastor was a good way of being included into the notices before or after the sermon". This would get the attention of the country folk that he was looking for singers and players. Art's ear was now getting fine-tuned to what was commercial. The travelling Art had done back home on his motorcycle through England Ireland Scotland and Wales selling tyres, introduced him to the people's music on a wide scale: the airs and ballads of England; the diddly music and dance of Ireland; the mouth music and bagpipes of Scotland; and those wonderful Welsh choirs.

All of what Art called "music from home" was here in the southern states, now being mixed and interwoven with black African and European folk music. The indigenous music of these countries had come together to form a recipe that was changing popular music forever. The "by the people for the people" approach taken by Art and Paramount was gaining more ground.

The piano company E. E. Forbes of Birmingham, Alabama, which covered thirteen states with its piano business, became a dealer. Not all the dealers were that big; many of them were small stores selling everyday items, but there were hundreds of them and the NYRL pressing plant was at full stretch to supply all the outlets. Paramount would sell masters to companies wanting to start their own catalogue, and such a deal was done with America's largest mail-order company Sears Roebuck. A different take of a hit on Paramount would be issued by Sears Roebuck, and the artists' or band's name changed. This was common practice by companies buying masters only.

Black Swan's parent company, the Fletcher Record Company, went bankrupt in 1923, so Harry C. Pace of Black Swan entered into negotiation with Paramount about taking over or merging the label and its artists. When this happened, it put Paramount way ahead of its rivals.

During World War I, radio was used for the first time. This newly invented technology was taken over by the American government. As in any war, technology moved forward quickly, and it was planned to release radio back to the private companies after the war but the US Navy had other ideas.

It had quietly bought coastal broadcasting stations, but the government ordered them returned to the original owners. Radio was up and running. The first commercial station licence was awarded on 2 November 1920 to the Westinghouse company in Pittsburgh, Pennsylvania. The call sign was KDKA, and its slogan was "the Pioneer Broadcasting Station of the World."

All of this could happen because of the advancements in electronics. Wireless first appeared as the wireless telegraph in which a spark jumped a gap, the length of which was determined by an operator with a keypad (Morse Code). This invention attributed to Guglielmo Marconi, an Italian inventor who, incidentally, had carried out experiments from Portishead on the coast of the Severn Estuary just a few miles from Bristol. However, history shows that Tesla had already patented the use of radio waves.

The most important advance was the invention of Ambrose Fleming, who realized that Edison's light bulb could do more than light a room. It was the thermionic valve, also called the vacuum tube, or electron tube, tube, or just plain valve, depending on where you live, that changed things. American inventor Lee De Forest moved things on even farther. The tube could amplify or switch (oscillate). A microphone produces a very small signal, but the tube could make the signal much bigger – big enough to drive a speaker. (That was an Idiot's Guide to electronics.)

The first patent for the loud speaker was by Ernst Siemens from Germany in 1877, and the microphone was adapted from the telephone invented by Alexander Graham Bell, or was it? Well, that's another story.

Recording studios were still all acoustic, but these advancements in electronics were about to make a big difference in the way sound made it to the disc. The first microphones were carbon types and were not at all successful in the studio. They were OK for a telephone, but they had only a narrow dynamic range and were temperamental during temperature changes, so many studios continued to use acoustic horns.

Electric motors were now available and fitted to the disc cutting equipment to drive the turntable, replacing the lead weights and springs or in some cases concrete blocks on the outside of the buildings that were wound up and released slowly on wire rope. It was just a matter of time before microphones would be the norm, and recording engineers would have to relearn their jobs.

The first radio equipment had a crystal diode with a few other components to tune the circuit. Add headphones and a battery, and there you are. Enter the valve, tube, this "thingy", a bottle with no air in it glowing dimly in a corner with a few friends doing the same but this time with a speaker. Now every one could hear, "C'mon every one gather round the radio and watch the valves glow." I can hear Granny say, " This new fangled 'lectric will never catch on" or "Give me a battery every time." Then, Great grandpa saying "Never mind batteries, you can't beat an oil lamp". Just think – if it wasn't for Edison we'd all be watching TV in the dark!

Thermionic tube/ valve 1920's (Authors collection)

Electrification did not take place overnight out in the backwoods. Some people were positively "agin it" (Granny again) and would not allow the cables in.

The record companies could not foresee how important radio was going to be. They could only see the negative from their point of view - fewer record sales – because you could tune in and listen for nothing. Radio stations were getting artists to sing and play live and not pay them!

"We're all doomed", was the thinking. Even Art with his forward thinking was not sure where this was going, but he was more worldly in his outlook and saw this development as just another opportunity.

The not-for-profit American Society of Composers, Authors and Publishers (ASCAP) was established in New York City on 13 February 1914 to protect the copyrighted musical compositions of its members. In 1919, ASCAP and the Performing Right Society of Great Britain signed the first reciprocal agreement for the representation of each other's members' works in their respective territories. Radio stations were appearing like mushrooms, linking city and rural communities alike.

Early on, founding member of ASCAP Victor Herbert brought a lawsuit against Shanley's Restaurant for refusing to pay royalties. The fight took two years and went to the Supreme Court. ASCAP won. Justice Oliver Wendell Holmes wrote the decision of the Court: "If music did not pay, it would be given up. Whether it pays or not, the purpose of employing it is profit and that is enough."

ASCAP issued the first radio licence to KFI in Los Angles on 1 November 1923, and others quickly followed, proving that the time of constant change was here to stay.

Technically, radio was leaping ahead of the studios and often had studios attached to main control rooms to record artists or go live. Music was filling the airwaves.

It was around this time that the American Federation of Musicians (AFM) was formed. James Petrillo became president of the Chicago local of the musician's Union in 1922 and was president of the AFM from 1940 to 1958. He continued being the prime force in the union for another decade. In the 1960s, he was head of the union's civil rights division, which saw to the desegregation of the local unions and the venues where musicians played.

Petrillo dominated the AFM on with absolute authority. His most famous actions were banning all commercial recordings by union members from 1942 to 1944 and again in 1948 to pressure record companies to give better royalty deals to musicians; these were called the Petrillo Bans. In an interview on a radio programme in 1978. When Art was a guest on KCLA with steel guitar player Leon McAuliffe, he said of Petrillo; "Petrillo wouldn't let any of the country musicians join the union, so I said we don't want you joining ours!" But of course later on they did join the union because their records were so successful.

The telephone company, AT&T, with its large research facilities had embraced and developed the new electronics, using it in telephone repeater stations to boost signals. One of their subsidiaries, Western Electric, had developed a electronic recording system for studios and players for the consumer. This was built under licence by Victor in1924 and called the

Orthophonic, (sounds a bit like a piece of medical equipment to me: "Now hold still whilst we insert the Orthophonic"). Orthophonic apparently means "straight sound", meaning better dynamics, frequency response, and higher fidelity. The slowness of the record industry to adapt to change has been seen all too clearly recently with the Internet, but I guess they will get there in the end. Meanwhile, "back at the ranch", television wasn't far away, where will it all end?

Until now, Arthur Satherley had been known as a record man, starting from the ground up and at the sharp end of the business, identifying the peoples music and getting it to them, through advertising and word of mouth. Sales of phonographs had peaked, the Roaring Twenties jazz and the blues kept it there. Art had his first million seller during this time; well, the term million seller is questionable; hit or sold a lot being closer. It was a gospel song by the Norfolk Jubilee Quartet called "My Lord Gonna Move This Wicked Race" (1923).

Art said in an interview with David Ferrell for the *Santa Ana Register*,

> I had an office in New York but I was never there. I was on the road. I had two secretaries; they knew where I was at all times, so they knew where to sent my checks (cheques). They would say "Art's freelance", and as long as I kept sending them records, they left me alone. I never followed a pattern. I

A rare photograph Art in his office 1140 Broadway New York 1923. He was seldom there.
Used with permission Judith Keigley and CMHF

was blessed with people who understood what I was doing. I must have cut eighty to ninety thousand records that way.

Art was trying to get the Wisconsin Chair Company to embrace the new recording technology, but the managers either wouldn't or couldn't. He wanted them to invest in the new portable recording equipment so he could go deeper into the hills and backwoods of the South to record more songs by unspoiled singers, real country folk, or hillbillies. The main distribution company's people in New York thought these recordings were absolute rubbish. They were so detached from rural America, let alone any music that might be happening there, that they told Art to get out and hit the road. So, he did just that! He knew what the people wanted. (Art detested the term "hillbilly"; he saw it as derogatory).

With his request denied, Art felt that, after fifteen years working for the WCC, it was time to move on. This was 1928.

The QRS company was formed in 1900 to make piano rolls ("pianola" also known as auto piano) and wanted to enter the record business. The company offered Art the job of setting up a label, but the quality was poor and he didn't stay long. He joined Plaza Music owned by Consolidated Film Industries (CFI), which processed movie film negatives. The purchase of the American Record Corporation (ARC) was arranged by CFI's Herbert Yates.

The Columbia Gramophone Company was also acquired, exactly how this came about isn't clear, even in the book by Gary Marmorstein, *The Label, The Story of Columbia Records* (Avalon Publishing Group), which states, "How Columbia ended up in the hands of Herbert Yates is a matter of some dispute." Yates promoted Art to vice president in charge of country dance and folk music. As A&R (artist and repertoire) man, Art could continue

Detail from the Country Music Hall of Fame diorama honoring Columbia Records A&R pioneer Arthur E. Satherley. The miniature scene depicts Satherley conducting a "field" recording session in the late 1920's. The figure of Satherley is approximately eight inches tall. Used with permission CMHF

to record those raw performances as he travelled, not with horn and wax equipment but with the new, but still primitive, electronics. This was the beginning of Art's twenty-year association with Columbia Records.

* * * * *

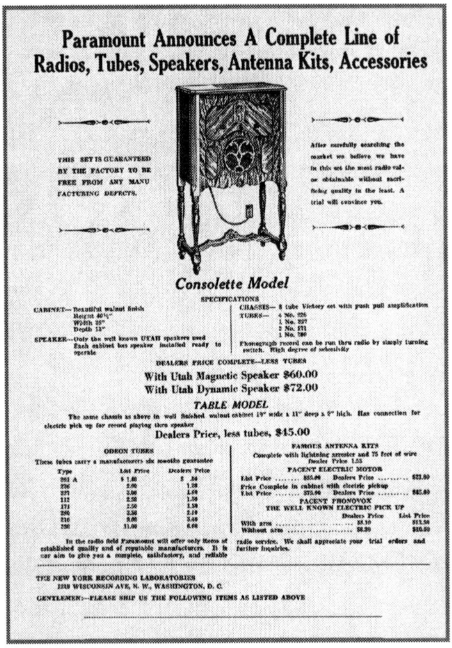

The impact of radio was being felt. The radio revolution had begun, and stations were springing up in every town and city. The National Life and Accident Insurance Company opened its radio station on the fifth floor of its downtown building in Nashville in 1925 with the call sign WSM ("We Shield Millions"). On 28 November 1925, they launched a programme called *Barn Dance* that presenter "Judge" George D. Hay had brought with him from station WLS in Chicago.

The seventy-seven-year old fiddler, Uncle Jimmy Thompson, from Tennessee joined the show, and in 1926, Uncle Dave Macon, a Tennessee banjo player, became its first real star.

The audiences attending the show were growing in number, and the studio on the fifth floor became too small, so in 1934, they moved out to Hillsboro to a theatre now known as the Belcourt. The show by then had been renamed by announcer Judge Hay, in a passing remark he made while taking a handing over from NBC's *Classical Music and Grand Opera Hour* to *Barn Dance* by saying, "Friends, from an hour of Grand Opera we are coming down to earth with three hours of *Grand Old Opry.*" The name stuck, and the show still is called *The Grand Ole Opry.*

With the audience numbers still growing, the station moved in 1936 to the Dixie Tabernacle in East Nashville, and again moved to the War Memorial Auditorium. In 1941, the Opry moved to the Ryman Auditorium, formally the Union Gospel Tabernacle. In 1974, the show moved out to the new Opryland complex. When I visited the Ryman before it was refurbished, it reminded me of the Wesleyan chapels back home in England.

WRR Texas was already on air in 1921, whilst over the border in Mexico, radio stations came on line nicknamed "border blasters" because they upped the power of their transmitters – one claimed a transmission power of a million watts – and covered the whole of North America without regulations. Some people in Texas complained they could hear the stations in their fencing wire and in their teeth because of the powerful transmissions! American regulations would not allow recorded music to start with, and the power of the station could not exceed fifty thousand watts, the stations were all AM transmissions – FM radio had yet to be invented. In 1937, W1XOJ was the first FM radio station granted a construction permit by the Federal Communications Commission (FCC). On 5 January 1940, FM radio was demonstrated to the FCC for the first time.

* * * * *

The challenges the record companies were facing because of radio were about to take second place to the stock market crash of 29 October 1929, "Black Tuesday", which was the start of the Great Depression. Virtually over night, the bottom fell out of the recording industry, in particular the New York Recording Laboratories' label Paramount. The company didn't have Art Satherley any more, and as the mail-order business dried up, it found it more and more difficult to survive. Just three short years, later the doors at the Grafton plant closed for good. The Wisconsin Chair Company kept going through the Depression by making furniture. The whole story is told in Alexander Van Der Tuuk's book *Paramount's Rise and Fall* (Mainspring Press). 2003.

The rise in popularity of hillbilly music or country music, as it became known during this time was due to Art out there recording and signing acts, as well as Victor's Ralph Peer, and the ever-growing "*Grand Old Opry*" radio show.

Speaking of Ralph Peer, the sessions he recorded in Tennessee in 1927 created "The Birthplace of Country Music". It was in a town called... wait for it... Bristol. Half the town is in Tennessee, and across Main Street the other half is in Virginia! Was there possibly some moonshine around when that happened, I wonder? (I'm only kidding.) So much was opening up in this new industry that many recordings had been made in various locations before that date, but does it matter? Ralph Peer certainly attracted singers and players to the sessions. These people were not well off by any means, and attracted to possible payment for singing and playing a few songs, they came from miles around. The most famous names were the Carter Family and Jimmy Rogers.

The
Bristol Sessions
Historic Recordings from
BRISTOL, TENNESSEE, featuring
The First Recordings By
The Carter Family · Jimmie Rodgers
and twenty · one additional artists
"the single most important event in the history of country music."
Johnny Cash

There's not too much known about the founding of this particular Bristol – it would appear not to have any links to Bristol UK – but seeing that Bristol Tennessee, was started by religious folk, could I offer up the suggestion that John Wesley's famous connection with Bristol UK had some thing to do with the naming, perhaps? Maybe – just a thought.

There are plans to forge closer links between the two Bristols, not just dignitaries from councils, etc. but musically as well. That'll be great: "Bristol to Bristol" – a great title don't you think?

Rural America was already in deep trouble before Black Tuesday. Agriculture had become the way of life for many families on the Great Plains, once called the Great America Desert because of the lack of surface water. Technology and invention had created a way of growing crops. Deep ploughing had been used over and over and had removed the natural grasses that had held the soil in place. With the government encouraging farming to feed the ever-growing population, loans were made to people to build homesteads and farm the land, and so the Great Plains were transformed. But, and it's a very big "but", the topsoil had become unstable and was about to turn into the Great American Dust Bowl.

The topsoil that would have remained in place with the roots of the grasses now took off in the wind, and big dust storms swept across the land with Oklahoma being particularly badly hit. Jim Rushing and Ricky Skaggs wrote a song in the 1980s called "A Hard Row to Hoe"' recorded by Ricky

Skaggs, on an album called *Love's Gonna Get Ya, Verse Three of the song sums it up.*

V3. The Final blow it came this morning in a note from the F H A
There'll be no more extensions on the note that I can't pay
They're gonna sell my farm at auction lock stock and cotton bow
And that leaves my wife and babies with a hard row to hoe

The appetite for country music was growing. The lost love and pain songs captured the imagination of people. Individuals realized it wasn't just their plight but others too, gained solace and comfort, knowing they weren't alone.

Art, having grown up in Windmill Hill and his relatives being Somerset farmers in the West Country of old England, would have felt the difficult way of life of the ordinary rural people, knowing the strong sense of community from his youth. He would talk of shucking the corn, cutting corn with a scythe, and sleeping under thatched roofs on dirt floors or flagstones – something we see as a picturesque setting today.

Traditional West Country thatched farm cottages. (Authors collection)

This personal experience was the driving force behind his actions: the continuous travelling to source and record the people's music, that music from home, hearing those different dialects, and then there was his plan to make maps of the movement of the early settlers from the east coast across America.

*****

Because of the plight of the farmers' claims and the counterclaims, the whole farm claims cases carry on unresolved to this day from 1933. In more recent times, country megastar Willie Nelson ran into difficulties with the Internal Revenue Service, after some bad advice. Willie founded Farm Aid in 1985. Nelson, one of the biggest earners as a songwriter and performer in country music, found himself with a $16 million tax bill. All of his possessions were sold at auction to pay money owed to the IRS, but Willie's fans bought it all and gave everything back to Willie. Nelson did a deal with the IRS by way of making an album, and the proceeds went to them. The IRS collected $3.6 million from the album called "Who'll Buy My Memories? (The IRS Tapes)" And the remaining debt? Willie agreed to pay only (only!) an additional $9 million over the next five years. This deal meant that instead of $16 million owed, only $12.6million was paid, a reduction of $3.4million, underlining the amount of money now flowing through the record business.

As the Depression took hold, agriculture and the stock market were in free fall. Unemployment and homelessness were going through the roof: one in six Caucasians and one in four African-Americans were out of work. That's a rise from 3.2 percent to 24.9 percent unemployment in three years, which was echoed internationally.

Columbia stopped production of records for a while: The Victor Company stopped producing Phonographs, concentrating on Radio, manufacturing both radios and programmes for the radio,

The great music city of Chicago found its music business almost totally collapsed, with musicians burning rubbish in the streets to keep warm, and the same being seen in every big city. People started looking for some escapism, gathering around radios listening to their favourite music and for those with a little money, the movies. This entertainment lifted the spirit and the morale to help people through those terrible times, a decade in all, but forever etched in their memory.

In the years between the late 1800s and 1929, a new industry had begun. The record business had come from wax cylinders with the very first words recorded "Mary had a little lamb" in Edison's lab, to classical music and music from vaudeville, and Emile Berliners flat disc, 78s with a song on each side. Blues, jazz, dance music, and the Roaring Twenties, to the sound of rural America, now being played on radio on a worldwide stage, even through World War I. It cannot be stressed enough that without the like of Arthur E

Satherley and a few more pioneers that can be counted easily on one hand, the multimillion dollar music business would not be what it is today. Big money was about to be made by stars of record, radio and Hollywood, and, as with any commodity, greed and abuse would join the game.

VERSE THREE

THE LIST

When articles have been written about Art and the people he recorded, they all have different names on the lists. The names that follow come directly from Art's office, (donated now to the Hall of Fame). Some are written in Art's handwriting, but most were roughly typed by Art. It's probably not a definitive list, but it's getting close. Art was ninety years old at this time, so it's possible there could be some errors due to memory but Art was still pretty sharp. The list was compiled, it seems, as the response to a request by Ken Kingsbury who interviewed Art on tape in 1979 (I listened to the whole interview). Kingsbury was researching for a book, Art had written a foreword, but the book never appeared.

The names are in no particular order. I could have listed just them, leaving the reader to research individuals. However, I try to join as many dots as possible, so those without access to the Internet for example can refer to the following names. Any one of the names could have become "big", you just can't tell until it's out there. This material was amongst the articles in Forrest White's office, now donated to the CMHF.

I include a small biography with each name. I couldn't find

information for some of the names, the problem being, that people used many different names to record at that time as they would record for anyone for the session fee. (There is an unknown names list at the back of this book.)

Some were members of well-known duos, trios, quartets, and bands and would use a pseudonym if they were recorded as an individual. The information was gathered from various sources including answers.com, Wikipedia, Tony Russell, John Rumble, and my own Collection.

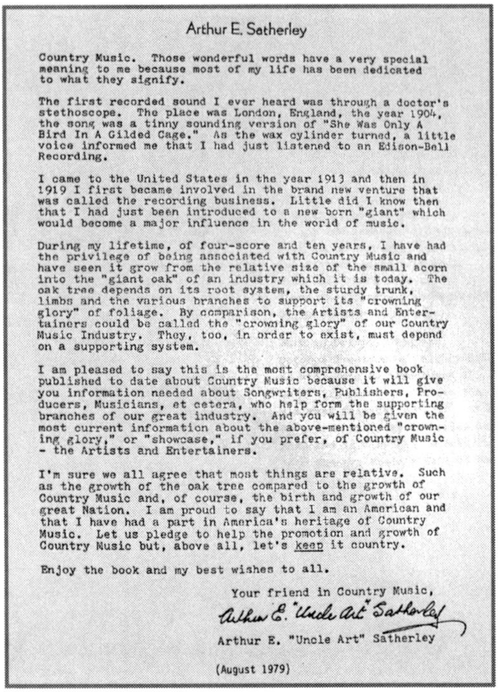

Arthur E. Satherley

Country Music. Those wonderful words have a very special meaning to me because most of my life has been dedicated to what they signify.

The first recorded sound I ever heard was through a doctor's stethoscope. The place was London, England, the year 1904, the song was a tinny sounding version of "She Was Only A Bird In A Gilded Cage." As the wax cylinder turned, a little voice informed me that I had just listened to an Edison-Bell Recording.

I came to the United States in the year 1913 and then in 1919 I first became involved in the brand new venture that was called the recording business. Little did I know then that I had just been introduced to a new born "giant" which would become a major influence in the world of music.

During my lifetime, of four-score and ten years, I have had the privilege of being associated with Country Music and have seen it grow from the relative size of the small acorn into the "giant oak" of an industry which it is today. The oak tree depends on its root system, the sturdy trunk, limbs and the various branches to support its "crowning glory" of foliage. By comparison, the Artists and Entertainers could be called the "crowning glory" of our Country Music Industry. They, too, in order to exist, must depend on a supporting system.

I am pleased to say this is the most comprehensive book published to date about Country Music because it will give you information needed about Songwriters, Publishers, Producers, Musicians, et cetera, who help form the supporting branches of our great industry. And you will be given the most current information about the above-mentioned "crowning glory," or "showcase," if you prefer, of Country Music - the Artists and Entertainers.

I'm sure we all agree that most things are relative. Such as the growth of the oak tree compared to the growth of Country Music and, of course, the birth and growth of our great Nation. I am proud to say that I am an American and that I have had a part in America's heritage of Country Music. Let us pledge to help the promotion and growth of Country Music but, above all, let's keep it country.

Enjoy the book and my best wishes to all.

Your friend in Country Music,

Arthur E. "Uncle Art" Satherley

Arthur E. "Uncle Art" Satherley

(August 1979)

ALBERTA HUNTER. (1 April 1895–17 October 1984) was a blues singer, songwriter, and nurse. Her career had started back in the early 1920s, and from there on, she became a successful international jazz recording artist, being critically acclaimed alongside Ethel Waters and Bessie Smith. In the 1950s, she retired from performing and entered the medi-

cal field, only to successfully resume her singing career in her eighties.

ALLEN BROTHERS. The Allen Brothers, Lee and Austin, were among the first of the fraternal duets that became popular in the 1920s and 1930s. They were known for their fast-paced, upbeat blues and old-time music-influenced songs. Offering sometimes bawdy good-time music, droll humour, and Lee Allen's delightful kazoo leads they created a unique blues-derived sound independent from that of country music's star bluesman of the day, Jimmie Rodgers. The Allen's made their recording debut on the Columbia label in 1926. Their first single was a version of "Salty Dog Blues" titled "Bow Wow Blues." It became quite popular, but when the label released their "Laughin' and Cryin' Blues" in its 14,000-numbered "Race" series instead of the 15,000 "Old-Time" series, the brothers were offended and threatened to sue the company if the records remained on the shelves. The mistake was probably an honest one on Columbia's part.

THE ALLEY BOYS OF ABBEVILLE. From the Abbeville area of Louisiana. Recorded between 1929 and 1939 on Vocalion; early roots Cajun.

SHELLY LEE ALLEY AND HIS ALLEY CATS. SHELLY **LEE.** (1894–1964). Shelly Lee Alley, fiddler and western-swing pioneer, was born in Alleyton, Texas, on 6 July 1894, the son of John Ross and Eliza (Hoover) Alley. Alley, considered one of the greatest bandleaders of the 1930s and 1940s, was descended from the original Austin colony settlers after whom Alleyton was named. His father owned a cotton gin. Alley learned to read music when he was a child. That skill enabled him during World War I to lead the orchestra where he was stationed in San Antonio. In the 1920s, he led several different orchestras that played primarily pop and jazz. He became a pioneer in radio broadcasting when his bands got airtime on numerous Texas radio stations, including KRLD in Dallas.

THE ANGLIN BROTHERS (TWINS). Red, Jim, and Jack Anglin, performing as the Anglin Twins and Red, billed themselves with some justification as "the South's favourite trio" in the 1930s. The group was something of an incubator for the next generation of country sounds, spawning the 1940s duo Johnnie & Jack and thence, indirectly, the career of Kitty Wells. The brothers were born in Franklin, Tennessee, into a large family, but grew up in Athens, Alabama. Befriended and influenced by northern Alabama's Delmore Brothers while they were still young, the Anglins moved to Nashville in 1930 and were inspired to think of a performing career themselves by a Delmore Brothers' performance on the *Grand Old Opry*. By 1933, they had formed a trio consisting of Jack on guitar, Jim on string bass, and Red singing vocal harmonies with the other two

THE ARKANSAS WOODCHOPPER or Arkie (b. Luther Ossenbrink, 2 March1906–23 June 1981) was born in the Ozarks near Kobnoster, Missouri, to a family who owned a farm and a general store. He learned to play guitar and fiddle, and his first job in music was performing on radio in Kansas City on KMBC in 1928. He started at WLS in 1930, performing on their *National Barn Dance*, and became one of the show's most popular performers, continuing there until 1959. During this time, he also released records for Columbia Records and Conqueror Records.

BOB ATCHER AND BONNIE BLUE EYES. Bob Atcher and Bonnie Blue Eyes were a husband-wife singing duo. Bob Atcher achieved a bit of fame as a singer and star of the WLS *National Barn Dance*. Bonnie Blue Eyes (her real name was Loeta Applegate) began her radio career by working with Bob Atcher in Louisville, Kentucky. It was then she changed her stage name to Bonnie Blue Eyes. In 1941, she toured with Gene Autry's "Melody Ranch". In 1935, she married Bob Atcher. They were both natives of the Kentucky hills.

ELDON BAKER AND HIS BROWN COUNTY REVELERS. This was one of those late 1930s country bands that was quite popular regionally (in this case, the Midwest) but left few records behind. The group made a name for itself in Kentucky, Ohio, and Indiana, played over WLW radio in Cincinnati, and cut eighteen songs for the Vocalion label in 1938—however, only four records (eight songs) were ever issued.

AL BERNARD. He recorded with Vernon Dalhart. In 1925, inspired by Dalhart, he began recording hillbilly songs. His 1930 version of "Hesitation Blues", recorded with the Goofus Five, is considered to predict the western swing style, with an intriguing combination of country and western and Chicago blues feels. Bernard continued to record into the 1940s and died in 1949 in New York City.

THE MINSTREL MAN. Emmett Miller (2 February1900–29 March 1962) was an American minstrel show performer and recording artist known for his falsetto, yodel-like voice. Little-known today, Miller was a major influence on many country-music singers, including Hank Williams, Jimmie Rodgers, Milton Brown, Tommy Duncan and Merle Haggard. Miller was born in Macon, Georgia. Though his early life is largely undocumented, it is generally acknowledged that he was performing in minstrel shows by his early twenties. In 1924, his first recordings appeared on the Okeh label. His backup group –The Georgia Crackers – included noted jazz musicians Tommy Dorsey, Jimmy Dorsey, Gene Krupa, and Eddie Lang. He continued to perform in minstrel shows well into his fifties, long after they fell out of fashion. Finally returning to Macon, he died there in 1962 and was buried in Fort Hill Cemetery. Miller's influence on early country is most apparent in Hank Williams' "Lovesick Blues", and Bob Wills' recording of "I Ain't Got Nobody", which closely resemble Miller's versions. Merle Haggard, Leon Redbone, Louis Prima, Van Halen, and Van Halen's frontman David Lee Roth have all recorded Emmett Miller songs.

BIG BILL BROONZY. Born William Lee Conley Broonzy in Scott County, Mississippi, one of Frank Broonzy and Mittie Belcher's seventeen children. Broonzy claimed he was born in 1893, and many sources report that year. But after his death his twin sister produced a birth certificate giving it as 1898. Big Bill Broonzy was probably the most important Chicago blues artist in the thirties and early forties (that's before the period of "Chicago Blues" represented by Muddy Waters, Willie Dixon, Little Walter, and Howlin' Wolf). Not only did he record frequently under his own name, he also accompanied numerous other artists on their recordings, and he acted as talent scout for record companies. In the fifties, he was probably the first to bring the blues to European audiences

CASEY BILL. He played a National steel guitar flat on his lap Hawaiian style. His slide guitar solos were emotional and unique. His style of playing was influential on the emerging Chicago Blues style.

BIG JOE AND HIS WASHBOARD BAND. McCoy played music under a variety of stage names but is best known as "Kansas Joe McCoy". Born in Raymond, Mississippi, he was the older brother of the blues accompanist Papa Charlie McCoy. As a young man, McCoy was drawn to the music scene in Memphis, Tennessee, where he played guitar and sang vocals during the 1920s. He teamed up with future wife Lizzie Douglas, a guitarist better known as Memphis Minnie, and their 1929 recording of the song "Bumble Bee" on the Columbia Records label was a hit . In 1930, the couple moved to Chicago where they were an important part of the burgeoning blues scene. Following their divorce, McCoy teamed up with his brother to form a band known as the Harlem Hamfats that performed and recorded during the second half of the 1930s.

BLACK BOY SHINE. Almost nothing is known of Black Boy Shine, aka Harold Holiday, except that he was based in a section of Houston, Texas, (which may have been his home) called West Dallas. In 1936 and 1937, he recorded for Vocalion in San Antonio and Dallas and left behind eighteen sides.

THE NORFOLK JUBILEE QUARTET. The section of Virginia known as the Tidewater region seems to have possessed some kind of magic when it came to the creation of male gospel quartets, at least in the 1920s and 1930s. These early years of the American recording industry were continually impacted by the public's realization that various genres of music might be entertaining to listen to at home, gospel among them. The Norfolk Jubilee Quartet were one of the Virginia groups that can be held responsible for these developments, releasing musical predictions such as the 1927 "You're Gonna Need That Pure Religion" that sold well beyond any bean counter's wildest expectations. "Standing by the Bedside of a Neighbour" was another of the group's standout efforts, originally produced in 1932.

MA RAINEY. Gertrude Malissa Nix Pridgett Rainey, better known as Ma Rainey (26 April 26– 22 December 1939), was one of the earliest known American professional blues singers and one of the first generation of such singers to record. She was billed as "The Mother of the Blues". She did much to develop and popularize the form and was an important influence on younger blues women, such as Bessie Smith.

THE WILLIAM BLEVINS QUARTET. A gospel quartet.

BLIND GARY. Reverend Gary Davis, also Blind Gary Davis, (30 April1896– 5 May 1972) was a blues and gospel singer and guitarist.

His unique finger-picking style influenced many other artists and his students in New York City.
BLIND JOHN DAVIS. (7 December 1913–12 October 1985 was an African-American, blues, jazz, and boogie-woogie pianist and singer.
BLIND MAC. Mac's real name is Lester McFarland; see Mac and Bob
BLIND WILLIE AND PIANO RED. Willie Perryman went by two nicknames during his lengthy career, both of them thoroughly apt. He was known as Piano Red because of his albino skin pigmentation for most of his performing life. But they called him Doctor Feelgood during the 1960s, and that's precisely what his raucous, barrelhouse-styled vocals and piano were guaranteed to do: cure anyone's ills and make them feel good.
THE BLUE RIDGE MOUNTAIN ENTERTAINERS, "Tom" Clarence Ashley, first recordings with Garley Foster and Doc Walsh in 1928. Throughout the late 1920s and early 1930s, Ashley recorded with Gwen Foster, and The Blue Ridge Mountain Entertainers.
ASHLEY AND FOSTER (same as above)
LUCILLE BOGAN. She was born Lucille Anderson in Amory, Mississippi, in 1897 and raised in Birmingham, Alabama. In 1916, she married Nazareth Lee Bogan, a railway man, and gave birth to a son. She first recorded vaudeville songs for Okeh Records in New York in 1923 with pianist Henry Callens. Later that year she recorded "Pawn Shop Blues" in Atlanta, Georgia, which was the first time a black blues singer had been recorded outside New York or Chicago. In 1927, she began recording for Paramount Records in Chicago, where she waxed her first big success, "Sweet Petunia", which was later covered by Blind Blake. She also recorded for Brunswick Records, backed by Tampa Red and Cow Cow Davenport.
LUCILLE BOGAN AND WALTER ROLAND. (piano player).
BOGAN'S BIMINGHAM BUSTERS. (Lucille's sons' band).
JOHNNY BOND AND HIS RED RIVER BOYS. Inducted to Nashville's songwriters Hall of Fame 1970, and the Country Hall of Fame 1999. Johnny Bond had several successful facets to a career that lasted over thirty years. As a member of the Jimmy Wakely Trio

and as a session musician, he was an important support musician in dozens of B Westerns, working alongside Jimmy Wakely, Tex Ritter, and Johnny Mack Brown. As a songwriter, he was responsible for several compositions that became country standards, including "Cimarron," "I Wonder Where You Are Tonight," "Conversation With a Gun," "Tomorrow Never Comes," and "I'll Step Aside," which became hits for everyone from Billy Vaughn & His Orchestra to Johnny Rodriguez. He also contributed mightily to the recorded music of Wakely, Ritter, and other country stars of the 1940s and 1950s. And his own recordings – which included work with such luminaries as Merle Travis – were popular from the 1940s onward and included several hits, but it wasn't until the 1960s that he had the biggest record of his career, "Ten Little Bottles."

J. H. BRAGG AND HIS RHYTHM FIVE. Jazz recordings.

BREAUX BROTHERS. Cajun recordings.

ELTON BRITT. Elton Britt parlayed his Jimmie Rodgers imitation -- with a yodeling ability and range that surpassed Rodgers' -- into country's biggest hit of the World War II era "There's a Star Spangled Banner Waving Somewhere," which sold four million copies in the early 1940s. He was born James Britt Baker in Zack, Arkansas, on 27 June 1913 and began playing guitar and singing around his hometown while in his mid-teens. Baker's career was made in 1930 when the Beverly Hill Billies returned from California to their Arkansas home to recruit a new vocalist. He won the talent search, and after being renamed Elton Britt, spent three years performing and recording with the Hill Billies. Britt moved to New York in 1933, initially playing in a quartet named Pappy, Zeke, Ezra & Elton. He recorded later in the 1930s as a solo act and also with the Wenatchee Mountaineers, Zeke Manners' Gang, and the Rustic Rhythm Trio.

BROTHER GEORGE AND SANTIFIED SINGERS. Gospel music.

BULL CITY RED. Gospel music.

BUMBLE-BEE SLIM. By 1931 he had moved to Chicago, where he first recorded as Bumble-Bee Slim for Paramount Records. The following year, his song, "B&O Blues", was a hit for Vocalion Records, inspiring a number of other railroad blues and eventually becoming a popular folk song. Over the next five years, he recorded over 150 songs for the Decca, Bluebird, and Vocalion labels, often accompanied by other musicians such as Big Bill Broonzy, Peetie Wheatstraw, Tampa Red, Memphis Minnie, and Washboard Sam

CHARLIE BURSE AND HIS MEMPHIS MUD CATS. Charlie Burse (25 August 190–20 December 1965) was an African-American blues musician best known for his skill with the ukulele. He was nicknamed "Uke Kid Burse" because of his talent, which extended to many other instruments as well. Burse learned to play banjo and regular guitar during his early life. He was also proficient with the tenor guitar and the mandolin. Additionally, Burse performed as a vocalist and could keep rhythm using the spoons. Burse began his own short-lived band, the Memphis Mudcats, in 1939. The Memphis Mudcats attempted to modernize the traditional jug band; a bass was used instead of the jug, and the saxophone replaced the harmonica. After the band's dissolution, Burse and Shade collaborated together until Burse's death on 20 December 1965; the two men would often play on street corners or at house parties. Their renown began to revive toward the end of their lives—especially triggered by their rediscovery by the blues researcher, Samuel Charters.

CALLAHAN BROTHERS. Joe and Bill made their debut in New York for American Record Company; they became the label's most popular duo during this era.

JUDY CANOVA. Judy Canova is best remembered today as a comic actress, but she cut her share of records from the early '30s and into the end of the '50s. As either actress or singer, however, she was a most unlikely success story. She was born Juliette Canova in Starke, Florida, in 1916. By the time she was twelve, she and her sister, Diane, and brother, Leon, were performing together, and she had adopted the stage name Judy. The trio, known as the Three Georgia Crackers, told jokes and sang songs on the radio in Jacksonville, which led to bookings for nightclub performances in New York. The trio was signed to the American Record Company in 1931, cutting hillbilly novelty songs, and they later appeared in a Broadway revue entitled "Calling All Stars".

CLIFF CARLISLE. White country bluesman Cliff Carlisle was

among the most prolific recording artists of the 1930s; a blues yodeller in the tradition of Jimmie Rodgers.

FRED KIRBY. Singing Cowboy, also songwriter, two cuts for Jimmy Dickens, kids TV entertainer from Charlotte, North Carolina.

BILL CARLISLE. Inducted into the hall of fame 2002, Bill Carlisle was a singer, a comedian, a superb guitarist; a gifted songwriter and a showman of the first order. Born William Toliver Carlisle in 1908, he was part of country music's first generation of professionals. By his early twenties, he and his brother Cliff were working in their family's band on radio station WLAP in Lexington, Kentucky. Beginning in the mid-1930s Bill and Cliff became two of country music's most popular performers, working solo and in tandem on a number of southeastern radio stations, most notably WNOX in Knoxville.

CARLISE AND BALL. Carlisle grew up in Kentucky and began performing locally with cousin, Lillian Truax, at age sixteen. Truax's marriage put and end to the group and following this, Carlisle began playing with Wilber Ball, a guitarist and tenor harmonizer. The two toured frequently around the U.S. playing vaudeville and circus venues in the 1920s. Carlisle and Ball first played at Louisville, Kentucky, radio station WHAS in 1930, which would make them local stars, and later that year, they recorded for Gennett Records and Champion Records. They recorded with Jimmie Rodgers in 1931. Toward the end of 1931, Carlisle signed with American Record Company and was offered performance slots on several radio stations nationwide, including WBT (Charlotte, North Carolina), WLS (Chicago), and WLW (Cincinnati). Cliff's brother Bill became his guitarist after Ball left in 1934. During the 1930s, Carlisle, who recorded a large amount of material despite a hiatus from 1934 to 1936, frequently released songs of a frankly sexual nature, including songs with barnyard metaphors (which became something of a trademark).

THE CAROLINA COTTON PICKERS. Hal Denman's Carolina Cotton Pickers was one of the more popular bands in Indiana in the 1920s, but they didn't record until 1931. Denman was from North Carolina and had been leading a band called the Carolina Cotton Pickers before joining a band called the Pirate Entertainers in 1923. When he moved to Indiana in 1924,he still had some old Carolina

Cotton Pickers stationery laying around, so he revived the band name. The band broke up sometime around 1932.

THE CAROLINA RAMBLERS STRING BAND. The North Carolina Ramblers, a banjo-guitar-fiddle trio with Poole's plain-spoken tenor voice in the lead, in great part created the musical templates for two giants: the bluegrass of Bill Monroe and, by extension, the lyrical aspects of the modern country music of Hank Williams. Bill C. Malone, in his important history of country music, *Country Music, U.S.A.* says, "The Rambler sound was predictable: a bluesy fiddle lead, backed up by long, flowing, melodic guitar runs and the finger-style banjo picking of Poole. Predictable as it may be, it was nonetheless outstanding. No string band in early country music equalled the Ramblers' controlled, clean, well-patterned sound."

LEROY AND SCRAPPER BLACKWELL. The term "urban blues" is usually applied to post-World War II blues-band music, but one of the forefathers of the genre in its pre-electric format was pianist Leroy Carr. Teamed with the exemplary guitarist Scrapper Blackwell in Indianapolis, Carr became one of the top blues stars of his day, composing and recording almost 200 sides during his short lifetime.

THE CARTER FAMILY. Originally recorded by Ralph Peer in Bristol Tennessee in 1927 (the now famous Bristol sessions). Peer later passed them to Uncle Art on American Record Company. The Carter Family were: Alvin Pleasant "A.P." Delaney Carter (1891–1960), his wife Sara Dougherty Carter (1898–1979), and his sister-in-law Maybelle Addington Carter (1909–978). Maybelle was married to A.P.'s brother Ezra (Eck) Carter and was also Sara's first cousin. All three were born and raised in southwestern Virginia, where they were immersed in the tight harmonies of mountain gospel music and shape-note singing. Maybelle's distinctive and innovative guitar playing style became a hallmark of the group.They were not with Art very long, moving on to Decca, but he did record or re-record "May The Circle Be Unbroken" and "Wildwood Flower" on 6 May 1935.

Author's note: In conversation with Chet Atkins at my home in Bristol, England in July 1994, I asked Chet if he had ever met Uncle Art. Chet replied:

"Oh, yes. I met him on more than one occasion. A very nice Englishman, white haired and well dressed. I was in the Carter Family's Band, and Uncle Art was with them, looking after them, but then I left the band."

(Me) "You left the band?"

(Chet) "Well, they fired me to tell the truth."

(Me) "Fired you, why"?

(Chet) "They just said 'is that it? Is that all you can do?' So that was me, gone"!

There was probably more to the story. It was Chet being light hearted about it. Chet recorded a lot of tracks with the Carter Sisters and Mother Maybelle, all now available as compilations.

CLAUDE CASEY. Songwriter ("Send Me the Pillow You Dream On"), composer, singer, guitarist, and bassist, he was a winner on the "Major Bowes Amateur Hour" programme and toured with the Bowes units. He had his own group in radio and television in North Carolina and Georgia and in films. He also worked as a disk jockey on an Augusta, Georgia, radio station. He joined ASCAP in 1951. His other song compositions include "Look In the Looking Glass"; "Journey's End"; "Days Are Long, Nights Are Lonely", "Juke Box Gal", and "Savannah River Rag".

CHICAGO RHYTHM KINGS. The New Orleans Rhythm Kings were one of the most influential jazz bands of the early-to-mid 1920s. The band was a combination of New Orleans and Chicago musicians most famous for their residency in Chicago, where they helped shape Chicago style jazz and influenced many younger musicians.

THE CHUCK WAGON GANG. A multi-award-winning Southern Gospel musical group that was formed in 1936 by founding member D.P. (Dad) Carter with his son Jim and daughters Rose and Anna. The "Gang" signed with Columbia Records and remained with them for over forty. At one point, they were Columbia's number-one selling group with record sales in excess of 37 million in record sales.

AL CLAUSER AND HIS OKLHOMA OUTLAWS. Born in Manitoa, Illinois, on 23 February 1911. A guitarist, songwriter, and engineer, Al may have originated the term "Western Swing," since he had used it as early as 1928. Clauser and his string band had a popular radio show in the mid-1930s on WHO in Des Moines, Iowa, where they were regulars until 1942, after which Clauser moved the band to Tulsa, Oklahoma, and began a regular weekly program on KTUL Radio. While at KTUL, Clauser added a teenage singer from Claremore, Oklahoma, named Clara Ann Fowler to his band, which was then called the Oklahoma Outlaws. Clara Ann later achieved international fame as Patti Page. The band specialized in Western swing, playing the popular songs of the day, with Al's original songs added in. Al Clauser and his Oklahoma Outlaws appeared in an early Gene Autry film, "Rootin' Tootin' Rhythm" and recorded a dozen tracks for the American Radio Company in the 1930s.

PETER CLAYTON. (Doctor). Blues and Gospel singer , friend of Big Bill Broonzy. First recordings 1935, later "Pearl Harbor Blues" was a hit.

COATES SACRED QUARTET. Gospel music.

SALTY DOG-SAM COLLINS. Sometimes known as Crying Sam Collins and also, according to one authoritative website, as Jim Foster, Jelly Roll Hunter, Big Boy Woods, Bunny Carter, and Salty Dog Sam. He was an early American blues singer and guitarist.

ARTHUR CORNWALL AND WILLIAM CLEARY. Recorded "Rock of Ages/Old Rugged Cross" on Conqueror Records.

THE COTTEN PICKERS QUARTET. Jazz, the Cotton Club. Duke Ellington may have been a member.

COX AND HOBBS. Bill Cox (see The Dixie Songbird) and Cliff Hobbs were teamed up by Uncle Art.

THE DIXIE SONG-BIRD. William Jennings Cox (1897–1968) Charleston, South Carolina. Songwriter, guitar, and harmonica. Got a job on WOBU, apparently unreliable through drink, made numerous recordings for both Gennett and the American Record Corporation between 1929 and 1940.

IDA COX WITH ALL STAR BAND WITH FLETCHER HENDERSON. One of the most popular blues singers of the 1920s, Ida Cox (born in 1889) ran away from home when she was fourteen to join travelling vaudeville shows such as Clark's Minstrels. Later, she moved to Chicago where she made her recording debut in June 1923 with Lovie Austin on Paramount. She made about a hundred recordings between 1923 and 1940 with some of the best jazz musicians accompanying her, such as Johnny Dodds; Buster Bailey; Charlie Green; Tommy Ladnier; Kid Ory; James P. Johnson; and Lester Young. She also wrote blues songs that were recorded by others such as Bessie Smith ("Nobody Knows You When You're Down And Out"). Fletcher Hamilton Henderson, Jr. (18 December 1897–28 December 1952) was an American pianist, bandleader, arranger and composer, important in the development of big band jazz and swing music. He was often known as "Smack" Henderson.

LIONEL HAMPTON. Lionel Leo Hampton (20 April 1908–31 August 2002) was an American jazz vibraphonist, percussionist, bandleader, and actor. Like Red Norvo, he was one of the first jazz vibraphone players. Hampton ranks among the great names in jazz history, having worked with a Who's Who of jazz musicians, from Benny Goodman and Buddy Rich to Charlie Parker and Quincy Jones. In 1992, he was inducted into the Alabama Jazz Hall of Fame.

ARTIE BERNSTEIN. Jazz Bassist.

CHARLEY CHRISTIAN. Legendary guitarist (29 July 1916–2 March 1942) was an American swing and bebop jazz guitarist.

HOT LIPS PAGE, AND J.C. HIGGINBOTTOM. See Ida Cox.

JIMMYJOHNSON. See Ida Cox.

THE CUMBERLAND RIDGE RUNNERS. This group was highly successful for several years with a stage show and series of radio broadcasts that combined top-flight musicianship with hillbilly dress up and hamming, although the players themselves certainly all had authentically rural backgrounds. Guitarist Karl Davis and mandolinist Hartford Taylor were a West Virginia duo act that often pretended to be brothers.

TED DAFFAN AND HIS TEXANS. Theron Eugene "Ted" Daffan (21 September 1912–6 October 1996), Daffan wrote "Truck Drivers' Blues" after he stopped at a roadside diner and noticed that every time a trucker parked his rig and strolled into the cafe, the first thing he did, even before ordering a cup of coffee, was push a coin in the jukebox. The song that was recorded by Cliff Bruner in1939 was a hit, starting a long line of truck-driving songs to the present day. The hit song brought Ted Daffan to the attention of Uncle Art who signed him. He scored a string of hits on his own with his band, The Texans, including "Worried Mind" and "Born to Lose". "Born to Lose" may have sold as many as 7 million copies. Daffan stopped performing in the 1960s, and founded a Nashville-based publishing house with Hank Snow. He retired to Houston, but retained interests in the publishing business for a time. He died in 1996 in Houston, Texas.

THE CRYSTAL SPRING RAMBLERS were one of the western swing bands to spring up in the wake of Bob Wills and His Texas Playboys and the Light Crust Doughboys. They recorded only four sides, all for Vocalion, of which "Fort Worth Stomp" is the most enduring. Their membership circa 1938 included Link Davis on vocals and fiddle; Earl Driver playing tenor sax; Joe Holley on fiddle; J.B. Brinkley on guitar; Morris Deason on banjo; Lauren Mitchell on piano; Jimmy Makado on bass; and Homer Kinnaird on the drums. The group took its name from the Crystal Springs Ballroom.

THE DALLAS JAMBOREE JUG BAND – JIMMY AND EDDIE DEAN. Briefly active in the mid thirties, the Dallas Jamboree Jug Band recorded a handful of sides that have shown up on quite a few reissue collections, sometimes under the band's name and sometimes under the name of some of its members.

JAMES DE BERRY AND HIS MEMPHIS PLAYBOYS. Jazz band local in Memphis.

AL DEXTER AND HIS TROOPERS. Born Clarence Albert Poindexter in Jacksonville, Texas, on 4 May 1902, Dexter began playing square dances around oil-rich eastern Texas during the 1920s. The Depression forced him to work as a house painter, but Dexter began moonlighting after he formed the Texas Troopers in the early thirties. The group recorded for Okeh and Vocalion during the rest of the thirties and into the forties. In 1944 – the first year when charts can be relied on -- Dexter scored four number ones on the country chart. "Pistol Packin' Mama" was re-released on the B-side of "Rosalita," and both songs hit number one in January 1944. His biggest hit of the year came in March, when "So Long Pal" spent thirteen weeks at number one on the country chart. Its

B-side, "Too Late to Worry, Too Blue to Cry," stayed at the top for two weeks.

THE DEZURIK SISTERS. The first women to become stars on both the National *Barn Dance* and the *Grand Old Opry*, largely a result of their original yodelling style. In 1938, the sisters recorded six songs for Vocalion: "I Left Her Standing There"; "Arizona Yodeler"; "Sweet Hawaiian Chimes"; "Guitar Blues"; "Go to Sleep My Darling Baby"; and "Birmingham Jail". Those six songs were the only tracks the duo would ever commit to vinyl, although some recordings exist of their appearances on Checkerboard Time.

THE BOSWELL SISTERS. The Boswell Sisters chalked up twenty hits during the 1930s, including the number-one record "The Object of My Affection" in 1935.The Andrews Sisters started out as Boswell Sisters imitators.

BRADLEY KINKADE. (1895 -1991) Sang sad, sweet songs on WLS. He was a quiet singer popular on the *Grand Old Opry*.

THE REV. EMMET DICKENSON AND CONGREGATION. Unlike the recordings of many contemporary black evangelists, Dickinson's records were all preaching with no musical accompaniment. A small congregation added vocal interjections on most sides, and several of the later recordings featured a woman moaning beneath the sermon. On other tracks, the congregation included a man impersonating a woman in a shrill falsetto. Dickinson recorded his final side in 1931, and his obscure identity continues to elude blues and gospel historians today.

THE DIXIE RAMBLERS. Original Dixieland Jazz band.

THOMAS DORSEY AND HIS GOSPEL SINGERS. (1 July 1899, Villa Rica, Georgia – 23 January 1993, Chicago) Known as "the father of gospel music". Earlier in his life he was a leading blues pianist known as Georgia Tom.

CHAMPION JACK DU PREE. Champion Jack Dupree was the embodiment of the New Orleans blues and boogie-woogie pianist, a true barrelhouse "professor". His father was from the Belgian Congo, and his mother was African-American and Cherokee. He was orphaned at the age of two and sent to the New Orleans Home for Colored Waifs (also the alma mater of Louis Armstrong). As a young man, he began his life of travelling, living in Chicago, where he worked with Georgia Tom, and Indianapolis, Indiana, where he hooked up with Scrapper Blackwell and Leroy Carr. While he was always playing piano, he also worked as a cook, and in Detroit he met Joe Louis, who encouraged him to become a boxer. He ultimately fought in 107 bouts and won Golden Gloves and other championships, and picking up the nickname Champion Jack, which he used the rest of his life.

EAGLE JUBILEE FOUR. Gospel quartet.

THE EDGE-WATER CROWS. "Hattiesburg has nurtured countless talented musicians whose work laid the foundation of rock and roll," Governor Haley Barbour said. "I am proud to celebrate the contributions of groups like the Mississippi Jook Band and the Edgewater Crows, who formed their sound here in South Mississippi."

FAIRVIEW JUBILEE QUARTET. Blues and Gospel.

THE GARLAND JUBLEE SINGERS. Gospel.

HOKUM BOYS. While the Famous Hokum Boys has turned up as a name for various regional old-time music and country-blues groups, the most famous group utilizing the name was a loose-knit aggregation of blues singers that were actually better known under their own names. Yet Georgia Tom, Tampa Red, and Big Bill Broonsy may have wanted the somewhat more anonymous cover of a combo name in order to release their raunchiest material, including the number "It's Tight Like That." By the time the latter ditty was cut in the late '20s, blues or so-called "race records" was established as an area where sexy, sometimes downright nasty lyrics, were a stock-in-trade. Georgia Tom, also known under his real name of Thomas Dorsey, particularly may have wanted some kind of a cover to prevent his high-profile gospel and religious singing career from being corrupted. The ruse hardly worked, however, but the result actually turned out to be a sort of a canonization of Dorsey and the Famous Hokum Boys by later advocates of what became known as "contemporary Christian music," in which it was alright, even desired, for the performer to touch on steamy subjects such as lust and adultery. "It's entirely arguable that Christian music would not exist if it were not for the Rev. Thomas A. Dorsey," a magazine devoted to the contemporary Christian genre even wrote. The term "hokum" is said to have been invented by the Famous Hokum Boys as a new descriptive term for the type of material the band was coming up with, but has since evolved into a minimally used expression for something corny, low-brow, or kitschy, with little reference to sex -- or gospel. ~ Eugene Chadbourne, Rovi.

PHIL AND DOC ROBERTS. One of the finest and most recorded old-time fiddlers of country music's golden era was Fiddlin' Doc Roberts of Madison County, Kentucky. In 1925, Roberts began his recording career with the aid of Edgar Boaz on guitar. In 1927, he recorded eighteen issued sides in Chicago for Paramount with a group known as the Kentucky Thorobreds, which also included Ted Chestnut on mandolin and Dick Parman on guitar. About this time, he is also believed to have recorded with another Madison County band known as Taylor's Kentucky Boys.

ARTHUR FIELDS OF THE AVON COMEDY FOUR. Vaudeville comedy.

FLEMING AND TOWNSEND. Old-time duo vocals, guitar, and mandolin.

RED FOLEY. For more than two decades, Foley was a major star of country music, selling in excess of 25 million records. He hosted the popular *Ozark Jubilee* ABC network radio and television programme between 1955 and 1960. During 1962-63, Foley was a regular cast member along with Fess Parker in *Mr. Smith Goes to Washington*, a television series based on the famous movie. Red Foley was elected to the Country Music Hall of Fame in 1967. For his contribution to the music industry, Red Foley also has a star on the Hollywood Walk of Fame at 6225 Hollywood Blvd.

FREENY HARMONIZERS. Formed about 1931 – a show band with brass, reeds, piano, and drums, but stripped down to a trio for the 1935 Jackson session. Ira Ellis was a hot, bluesy fiddler.

FUNNY PAPER SMITH. J.T. "Funny Paper" Smith was a pioneering force behind the development of the Texas blues guitar style of the pre-war era. In addition to honing a signature sound distinguished by intricate melody lines and simple, repetitive bass riffs, he was also a gifted composer, authoring songs of surprising narrative complexity. A contemporary of such legends as Blind Lemon Jefferson and Dennis "Little Hat" Jones, next to nothing concrete is known of John T. Smith's life.

LITTLE BILL GAITHER. Sometimes known as "Little Bill" Gaither or Leroy's Buddy, was a blues guitarist and singer. Gaither recorded hundred of songs for labels such as Decca, Arhoolie, and Okeh.

GENE AND GLEN. Old time.

CURLY WEAVER. "The Georgia Guitar Legend" was, rather unfairly, better known as Willie McTell's partner than as an artist in his own right.

BUDDY MOSS AND BLIND WILLIE. McTell worked under a variety of names and with a multitude of partners, including his one-time wife, Ruthy Kate Williams (who recorded with him under the name Ruby Glaze) and also Buddy Moss and Curley Weaver. McTell cut some of his best songs more than once in his career. Like many bluesmen, he recorded under different names simultaneously and was even signed to both Columbia and Okeh Records, two companies that ended up merged at the end of the 1930s, at the same time under two names. His recording career never gave Willie quite as much success as he had hoped, partly due to the fact that some of his best work appeared during the depths of the Depression.

THE GEORGIA GRINDER. Charles Edward Devonport recorded under many names; his song "Cow-cow Blues" was a hit and became a nickname. It's also believed that he was first to use the term "boogie-woogie".

GEORGIA SLIM. Robert Rutland, a very fine fiddler; some of his best work was an album called "Georgia Slim, Raw Fiddle".

CLARA BELLE GHOLSTON AND CHORAL Gospel. Known as the Georgia peach.

GIRLS OF THE GOLDEN WEST. The Girls of the Golden West were originally from Mt. Carmel, Illinois. They had entertained friends and family in their early years before they worked on a radio station in St. Louis, Missouri, and then later moving to the WLS's *National Barn Dance* in 1933. Gene Autry, Patsy Montana and Bradley Kincaid, would later work with the girls in their recordings. They first started recording for Bluebird Records in 1933, where they stayed for quite some time. "Put My Little Shoes Away" and "Ragtime Cowboy Joe" were just two of their hits, and these made them stars.

LONNIE GLOSSON. (1908 - 2001) Known nationally for his harmonica playing. He also played guitar, sang, and even wrote songs. He was often a guest on live radio shows such as: the *Louisiana Hayride* in Shreveport, Louisiana; *Grand Old Opry* on WSM in Nashville, Tennessee; *Renfro Valley Gang* on the Mutual Radio Network, and *Saturday Night Barn Dance.* Several of the shows he performed on aired on many radio stations. A short list includes; KMOX in Saint Louis, Missouri; WLS in Chicago, Illinois; WLW in Cincinnati, Ohio; KARK in Little Rock, Arkansas, and KWHN in Fort Smith, Arkansas. Later, he would even have his own regular radio shows. Some of these shows were recorded and aired on as many as 200 radio stations around the country.

GEORGE GOBEL. "Lonesome" George Gobel was barely of voting and drinking age when he was first hired as a musician/comic on the WLS radio *Barn Dance* in his native Chicago. True stardom eluded Gobel until 1954, when he debuted in his own variety series on NBC television. Historians have compared Gobel's low-key, self-effacing style to that of Herb Shriner and Johnny Carson, but anyone who's ever seen him in action will agree that he was in a class by himself.

THE GOLD STAR QUARTET. Gospel.

COOTS GRANT AND SOCKS WILSON. Leola B. Pettigrew, was a classic blues singer and guitarist from Alabama whose legal name became Leola Wilson following her marriage to performing partner Wesley Wilson. The pair, who were born in the same year 1893, met and began performing together in 1905 and were wed seven years later. Pettigrew was already known as Coot Grant by this time, the name representing some kind of word play on the nickname "Cutie." She had been involved in show business since she was a child, beginning as a dancer in vaudeville. Prior to the beginning of the World War I, she had already toured both Europe and South Africa, sometimes appearing under the name of Patsy Hunter. Her husband, who played both piano and organ, also performed under a variety of bizarre stage names including Catjuice Charlie, in a gross-out duo with Pigmeat Pete, as well as Kid Wilson, Jenkins, Socks, and Sox Wilson.

ROOSEVELT GRAVES AND BROTHERS. On all his recordings, Roosevelt played with his brother Uaroy Graves, who was also nearly blind and played the tambourine. They were credited as "Blind Roosevelt Graves and Brother". Their first recordings were made in 1929 for Paramount Records. Theirs is the earliest version recorded of the famous tune "Guitar Boogie", and they exemplified the very best in gospel singing with the classic "I'll Be Rested".

ROY HALL AND HIS BLUE RIDGE ENTERTAINERS. Early Bluegrass string band.

THE HARLEM HAM-FATS, was a Chicago jazz band formed in 1936. Initially, they mainly provided backup music for jazz and blues singers, such as Johnny Temple, Rosetta Howard, and Frankie Jaxon for Decca Records but when their first record "Oh! Red!" became a hit, it secured them a Decca contract for fifty titles They launched a successful recording career performing danceable music.

HATTIE HART. Blues singer Hattie Hart recorded with the Memphis Jug Band in the 1920s. During this time, she was also known for the parties she threw. Hart went on to record contemporary blues after moving to Chicago in the mid 1930s, then disappeared from the public eye

ADOLPH HOFNER AND HIS SAN ANTONIANS. Bandleader

and vocalist Adolph Hofner was a durable musical icon of south Texas who helped shape Western swing and whose dual career as a swing bandleader and Czech dance musician showed the ways in which Western swing had roots in Central European dance traditions. Hofner was raised on a farm in Lavaca County, Texas, and like many other rural Texans his ethnic background was German and Czech. While growing up, Hofner heard polkas, schottisches, and other forms of local dance music. He and his family moved to San Antonio in 1928, where, four years later, Adolph and his steel guitar-playing brother, Emil, began performing in local clubs. Their sound reflected several strands of the Texas musical mosaic. Adolph was a crooner in the Bing Crosby mould.

TONY HOLLINS. Delta blues singer/guitarist Tony Hollins was born in Clarksdale, Mississippi, around the turn of the twentieth century. Few details are known of Hollins' life; he cut his first recordings for OKeh in 1941, with his fluid, insistent performance of "Crawlin' King Snake" serving as the blueprint for John Lee Hooker's later rendition. "Travelling Man Blues" was also later appropriated by Hooker for his "When My Wife Quit Me"; clearly admired by his peers.

DOC HOPKINS. Real name: Doctor, but not a medical doctor. He did the old folk songs and ballads. Back then, some thought he was the best thing going for old-time folk music of the mountains where he grew up. He grew up in Harlan County, Kentucky; raised on corn bread.

THE HUMBARD FAMILY. Rex became a well-known televangelist, the family were Pentecostal Evangelists Gospel singers.

ANDY IONA AND HIS ORCHESTRA. Andy Iona (1902–1966) was an American musician and one of Hawaii's most influential musicians. He was a composer, songwriter, conductor, saxophonist, and steel guitarist He went to the Kamehameha School for Boys. He was also educated at Henri Berger's Private School of Music in Honolulu. He was a member of the radio station KHS staff orchestra. He went on to form his own group called Andy Iona and His Islanders, and they appeared in films, hotels, theatres, and on records. He toured with Sonja Henie for twelve years. He composed songs for the American Society of Composers, Authors, and Publishers after joining in 1940.

JAKE AND CARL THE NIGHT HERDERS. Cowboy songs.

JAZBO TOMMY AND HIS LOW LANDERS. Jazz and Western Swing.

LIL JOHNSON. Lil Johnson made use of one thing that always sells in music, every time: sex. She eventually toned down her lyrics somewhat, since record company censorship was beginning to plague her as well as shifting public taste. Nonetheless, she recorded quite a few sides between the late 1920s, when she first appeared in the recording studios, and 1937, when she performed on her last known songs. Like many pianists and singers from this period, her recordings fell into a state of copyright limbo in which just about anyone capable of sequencing a series of tracks was able to release her songs on anthologies relating to the blues and boogie-woogie piano.

ROBERT JOHNSON. Robert Leroy Johnson (8 May 1911–16 August 1938) is among the most famous of Delta blues musicians. His landmark recordings from 1936–37 were arranged and supervised by Uncle Art Satherley, and produced by Don Law. He displays a remarkable combination of singing, guitar skills, and songwriting talent that have influenced generations of musicians. Johnson's shadowy, poorly documented life and death at age twenty seven have given rise to much legend. Considered by some to be the "Grandfather of Rock 'n' Roll", his vocal phrasing, original songs, and guitar style have influenced a broad range of musicians, including Muddy Waters,

Bob Dylan, Jimi Hendrix, Led Zeppelin, The Rolling Stones, Jeff Beck, Jack White, and Eric Clapton, who called Johnson "the most important blues musician who ever lived". He was also ranked fifth in *Rolling Stone's* list of 100 Greatest Guitarists of All Time. He is an inductee of the Rock and Roll Hall of Fame.

CURTIS JONES. (18 August 1906, Naples, Texas–11 September 1971, Munich, Germany) was an American blues pianist. Jones played guitar while young but switched to piano after a move to Dallas. In 1936, he relocated to Chicago, where he recorded between 1937 and 1941 on Vocalion Records, Bluebird Records, and Okeh Records. Among his best-known tunes from these recordings were the hit "Lonesome Bedroom Blues".

CHARLIE JORDON. Jordan recorded numerous singles for Vocalion and Decca between 1930 and 1937 and also performed with some well-regarded bluesmen from the 1920s to the 1940s. Jordan recorded with Peetie Wheatstraw, Roosevelt Sykes, Casey Bill Weldon, and Memphis Minnie. He had most of his biggest hits, including "Keep It Clean", in the early to mid 1930s. Later in that decade and into the 1940s, he worked frequently with Big Joe Williams. His most appreciated number, however, seems to have been "Keep It Clean", a selection of mildly suggestive traditional jokes strung along on the melodic thread of a blues, to which he added several sequels.

JUBILEE GOSPEL TEAM. Plantation gospel choir.

KARL AND HARTY TAYLOR. This group had quite a history and saw several changes in makeup. In a folio called "Doc Hopkins and Karl and Harty of the Cumberland Ridgerunners" published back in 1936 seems to detail the roots of this group. As fate would have it, Doc Hopkins, Karl, and Harty all attended the infamous "Red Bud School" near Mt. Vernon, Kentucky in the Renfro Valley area where another infamous barn dance started and still exists today. The folio says that Doc, Karl, and Harty took to "mountain music" at an early age and could often be seen together at the Davis' barn or the Taylor's blacksmith shop playing their tunes on their guitar and mandolin. In this case, it was birds of a feather did indeed flock together. When Doc returned from World War I, the three boys formed a string band and called themselves the Krazy Kats. They got themselves quite a following in central and eastern Kentucky. Later, they were heard singing over radio station WHAS in Louisville, Kentucky.

W. C. HANDY.1873 – 1958

Referred to as the father of the blues. Musician, composer and music publisher "Saint Louis Blues" just one of many that he wrote. He moved to New York in 1918 promoting blues to mainstream audiences. Handy was responsible for the first blues performance in New York City's Carnegie Hall. Handy who went blind in his later years had his autobiography "Father of the Blues" turned into a film of the same name shortly after his death. Nat King Cole played Handy

HUDDIE LEDBETTER (LEADBELLY). Huddie Ledbetter, better known as Leadbelly, was one of the most powerful figures in the early years of the American folk music movement. He wasn't tall or muscular, but his steel-wire energy as a "cotton-chopper" gave him the nickname he bore most of his life. His performances radiated an overwhelming intensity that few artists have ever matched. His recordings were instrumental in the creation of Britain's Skiffle movement, which produced the Beatles and many of the other rhythm and blues artists. He was born Huddie William Ledbetter on Jeder Plantation, a farm in Mooringsport, Louisiana. His birth date has been variously listed as 20 January 1889, 21 January 1885, or 29 January 29 1885. During his early years, his family appears to have lived in a number of locations in western Louisiana and eastern Texas. As a young man, Huddie Ledbetter mastered the twelve-string guitar which sounded in his hands like a small orchestra. He became known as "King of the Twelve-String Guitar", and formed a duo with the legendary blues musician Blind Lemon Jefferson. He teamed up with folk song gatherers John and Alan Lomax for a short time. Leadbelly had a song that although he didn't write it became his signature tune, "Goodnight Irene". Ironically Uncle Art recorded Leadbelly performing "Goodnight Irene", a song that is still sung by fans of Bristol Rovers Football Club back in Art's hometown.

BLIND LEMON JEFFERIES. Jefferson had an intricate and fast style of guitar playing and a particularly high-pitched voice. He was a founder of the Texas blues sound and an important influence on other blues singers and guitarists, including Leadbelly and Lightnin' Hopkins. The white North Carolina performer Arthel "Doc" Watson credited listening to Jefferson's recordings as his first exposure to the blues, which would powerfully influence his own style. He was the author of many tunes covered by later

musicians, including the classic "See That My Grave Is Kept Clean". Another of his tunes, "Matchbox Blues", was recorded more than thirty years later by the Beatles, albeit in a rockabilly version credited to Carl Perkins, who himself did not credit Jefferson on his 1955 recording. Given this influence, it is unfortunate that many of the details of his life remain shrouded in mystery, perhaps forever; even the only known picture of him, shown here, is heavily retouched, with a fake tie painted in by hand. However, at the time, "race music" and its white cousin, "hillbilly music," were not considered to be worthy of consideration as art, rather as a low-cost product to be sold and soon forgotten. Today, Blind Lemon Jefferson is the featured musician on a State of Texas license plate. B. B. King has always maintained that Jefferson was a huge influence on his singing and guitar playing. Uncle Art would whisper the lyrics to Jefferies as he recorded them.

BESSIE SMITH. After singing with "Ma" Rainey's Rabbit Foot Minstrels travelling show for several years, Bessie Smith went solo and signed with Columbia Records. Her songs, the best known of which included "Down Hearted Blues", "Gulf Coast Blues", "Jealous Hearted Blues", and "Cold in Hand Blues", were about poverty, oppression, and unrequited love and touched the hearts of thousands. Her records sold excellently, and she became a major attraction in vaudeville. Changing tastes in music as well as alcoholism caused Bessie Smith's career to fade out by the end of the 1920s. Nevertheless, her singing talent did not diminish.

From 1933, she was gradually making a comeback with a recording session and an appearance at the Apollo Theatre. This was all cut short by her tragic death in an automobile accident. Uncle Art commented that he thought she was the best of all the black blues singers he recorded.

LAWRENCE LOY. Columbia was one of the first labels to recognize the potential of square-dance records. In 1941, Carson Robinson was contracted to make square-dance recordings. Of course, they needed a caller for the records. Lawrence Loy, who by now was an experienced caller, did the calls at the recording session on 17 February 1941. Of this session, eight tracks were released on four 78 rpm records (Columbia 36018 through 36021). These records were reissued in 1953, when the square-dance boom was at a peak, in an album (C 47), and on a ten-inch LP called "Square Dances" (CL 6029), which two years later was reissued.

JOHNNY MASTERS (THE MASTERS FAMILY). Their music took them to Nashville, Tennessee, in April 1950 where they appeared on the WSM *Grand Old Opry* for three months. While there, they obtained their release from the Mercury label and were signed to Columbia by the Art Satherley and Don Law. At the same time, Johnnie Masters gave his songwriting to the Peer-Southern publishing company.

MELISSA MONROE. Mother of Bill Monroe, Melissa Vanderver Monroe, sang and played the fiddle, harmonica, and accordion. Her brother Pendleton Vanderver was a fiddler of considerable talent and local renown who taught Bill the essentials of the mandolin, fiddle, and guitar.

GEORGE MORGAN. George Morgan was a member of the *Grand Old Opry* from 1948 and is best remembered for the Columbia Records song "Candy Kisses", which was a number-one hit on the *Billboard* country music charts for three weeks in 1949. He also had several hits based on a "rose" theme, like "Room Full of Roses", "Red Roses for a Blue Lady", and "Red Roses from the Blue Side of Town". His daughter, Lorrie Morgan, is also a country-music singer. Using modern technology, Lorrie recorded a duet with her late father entitled "From This Moment On". In 1974, George Morgan was the last person to sing on the stage of the Ryman Auditorium before the *Grand Old Opry* moved to the new *Grand Old Opry* House. A week later, he was the first to sing on stage at the new *Grand Old Opry.*

LEON MCAULIFFE. (1917–1988) was a Western swing musician from Houston, Texas. He is famous for his steel guitar solos with Bob Wills and His Texas Playboys, inspiring Wills' phrase "Take it away, Leon." McAuliffe, at age sixteen, first played with the Light Crust Doughboys, playing both rhythm guitar and steel guitar. In 1935, at age eighteen, he went on to play with Bob Wills in Tulsa. He stayed with Wills until World War II. While with Wills, he helped compose "San Antonio Rose". He is more noted, however, for his most famous composition, "Steel Guitar Rag", and his playing, along with that of Bob Dunn (Light Crust Doughboys), that popularized the steel guitar in the United States. His playing (and Dunn's) is also credited with inspiring the rhythm and blues electric guitar style occurring some twenty years later.

After the war, McAuliffe returned to Tulsa, forming his Western swing band and releasing a number of recordings, including "Panhandle Rag" (Columbia 20546) which reached number six in 1949. McAuliffe soon opened his Cimarron Ballroom in the remodelled Akdar Shrine Mosque in Tulsa. He and his band recorded several songs as Leon McAuliffe and his Cimarron Boys named for the ballroom. He also opened a recording studio, Cimarron Records.

SHENANDOAH VALLEY (trio). The Shenandoah Valley Trio was a glorified example of a tradition in country music which began sometime in the 1940s, namely an opening act in a country show that is actually made up of membership drawn from the headlining group. The most common examples of this practice – which has also provided a way of creating warm-up acts for soul and blues shows as well – would involve an individual performer from the star's group who gets a twenty-minute slot in which to perform as lead vocalist. Some country stars such as Cal Smith got their start this way, while plenty of others found it a defining experience in their decision to remain a sideman. Bill Monroe did the entire tradition one better, or perhaps three better would be more accurate, by creating a vocal trio from the membership of his Bluegrass Boys, but the resulting ensembles were popular enough to warrant recording activity on their own. The membership of the vocal trio was subject to the same sort of sometimes rapid turnover as the band proper, but the most famous version of this trio featured lead vocalist Joel Price, guitarist and baritone Jimmy Martin, and the fiddle and tenor vocal of Merle "Red" Taylor. This line-up recorded for Columbia in the early 1950s, augmenting the basic trio sound with a fine steel guitarist who unfortunately has never been properly identified, although guesses are that it is Jimmie Selph from Red Foley's band. Despite founding-father Monroe's status in bluegrass, the recordings of the Shenandoah Valley Trio fit snugly in the mainstream country tradition. Monroe's daughter Melissa Monroe also recorded for Columbia around this time, and it seems as if the Shenandoah Valley Trio provided both instrumental and vocal backup on these sessions as well. By the early 1960s, business was down in both the bluegrass and country genres, meaning promoters decided the only way to sell tickets was to create package shows. Just Bill Monroe's band plus whatever subdivisions might come out of that weren't good enough; in the new style of lavish spectaculars, three or four "name" country or bluegrass acts were on the bill, one of them getting the traditional warm-up slot. As a result, there was no longer a need for Monroe to provide such groups, and the vocal trio idea fell by the wayside.

CARL SMITH. Carl Smith was one of country music's most popular singers during the 1950s. Over the course of the decade, he racked up thirty Top Ten hits, and his success continued well into the 1970s, where he had a charting single every year (except one). Smith was born in Tennessee in 1927. He grew up in the town of Maynardville, the hometown of another leading country singer, Roy Acuff. During Smith's childhood, he idolized Acuff, Ernest Tubb, and Bill Monroe. In his teenage years, he taught himself to play the guitar. According to legend, he bought his first guitar with money earned by selling flower seeds. At age fifteen, he started performing in a band, called Kitty Dibble and Her Dude Ranch Ranglers. By the age of seventeen, he had learned to play the string bass and spent his summer vacation working at the radio station WROL in Knoxville, Tennessee. After graduating from high school, he briefly served in the U.S. Navy.

He went back to the radio station (WROL) and played string bass for country singers, Molly O'Day and Skeets Williamson. He also started singing at this time. One his colleagues at the station sent an acetate of his singing to WSM (the radio station of the *Grand Old Opry*) in Nashville, Tennessee. WSM soon signed Smith to a contract, and he was soon working for WSM and the *Grand Old Opry*. In 1950, Smith was finally signed to a recording contract with Columbia Records by producers Uncle Art and Don Law. He was inducted in to the Hall of Fame in 2003.

STAMPS QUARTET. In 1924, when V. O. Stamps formed the V. O. Stamps School of Music, Stamps' brother Frank formed the first Stamps Quartet around the same time. Then in 1926, V. O. partnered with J. R. Baxter to form the Stamps-Baxter Music and Printing Company. They would become the most successful publisher of shape-note hymn books in the United States. V. O. Stamps also formed a quartet of his own.

CURT MASSEY. Curt Dott Massey was part of a group called the Westerners. He appeared on radio WLS's *Barn Dance* and, as a songwriter, wrote theme tunes for TV, notably The Beverly Hillbillies.

CARSON ROBINSON. Columbia was one of the first labels to recognize the potential of square-dance records. In 1941, Carson Robinson was contracted to make square-dance recordings.

WILMA LEE AND STONEY COOPER. Wilma Lee Cooper (born Wilma Lee Leary, 7 February 1921 in Valley Head, West Virginia), is a bluegrass-based country-music entertainer. As Wilma Lee Leary she sang in her youth with her family's gospel music group, The Leary Family, which included her parents and sisters. Wilma Lee and Stoney Cooper had remarkable record success in the late 1950s and early 1960s on Hickory Records given both their bluegrass sound (which has rarely been so commercially successful) and the damage rock-n-roll was doing to country music's popularity at the time. They scored seven hit records between 1956 and 1961, with four top ten hits in Billboard, notably "Big Midnight Special "and "There's a Big Wheel". They remained connected to the Leary Family tradition as well, recording popular gospels songs like"Tramp on the Street" and "Walking My Lord Up Calvary's Hill".

MAC AND BOB. Lester "Mac" McFarland was from Gray, Kentucky, and Robert "Bob" Gardner was from Oliver Springs, Tennessee. They met at around 1916 where they were both studying music at the Kentucky School for the Blind. Mac played the piano, cornet, trombone, guitar, and mandolin and later became a music teacher. Bob made a living as a piano tuner with a perfect ear for pitch and tone. They teamed up as a harmony duo and recorded about 200 songs with sales totalling over a million. When Mac and Bob learned a new song, the notes and words were read to them and they punched them out on a sheet using the "point system".

SMILEY BURNETT. Lester Alvin (Smiley) Burnette (18 March1911–16 February 1967) was an American singer-songwriter who could play as many as 100 different musical instruments and was a successful comedy actor in Western films over three decades. Burnette was born in Summum, Illinois. He began singing in childhood and learned to play a variety of instruments while still a boy. In his teens, he worked in vaudeville and at a local radio station. His break came when he was hired to perform on the *National Barn Dance* on Chicago's WLS radio station where Gene Autry was the show's major star. At a time when Hollywood was searching for talent for Western films, Burnette and Autry got their first small role in the 1934 Ken Maynard Republic Pictures film *In Old Santa Fe.* Burnette appeared in several bit parts until the following year's release of the Rin-Tin-Tin-hit film *The Adventures of Rex and Rinty* in which he had a secondary but more prominent role. By then, Autry was already being cast in a lead role and the rotund Burnette would team up with him as a lovable comedy sidekick named Frog Millhouse (or plain Frog and sometimes as Smiley). Their association would produce more than sixty feature-length musical Westerns.

FRANK LUTHER. One of the first urban cowboys, Frank Luther made a career out of supplying urban listeners with their fix of traditional country music. A Kansas native, Luther was a professionally trained pianist who played in several vocal groups in his home state before moving to New York in 1928 and meeting fellow Kansas transplant Carson Robinson. The duo wrote and recorded several songs targeted at urbanites and regularly were guest on a country-radio programme hosted by Ethel Park Richardson. When Luther met and married a fiddler Zora Lyman who had once played with Robinson, he began to move away from country music, preferring to write and perform children's music.

FRANKIE MARVIN. Songwriter/steel guitarist Frankie Marvin (born Frank James Marvin) was a highly visible member of Gene Autry's onscreen coterie. Marvin, who had earlier performed with Autry on radio, would occasionally play a minor role as well, often as Gene's foreman, a ranch hand, or a cowboy. He would even join the bad guys in non-Autry vehicles such as the 1941 serial "*Adventures of Red Ryder*, in which he attempted to poison the Circle R's water supply. In all, Marvin appeared in more than eighty feature Westerns and at least six serials.

BLUE RIDGE PLAYBOYS. Leon Selph was one of the pioneers of Western Swing and Texas Swing. He was there at the beginning, even before it was called Western or Texas Swing. In 1934, after playing fiddle for Bob Wills, he started his own group the Blue Ridge Playboys. The Blue Ridge Playboys gained quite a following and were responsible for starting the careers of Western Swing legends Floyd Tillman, Moon Mullican, and Ted Daffan.

TEXAS JIM LEWIS.A Western swing musician, he formed the Lone Star Cowboys, a group that worked mainly in and around New York. From 1937 to 1939, he recorded for Vocalion, helping to popularize the Western Swing genre in the eastern USA.

TARLTON AND DARBY. Singer Tom Darby and slide guitarist Jimmie Tarlton were not only legendary bluesmen, but also pioneers of country music. Although they were only together for a brief time during the late 1920s and early 1930s, they popularized the steel slide guitar in the genre and exerted a heavy influence on the Allen Brothers and the Delmore Brothers.

ROY SMECK. (6 February 1900 – 5 April 1994) His skill on the banjo, guitar, steel guitar, and especially the ukulele, earned him the nickname "Wizard of the Strings". Born in Reading, Pennsylvania,

Smeck started on the vaudeville circuit. His style was influenced by Eddie Lang, Ikey Robinson, banjoist Harry Reser, and steel guitarist Sol Hoopii. Smeck could not sing well, so he developed novelty dances and trick playing to supplement his act.

PRAIRIE RAMBLERS. Especially with the presence of the word "ramblers" in the name, this group which originated in Kentucky may seem on the surface like just another old-time music or traditional country band. But judging from the group's versatility and the number of different genres they were comfortable with, the Prairie Ramblers have more in common with groundbreaking music groups such as the Beatles. One of the group's recordings, featuring its female vocalist Patsy Montana, was the first record by a female country artist to sell a million copies, so hit-parade gold dust was hardly out of this band's reach. The Prairie Ramblers were originally formed as the Kentucky Ramblers by mandolinist Charles Chick Hurt, and "Happy" Jack Taylor, who played both bass and tenor banjo. Both men hailed from the Summershade area near Glasgow, Kentucky. Relocating to Illinois, the two wound up collaborating with another pair of Kentucky players. These were fiddler and lead vocalist Tex Atchison and Floyd "Salty" Holmes, a multi-instrumentalist who beside his spicy nickname was also known as the "maestro of the harmonica." The group began working together at the outset of the 1930s and within a few years had made their radio debut on WOC out of Davenport, Iowa. Later, in 1932, the group moved to WLS Chicago, a station that would make country music history with innovative programs such as *Merry Go-Round* and *National Barn Dance*". Signed by Uncle Art in the mid thirties, one song that stood the test of time is "When I Grow Too Old To Dream".

LULU BELLE AND SCOTTY were one of the major country music acts of the 1930s and 1940s, known as "The Sweethearts of Country Music". Lulu Belle was born Myrtle Eleanor Cooper, 24 December 1914 in Boone, North Carolina. She died 8 February 1999. Scotty Wiseman was born 8 November 1909, in Spruce Pine, North Carolina. He died of a heart attack on 1 February 1981. Lulu Belle and Scotty enjoyed enormous national popularity thanks to their regular appearances on the *National Barn Dance* which was broadcast on WLS Radio in Chicago and was a serious rival to the *Grand Old Opry*. In fact, the *Barn Dance* enjoyed a large radio audience in the 1930s and early 1940s with some 20 million Americans regularly tuning in. The duo married in 1934, one year after Scotty became a regular on the *Barn Dance* (Lulu Belle had been a solo performer there since 1932). The duo is best known for their self-penned classic "Have I Told You Lately That I Love You?", which became one of the first country songs to attract major attention in pop circles and was recorded by many artists in both genres. Lulu Belle was the somewhat dominant star of the group with a comic persona as a wisecracking country girl. Her most famous novelty number was "Does Your Chewing Gum Lose its Flavor on the Bedpost".a song that was a big hit in1959 for skiffle artist Lonnie Donegan in England. In 1938, she was named Favorite Female Radio Star by the readers of *Radio Guide* magazine, an amazing feat for a country performer. Lulu Belle and Scotty recorded for many record labels over the years, including Vocalion Records, Columbia Records, Bluebird Records, and finally Starday Records.

SALTY HOMES. Floyd "Salty" Holmes (6 March 1909 – 1 January 1970) was an American country musician. Holmes was born in Glasgow, Kentucky. He became a virtuoso on the harmonica, specializing in the style known as "talking harp" which imitated the human voice (much like Sonny Terry). He also played the jug and guitar. He formed the group The Kentucky Ramblers in 1930, who changed their name to The Prairie Ramblers in 1933 and began broadcasting on Chicago radio station WLS with new vocalist Patsy Montana. They continued performing and recording under this name until 1952, playing country, hillbilly music, gospel, and pop songs. They were the backing group on Montana's platinum hit "I Want to Be a Cowboy's Sweetheart". Group members included Jack Taylor on bass, Chick Hurt on mandolin and Alan Crocket and, later, Tex Atchison on fiddle. They made over 100 recordings between 1933 and 1940, including as session musicians.

While a member of the Prairie Ramblers, Holmes befriended Gene Autry, who invited him to Hollywood to star in Westerns in 1936 and 1944; among the films Holmes appeared in are *Arizona Days* and

Saddle Leather Law. In a scene in *Arizona Days*, Holmes plays two harmonicas using both his mouth and nose. The Prairie Ramblers also backed Autry on some of his recordings in the 1930s. He collaborated with Jean Chapel as "Mattie and Salty", playing regularly on the *Grand Old Opry*; the two married in 1947 and divorced in 1956.
JOE KELLY. One of Chicago radio's most beloved personalities, Joe Kelly for a number of years hosted the WLS *National Barn Dance* as well as NBC's *Quiz Kids* broadcast. In the mid and later 1950s he hosted *The Totem Club* on WTTW television.
FRANK AND JAMES McGRAVEY. Folk music.
TEXAS RUBY. She made her first breakthrough in the music industry working with country bandleader, Zeke Clements, but by the mid-forties she and husband Curly Fox had developed their own stage act and were much in demand, including a stint as regulars on the *Grand Old Opry* from 1944 to 1948. The Foxs left the Opry and moved to Texas, where most of their concert dates were. The move seemed to push national stardom further away from the duo, who eventually in the early 1960s moved first to Los Angeles (appearing on the *Town Hall Party* country-music television series) and then back to Nashville in attempts to get back into the limelight.
CURLY FOX. Arnim LeRoy Fox was born in Graysville, Tennessee, 9 November 1910 and died 10 November 1995. In 1937, Fox, a fiddler, met singer Texas Ruby (Ruby Agnes Owen), sister of Tex Owens. They married shortly thereafter and began playing together professionally on the *Grand Old Opry* (where they performed from 1937 to 1939 and 1944 to 1948. They also performed together on various radio programmes nationwide. They occasionally recorded together, including a session for King Records in 1947. In 1948, Curly and Ruby moved to Houston, Texas, where they remained for over a decade, working in radio and television.

ZEKE WILLIAMS. A singing cowboy.
EZRA PAULETTE (BEVERLY HILLBILLIES). Ezra (longnecker) Paulette was the main vocalist of the cowboy-western Hillbillies.
ROY NEWMAN BAND. Roy Newman was a western-swing bandleader whose outfit was making records before Bob Wills and

was already broadening the boundaries of western swing before they were defined. Roy Newman & His Boys had a sound was also just about the least countrified of major western swing artists, being more Dixieland in character, especially in their use of the clarinet. Their singles were on Vocalion.

ASA MARTIN. Old-time Kentucky singer Asa Martin made many records during the 1920s and 1930s and was closely associated with the famed fiddler, Doc Roberts, for whom he played rhythm guitar. In turn, Roberts frequently played mandolin on Martin's recordings; Roberts' son James even sang duets with Martin under the name Martin and Roberts.

FIDDLING DOC ROBERTS. Doc Roberts was born in 1898 near Kirksville, Madison County, Kentucky and recorded more than eighty traditional tunes over a course of ten years with Gennett, American Record Company, and Paramount. He played in a bluesy style, which is attributed to his mentor, Owen Walker, a black fiddler born in 1857 who taught Roberts most of his tunes.

RILEY CRABTREE. (1912–died 1984) was a fan of both Hank Williams and Jimmie Rodgers. His first two sessions consisted of Jimmie Rodgers' songs with beautiful yodelling. Later, he seemed to be more impressed with Hank's style. He didn't copy either of the two. He soon developed his own country-blues voice, with so much feeling that the *Grand Old Opry* wanted him as a regular in the early 1950s. If he hadn't turned down that offer and not decided to stay near his home in the Dallas area to become a regular at the *Big "D" Jamboree*, he might have been a second Hank Williams. Riley did the tribute song "When Hank Williams Met Jimmie Rodgers" (1953).

BILLY WALKER. A native of west Texas who was active on the *Grand Old Opry*, Billy Walker emerged from the talent-rich Dallas scene of the late 1940s and early 1950s. After a brief stint on Capitol, he was signed to Columbia in 1951 at almost exactly the same time as Ray Price. For a while, Walker, Price, and Lefty Frizzell were all recording at the legendary Jim Beck studio in Dallas, which did for 1950s honky-tonk what Sun Studio in Memphis did for rockabilly. Nevertheless, Walker enjoyed his greatest success ten years later in Nashville, where the studio sound was perhaps more suited to his smooth tenor voice. Walker died 21 May 2006, in an automobile accident in Alabama. – Dan Cooper, *All Music Guide*

EDDIE DEAN. Eddie Dean made his name as a country-western singer on radio in the 1930s. He journeyed to Hollywood to make it in western movies, debuting in *Manhattan Love Song* (1934), but he could only land bit parts in features and musical shorts. His career started to take off in the early 1940s, though, and by 1945, he was among the more popular of the cowboy stars.

Jimmie Davis. Rose to prominence in the 1930s with a smooth vocal style that helped popularize country music far beyond its original rural, southern audience. In many ways, his music was a harbinger of Eddy Arnold's broadly accessible style. Davis's best-selling records –particularly "Nobody's Darling But Mine" and "You Are My Sunshine" –not only made him a wealthy and well-known singer but also carried him to the governorship of Louisiana. He was inducted into the Hall of Fame in 1972. – Country Music Hall of Fame and Museum

TEX WILLIAMS. Sol "Tex" Williams was born in Ramsey, Illinois. In the 1940s, western swing music was at its peak, and among the more popular performers were Bob Wills and Spade Cooley. Tex Williams was the lead vocalist and guitar player with Cooley's band, and he and several of the members left to form an outfit called Tex Williams and the Western Caravan around 1946. Their biggest hit, "Smoke! Smoke! Smoke (That Cigarette)" came out a couple years later. "Smoke" was written by Merle Travis for Williams.

SMOKEY ROGERS. For his many years playing in California's western-swing scene, is best known for penning the classic ballad "Gone". The song went nowhere when Ferlin Husky first recorded it in 1952, but when Husky re-recorded "Gone" in 1956, it went straight to the top of the country charts, where it stayed for eight weeks and even crossed over to the pop charts. Rogers also co-wrote "Spanish Fandango" with western-swing king Bob Wills, which was released in 1947. In 1949, Rogers had a modest hit with "A Little Bird told Me." Beginning in 1949, Rogers appeared in some of Universal's pre-music video "musical featurettes" along with Tex Williams. Rogers worked for years with Williams, as he also did with

Spade Cooley. Never camera shy, Rogers hosted his own TV show in San Diego in the 1950s.

MADDOX BROTHERS AND ROSE. Rose Maddox exerted a heavy influence on honky-tonk females through her recordings with the Maddox Brothers but later turned to traditional bluegrass forms as well to inspire folk revivalists of the 1960s and 1970s. Born Roselea Brogdon on 15 August 1925, she moved from Alabama to Modesto, California, with her family to make a better living as farm labourers. After several years of hard work and occasional amateur musical appearances, Fred Maddox lobbied KTRB-Modesto to give a time slot to him and his brothers Cliff, Cal, Don, and Henry. The radio station agreed, but on the condition that the Maddoxes include a female singer. Rose was recruited-as an eleven-year-old, and the group soon appeared in bars as well as on the radio show. They won a contest at the California State Fair in 1939, and began to broadcast at KFBK in Sacramento, which included several stations in nearby states as part of its coverage. They recorded for 4 Star and Columbia, making annual trips east to appear on the *Louisiana Hayride* and *Grand Old Opry*.

JOHNNY MARVIN. Marvin signed with Columbia Records in the mid-1920s recording as Johnny Marvin, The Ukulele Ace. The contract was not exclusive, and he also made recordings for other record labels and their dime-store subsidiaries under many pseudonyms, such as Jimmy May and His Uke, Ukulele Luke, George Thorne, Billy Hancock, Ken Wallace, Elton Spence and His Uke, and Jack Lane and His Uke. The most popular of his pseudonyms was Honey Duke and His Uke on the Harmony label. Interestingly, he had recorded under his own name, Johnny Marvin, on Edison wax cylinders.

JIMMY LONG. Jimmy Long was a railroad man with a knack for singing and playing the guitar who emerged on radio and then on records in the 1920s and early 1930s. If that background sounds a little like the early biography of Gene Autry, it's no accident -- Long worked the railroads at the same time that Autry did, and the two ended up becoming performing and recording partners. Long also co-wrote the song that became Autry's signature tune, "That Silver

Haired Daddy of Mine"; and Autry married Long's niece Ina in 1930.

PATSY MONTANA. She was inducted into the Country Music Hall of Fame in 1996. Born Ruby Blevins in Hot Springs, Arkansas, the eleventh child and first daughter of a farmer, she attended schools in her hometown of Hope. She was influenced early on by the music of Jimmie Rodgers, and as a child she learned to yodel and play organ, guitar, and violin. Patsy was the first woman in country music to have a million-selling single – 1935's "I Want to Be a Cowboy's Sweetheart" – and was a mainstay on the *National Barn Dance* on Chicago radio station WLS for many years. She might also have been country music's first female session musician. In the 1930s and 1940s, she recorded in New York on the ARC label. Her other hits included "Rodeo Sweetheart", "Montana Plains", and "I Want to Be a Cowboy's Dream". In 1939, she made her full-length feature-film debut with Gene Autry in *Colorado Sunset.*

MOLLY O'DAY. Her career was relatively brief, but her lasting influence has proven massive. Born Lois LaVerne Williamson on 9 July 1923 to a coal-mining family living in a remote Appalachian community in Eastern Kentucky. She spent her childhood enamoured of cowgirl singers like Patsy Montana,, Lulu Belle Wiseman, Texas Ruby Owens, and Lily May Ledford and eventually began singing and playing guitar in a string band with her brothers Cecil ("Skeets") on fiddle and Joe ("Duke") on banjo. In 1939, Skeets began playing on a radio station in Charleston, West Virginia, and his sister soon followed, adopting the stage name "Mountain Fern". A year later, now under the name "Dixie Lee Williamson,," she joined guitarist Lynn Davis' band the Forty Niners, and in 1941, she and Davis married. It was her deeply felt solo performances of inspirational songs that had the biggest impact and that led writer/publisher Fred Rose to sign the singer to Columbia Records. There, O'Day performed a number of songs written by a young Hank Williams, who she had already known from their days on the radio circuit; in fact, it was Williams who taught O'Day her best-loved song, "Tramp on the Street," one of eight tunes she cut during her first studio session in late 1946. Backed by Davis, her brother Skeets, bassist Mac Wiseman, and George

"Speedy" Krise on the dobro, the recordings gave a further boost to O'Day's surging popularity, but already she was having trouble coping with her success. O'Day and Davis spent much of 1947 out of music, but in December of that year she returned to the studio, where she recorded her crowd-pleaser "Matthew Twenty-Four". She and Davis spent much of the next several years on the road, where she began performing religious material almost exclusively; in mid-1949, she cut another session, recording songs like "Teardrops Falling in the Snow", "Poor Ellen Smith", and Williams' "On the Evening Train". In the latter half of the year, O'Day suffered a nervous breakdown and was hospitalized; although she did record again in 1950 and 1951, she largely turned her back on show business afterward.

STANLEY BROTHERS. Ralph and his brother Carter performed as the Stanley Brothers with their band the Clinch Mountain Boys from 1946 to 1966. After Carter's death in 1966, Ralph continued to perform, eventually reviving the Clinch Mountain Boys. Larry Sparks, Roy Lee Centers, Ricky Skaggs, Keith Whitley, and Charlie Sizemore were among those who played in the revived band. Stanley has maintained an extensive touring schedule. His work was featured in the 2000 film *O Brother, Where Art Thou?* in which he sang the dirge "O Death". Stanley was inducted into the International Bluegrass Music Hall of Honor in 1992 and has come to be known in the world of bluegrass music by the popular title, "Dr. Ralph Stanley" after being awarded an honorary doctorate of music from Lincoln Memorial University in Harrogate, Tennessee, in 1976.

SONS OF THE PIONEERS. America's premier western singing group was formed in 1933 by Ohio-born Leonard Franklin Slye (later Roy Rogers) and was initially called the Pioneer Trio. The group included Canadian-born Bob Nolan and Tim Spencer of Oklahoma. In late 1933 or early 1934, the trio added Hugh Farr, one of the finest country fiddlers of that era, and in mid-1935 guitarist Karl Farr, Hugh's brother, joined the quartet, bringing with him a unique skill that would influence musicians for years to come. Slye, Spencer, Nolan, and Hugh and Karl Farr are referred to by some as the "original" Sons of the Pioneers. Uncle Art recorded them for ARC in 1936. In 1980, they were inducted into the Hall of Fame.

ROY ROGERS. Born Leonard Franklin Slye (5 November 1911 – 6 July 1998), was a singer and cowboy actor. He and his third wife Dale Evans, his golden palomino Trigger, and his German Shepherd Bullet, were featured in over 100 movies and *The Roy Rogers Show*. The radio show ran on radio for nine years before moving to television from 1951 through 1957. His productions usually featured two sidekicks, Pat Brady, (who drove a jeep called "Nellybelle"), and the crotchety Gabby Hayes. Roy's nickname was "King of the Cowboys". Dale's nickname was "Queen of the West". For many Americans (and non-Americans), he was the embodiment of the all-American hero.
JIMMY DICKENS. Born into a large West Virginia family, Dickens got his early radio experience on local radio station WJLS with performers like Mel Steele, Molly O'Day, and Johnnie Bailes. Through the 1940s, he had his own radio programs in such spots as Fairmont, West Virginia; Indianapolis; Cincinnati; Topeka; and Saginaw, Michigan. Roy Acuff heard him for the first time in Cincinnati in 1947 and brought him to the attention of both *Grand Old Opry* officials and Art Satherley at Columbia Records. After guest appearances he signed with Columbia on 16 September 1948, and joined the Opry shortly thereafter. Dickens became an instant success for both, beginning in early 1949.

LESTER FLATT. Lester Flatt was born in Tennessee in 1914 and learned to play banjo from his father at an early age. He didn't particularly like the banjo, so quit that to pick up guitar before he was seven. By the age of ten, Flatt was playing guitar and singing in local schools and churches. As a teenager, he moved to North Carolina to work in a silk mill. While there, he married his wife, Gladys, with whom he began performing as a duo. When the mill shut down, the Flatts returned to Tennessee for a short time before moving to Virginia. As the result of a bout of rheumatoid arthritis, Flatt quit millwork permanently to focus on a career in music. He played with a handful of groups before being invited by Charlie Monroe to join the Kentucky Pardners in North Carolina. Charlie had Flatt playing mandolin and singing tenor, neither of which pleased Flatt too much. Upon finally leaving the Kentucky Pardners, Charlie's brother Bill

Monroe immediately invited Flatt to join his Blue Grass Boys as a guitar player and lead singer. His first gig with the band was in 1945 at the *Grand Old Opry*, with no prior rehearsal. Soon after, banjo player Earl Scruggs joined the Boys.

LEFTY FRIZZELL. He was inducted into the Nashville Songwriter's Hall of Fame in 1972 and the Country Music Hall of Fame in 1982. He has been called the most influential singer/stylist in the history of country music. He was born William Orville Frizzell on 31 March 1928 in Corsicana, Texas. His father was an oil driller who moved the family from Texas to El Dorado, Arkansas, shortly after his birth. His uncle Lawrence bought him his first guitar from an old black farmer for two dollars. With that guitar and an old Victrola, he learned every song of his hero and greatest influence, Jimmie Rodgers. During this time, Frizzell developed the style of singing that would revolutionize how country songs would be sung. By age twelve, Frizzell, who was called Sonny by his family and close friends, had his own spot on a children's show at an El Dorado radio station. Moving back to Texas in the early 1940s, Frizzell earned his nickname Lefty, following a schoolyard fight when he was 14.

By his early twenties, Frizzell was a regular at the Ace of Clubs in Big Springs, Texas, and after spending years singing in other various honky tonks, barn dances, and parties, Lefty got the attention of Columbia Records. Lefty had a heart slightly bigger than Oklahoma, but some say his personal opinion of his own talent was not so big. Merle Haggard has publicly told the world how he loved Lefty; he was the first person to put him on the stage as a teenager. How nervous Merle was to open for his hero, Lefty Frizzell! Merle says "When I was fifteen years old, I thought Lefty hung the moon. You know – I'm not sure he didn't." Haggard recorded his own tribute single, "That's The Way It Was In '51". Willie Nelson cut a tribute album entitled, "To Lefty, From Willie" in 1977 in honour of his friend.

STUART HAMBLEN (Carl). He was inducted into the Country/ Western Songwriters Hall of Fame in 1970, was presented the ACM Pioneer Award in1972, received the Gene Autry Golden Boot Award 1988, and was inducted into Texas Country Music Hall of Fame 2001. He later received a star on Hollywood's Walk of Fame. A radio cowboy between 1931 and 1952, Hamblen had a series of highly popular radio programmes on the West Coast of the United States. He composed music and acted in motion pictures with such other stars as Gene Autry, Roy Rogers, and John Wayne. In 1949, he underwent a religious conversion at a Billy Graham revival in Los Angeles. He soon gave up his secular radio and film career to enter Christian broadcasting with his radio show, *The Cowboy Church of the Air,*

FLOYD TILLMAN. Inducted into the Country Music Hall of Fame in 1984, Floyd was the youngest of eleven children born to a sharecropping family in Ryan, Oklahoma. He was three months old when his family moved to Post, Texas. He learned banjo, mandolin, and guitar, and by age eighteen, he was playing in the popular German-Czech swing band of Adolph and Emil Hofner in San Antonio. He also played in a Houston dance band. Bandleader-fiddler Leon "Pappy" Selph recruited Floyd as lead singer for the Blue Ridge Playboys, which included pianist Moon Mullican and steel guitarist Ted Daffan. "It Makes No Difference Now" was the first of his many songs covered with great success by mainstream artists. Years later, Diana Ross and the Supremes and Ray Charles recorded versions of the song.

RAY PRICE. He was inducted into the Country Music Hall of Fame in 1996. Ray became one of the stalwarts of 1950's honky-tonk music, with such songs as "Talk To Your Heart" (1952) and "Release Me". He later developed the famous "Ray Price Shuffle", a 4/4 arrangement of honky tonk with a walking baseline, which can be heard on "Crazy Arms" (1956) and many of his other recordings from the late 1950s. Ray met Uncle Art in 1951 when he signed for Columbia Records, Don Law was given the job of producing Ray by Art, as Ray said in an interview with me in October 2008. "Art was already a legend by then; he would bring me songs to look at and was always friendly, kind and considerate. Uncle Art should be held in highest respect as the man who single-handedly did so much for the music industry. Not forgetting Don Law, also an Englishman, who succeeded Art at Columbia. He was a great guy who did so much for me and my career." Other hits included, "Make the World Go Away",

"She Wears My Ring", "Heartaches By The Number", "Danny Boy", "For the Good Times". There are many, many more.

MARGE TILLMAN. A member of her husband Floyd's band

FRED ROSE. Knowles Fred Rose was a principal figure in the rise of the Nashville music industry between 1942 and 1954 in his roles as music publisher; songwriter; producer, and talent scout. Rose's parents separated soon after he was born, and he grew up with his mother and other relatives in St. Louis. There he supplemented the family income by playing piano and singing for tips in local saloons. By 1917, he had moved to Chicago, where he found similar work in rough-and-tumble clubs and bars of the South Side. During the 1920s, Rose made his name as a successful songwriter, authoring or co-authoring pop and jazz hits such as "Red Hot Mama", "Deed I Do", and "Honest and Truly". During these same years, he also made piano rolls; broadcast on Chicago radio stations KYW, WLS, and WBBM; and recorded for the Brunswick label. In 1933, having lost his Chicago radio job because of a drinking problem, Rose moved to Nashville to work on WSM. Between 1933 and 1938, he divided his time mostly among Nashville, Chicago, and New York, performing on live radio shows and shopping his songs to music publishers. While continuing to write pop material, he also began to work closely with the Vagabonds and the Delmore Brothers of WSM's *Grand Old Opry* and also wrote songs for cowboy singer Ray Whitley, then working in New York. In about 1935, in New York, Rose converted to Christian Science, a faith that would guide his personal and professional life from then on. In 1936 he scored his first pop-western hit, "We'll Rest at the End of the Trail", recorded by Tex Ritter, the Sons of the Pioneers, and Bing Crosby. Rose spent most of the years 1938 to 1942 in Hollywood penning a series of hits for cowboy film stars Gene Autry, Ray Whitley, and Roy Rogers. In 1942, Rose joined Roy Acuff in founding Acuff-Rose Publications, Nashville's first major country publishing house. Rose continued to write or co-write country standards such as "Wait for the Light to Shine", "Afraid", and "Blue Eyes Crying in the Rain" while serving as an expert editor, most notably for his protégé Hank Williams. Rose also made Acuff-Rose a solid institutional base for aspiring songwriters such as Boudleaux and Felice Bryant. In addition, Rose served as MGM Records' unsalaried, Nashville-based A&R man. For this label he supervised sessions for Williams, the Louvin Brothers, Red Sovine, Bob Wills, and many other acts. For all of these efforts and for his tireless promotion of country music within the American music industry, Rose was elected to the Country Music Hall of Fame in 1961 – the first year the honour was bestowed by the Country Music Association (CMA). Rose died of heart failure on 1 December 1954.

– John Rumble, Adapted from the Country Music Hall of Fame® and Museum's *Encyclopedia of Country Music*, published by Oxford University Press. (In the following chapters there will be more on Fred Rose as he was a close associate of Uncle Art.)

MERLE TRAVIS. He was inducted into the Nashville Songwriters Hall of Fame in 1970 and elected to the Country Music Hall of Fame in 1977.The son of a tobacco farmer-turned-coalminer, Merle Travis spent most of his childhood in the small town of Ebenezer, living amongst conditions of extreme poverty. His father played the five-string banjo, and for a while Merle also took up the instrument but by the age of 12 he switched over to guitar, after being presented a non-descript model by his brother. From some of his coalmining neighbours (one of whom was the father of two boys who later became known as The Everly Brothers) he learned a picking technique that used the thumb and two fingers to play bass and melody lines simultaneously – a technique that was responsible for much of his later fame, due to both the incredible technical prowess he achieved through its use and the variety of musical styles to which it could be applied. By his late teens, Travis hit the road, busking around the country and eventually landing a job with The Tennessee Tomcats, followed by a period with the higher-profile group Clayton McMichen's Georgia Wildcats, beginning in 1937. A year later, he had secured a regular spot on WLW in Cincinnati as part of The Drifting Pioneers – an opportunity brought to an end by the outbreak of World War II, but as a result of which he managed to broaden his exposure to a national audience.

At the same time as his membership in the Pioneers, Travis began collaborating with old-style banjo performer Grandpa Jones and The Delmore Brothers in a gospel group named The Brown's Ferry Four. By 1943, he and Jones were recording as The Shepherd Brothers for the King Records label, with whom Travis also produced solo material under the name Bob McCarthy. A brief period with the Marines was soon followed by a move to Los Angeles, where he worked in a variety of country bands and even launched an acting career with roles in Westerns like *The Old Texas Trail* (1944) and *Beyond the Pecos* (1945). After making the acquaintance of Tex Ritter and securing a record deal with the newly-founded Capitol Records label, Travis' recording career finally began to make some progress: his first release "No Vacancy" scored reasonable success with both sides, and follow-up songs "Divorce Me C.O.D", "Missouri", and "So Round, So Firm, So Fully Packed" went even further, with "So Round" climbing to the number one position on the country charts. For Ritter he penned "Smoke, Smoke, Smoke That Cigarette", which went on to become Capitol's first million-selling release. A less immediately popular venture was "Folk Songs From The Hills", an eight-song collection themed around the plight of the coal-mining community. Tracks such as "Sixteen Tons" and "Dark as a Dungeon" have since become classics. Around 1948, Travis met machinist and instrument-maker Paul Bigsby, whose skills he enlisted to realize a design he had created for a solid body electric guitar. The result later attracted the attention of guitar manufacturer Leo Fender, who adapted and simplified the design into what he called the Fender Broadcaster, issued in 1950 as the first commercially available solid body guitar. By this time Travis' time as a hit-making songwriter had more-or-less passed, and he turned his attention back towards his playing, taking a job as lead guitarist for Hank Thompson's Western Swing Band. Alcoholism was beginning to impact on both his personal and professional life but his career was far from over: in 1953 his film work reached its peak with an appearance in *From Here To Eternity*, and in 1955, Tennessee Ernie Ford turned his anthem "Sixteen Tons" into a crossover hit. In the 1960s, Travis moved his base of operations out of California and for the first time began working in Nashville, Tennessee. Aside from a second folk song collection, "Songs of the

Coal Mines" in 1963, his recorded output focused primarily on instrumental material, showcasing a technical prowess on the guitar that remained undiminished through the years. Incidents of public drunkenness cast a pall over his reputation, however, and it wasn't until his collaborative record and tour with Chet Atkins in 1974 that he began to put his life back together. (NNDB. com)

SPADE COOLEY. His parents were a mix of Anglo and Native American, and Cooley attended Indian school. His father, John, was an amateur fiddler. Spade took on the title of "King of Western Swing".

Here's a brief biographical sketch from www.bakersfield.com. If you want to know more see David Krajicek's piece on www.trutv.com

> Born Donnell Clyde Cooley to an impoverished family; moves to Oregon at age 4.
>
> Family moves to Modesto in 1930; by this time Spade, trained in classical violin and cello, is playing at dances.
>
> Gets established as a movie stand-in for Roy Rogers, whom he resembled, in 1934. He earns his nickname from his prowess at poker.
>
> Starts his own band, becomes a star at the Venice Pier Ballroom near Los Angeles, and lands a recording contract.
>
> His first hit, "Shame, Shame on You," recorded in the early '40's, becomes his theme song. As a Western Swing star, Cooley now rivals Bob Wills.
>
> Band rises to headliner-status at the prestigious Santa Monica Ballroom. Cooley appears in numerous movies, including *Chatterbox, The Singing Bandit*, *The Singing Sheriff*, *Outlaws of the Rockies*, and *Texas Panhandle.*
>
> Spade gets his own TV show on KTLA, "The Hoffman Hayride," named for a sponsoring TV manufacturer, in 1947. The shows attract 75 percent of the viewing audience throughout the late '40s. Ratings eventually dwindle and show goes off the air in the early '50s.
>
> Spade, still a popular live performer, tours extensively throughout the mid- and late-50s. He plays at the Blackboard on numerous occasions.

In July 1961, Spade, living in the Mojave area, attacks his estranged wife, beating and kicking her to death.

(More in Verse Six)

HOOSIER HOT SHOTS. The Hoosier Hot Shots were an American quartet of madcap musicians who entertained on stage, screen, radio, and records from the mid 1930s into the 1970s. The group initially consisted of players from Indiana. Beginning on local Indiana radio in the early 1930s, the Hot Shots went on to a successful national radio career on the *National Barn Dance* at WLS in Chicago, Illinois, and a successful and prolific recording career, before moving to Hollywood to star in many feature-length western movies. Over their career, the Hoosier Hot Shots recorded hundreds of seventy eights for such labels as Banner, Conqueror, Decca, Melotone, Oriole, Perfect, Romeo, and Vocalion. Some of these releases have made it to LPs, cassettes, and compact discs. Recordings of songs made by the Hoosier Hot Shots often include the signature spoken (by Ken Triesch) intro, "Are you ready, Hezzie?" followed by the sound of the bustle of the musicians preparing to play their instruments. However, the tightly-rehearsed skill of the performers lets the listener in on the joke as soon as the song actually begins. Their producer (Uncle Art) avoided recording too many takes of their performances, preferring a spontaneous sound: according to one member, Uncle Al would record at most two takes of a particular song, and use the one that sounded worst. Between 1937 and 1950, the Hot Shots appeared in more than twenty movies, sharing billing with the likes of Gene Autry, Dale Evans, Bob Wills, and Merle Travis. During the mid- to late 1940s they starred in their own series of musical westerns for Columbia Pictures. During the World War II era, their popularity was at its peak and, in addition to their normal pursuits, they toured with the USO in North Africa and Italy. Frank Kettering was drafted in 1943 and replaced by singer-bassist Gil Taylor. They moved to the West Coast where they continued to make movies, records, stage, and radio appearances. They made the transition to television easily and were seen on such TV shows as the Tex Ritter "Ranch Party." Signed by Uncle Art in the Mid 1930's.

TEX RITTER. Inducted into the Hall of Fame in 1964, he was

born Woodward Maurice Ritter in Murvaul, Texas, the son of James Everett Ritter and Martha Elizabeth Matthews. He grew up on his family's farm in Panola County and attended grade school in Carthage. He then attended South Park High School in Beaumont. After graduating with honours, he entered the University of Texas at Austin. He studied pre-law, majoring in government, political science, and economics. One of the early pioneers of country music, Ritter soon became interested in show business. In 1928, he sang on KPRC Radio in Houston, a thirty-minute show featuring cowboy songs. In that same year, he moved to New York City and quickly landed a job in the men's chorus of the Broadway show "The New Moon" (1928). He appeared as "The Cowboy" in the Broadway production "Green Grow the Lilacs" (1930), which was the basis for the later musical Oklahoma!. He also played the part of Sagebrush Charlie in "The Round Up" (1932) and "Mother Lode" (1934). Ritter also worked on various radio programs.. In 1932, he starred on the WOR Radio show *The Lone Star Rangers*, which was New York's first broadcast western. He sang songs and told tales of the Old West. Ritter wrote and starred in *Cowboy Tom's Roundup* on WINS Radio in New York in 1933. This daily children's cowboy radio programme aired over three stations on the East Coast for three years. These shows marked the beginning of Ritter's popularity in radio, which paved the way for his upcoming singing career. He also performed on the WHN Radio show *Barndance* and sang on NBC Radio. He appeared in several radio dramas, including CBS's *Bobby Benson's Adventures* and *Death Valley Days*.

Ritter began recording for American Record Corporation (Columbia Records) in 1933 when he was signed by Uncle Art. His first released recording was "Goodbye Ole Paint." He also recorded "Rye Whiskey" for that label. In 1935, he signed with Decca Records, where he recorded his first original recordings, "Sam Hall" and "Get Along Little Dogie." In 1936, he moved to Los Angeles, California. His motion picture debut was in *Song Of the Gringo*" (1936) for Grand National Pictures. He starred in twelve movies for Grand National, "B" grade Westerns, which included *Headin' for the Rio Grande* (1936), and *Trouble in Texas* (1937) co-starring Rita Hayworth (then known as Rita Cansino). After starring in *Utah Trail* (1938), Ritter left the financially troubled Grand National. Between 1938 and 1945, he starred in around forty "singing cowboy" movies, mostly to critical scorn. Ritter made four movies with actress Dorothy Fay at Monogram Pictures: *Song of the Buckaroo* (1938), *Sundown on the Prairie (*1939*), Rollin' Westward* (1939) and *Rainbow Over the Range* (1940). He recorded a total of twenty-nine songs for Decca, the last being in 1939 in Los Angeles as part of Tex Ritter and His Texans. Tex helped start United Cerebral Palsy Associations, Inc, after his son, Thomas, was found to have cerebral palsy. Tex, Thomas, and John spent a great deal of time raising money and public awareness to help others with cerebral palsy. Ritter was the first artist signed with the newly-formed Capitol Records as well as being their first western singer. His first recording session was on 11 June, 1942. His music recording career began what was his most successful period. In 1952, Ritter recorded the movie title-track song "High Noon (Do Not Forsake Me, Oh My Darlin')", which became a hit. He sang "High Noon" at the first Academy Awards ceremony to be televised in 1953, and he recorded the song a number of times. It received an Oscar for Best Song that year.

MARTY ROBBINS. Martin David Robinson (26 September – 8 December 1982) was inducted into the Nashville Songwriters Hall of Fame in 1975, and the Country Music Hall of Fame in 1982.Robbins has a star on the Hollywood Walk of Fame at 6666 Hollywood Boulevard. One of the most popular and successful American country and western singers of his era, Robbins' songs were often eclectic, touching notably on an array of world music. For most of his nearly four decade career, Robbins was rarely far from the country-music charts, and several of his songs also became pop hits. Robbins was born in Glendale, a suburb of Phoenix, in Maricopa County, Arizona. He was reared in a difficult family situation. His father took odd jobs to support the family of ten children. His father's drinking led to divorce in 1937. Among his warmer memories of his childhood, Robbins recalled having listened to stories of the American West told by his maternal grandfather, Texas Bob Heckle, a former Texas Ranger and medicine show performer. Robbins left

the troubled home at the age of seventeen to serve in the United States Navy as an LCT coxswain during World War II. He was stationed in the Solomon Islands in the Pacific. To pass the time during the war, he learned to play the guitar, started writing songs, and came to love Hawaiian music. After his discharge from the military in 1945, he began to play at local venues in Phoenix, then moved on to host his own radio station show on KTYL. He thereafter had his own television show on KPHO in Phoenix. After Little Jimmy Dickens made a guest appearance on Robbins' TV show, Dickens got Robbins a record deal with Columbia Records. Robbins became an immensely popular singing star at the *Grand Old Opry* in Nashville, Tennessee. He was especially known for his kindness toward his many fans.
VERNON DALHART. (1883-1948_. Inducted into the Hall of Fame in 1981,he was one of the most productive and versatile figures of the early recording industry, who by chance slipped into the role of a singer of hillbilly songs and became by far the most prolific recorder of such material in the 1920s. Born Marion Try Slaughter, he derived his professional name from a couple of Texas towns where he worked as a cattle puncher in his teens before studying voice at the Dallas Conservatory of Music. By 1910, he was pursuing his career in New York, where he filled roles in opera and operetta productions. His first recording, "Can't You Hear Me Callin', Caroline?" (Edison, 1917), revealed his skill with dialect songs and for some years he was busy making records for Edison, Columbia, and other labels as a journeyman studio artist handling every kind of repertoire required by the popular disc market, from "coon song" to Hawaiian.
His 1924 Victor recording of "The Wreck of the Old '97" coupled with "The Prisoner's Song" became country music's first million-seller and redirected the course of his career. Over the next nine years, he devoted himself primarily to hillbilly songs, of which he recorded several hundred, routinely cutting the same material for half a dozen or more different companies. Since many of these recordings would then be released on subsidiary labels, a collection of all his distinct issues would run into thousands, though this near-domination of the hillbilly disc market was somewhat masked by an extensive use of pseudonyms such as Al Craver (Columbia), Tobe Little (OKeh)

and Jeff Fuller (Vocalion). A typical Dalhart recording featured a studio violinist, his own harmonica and sometimes Jew's harp, and the guitar of Carson Robison, Dalhart's regular partner from 1924 to 1928, who also frequently sang a tenor part and wrote much of his material. They were joined in trio performances by the singer and violinist, Adelyne Hood. Though Dalhart drew on minstrel-stage repertoire like "Golden Slippers" and cowboy songs like "Bury Me Not on the Lone Prairie," which he had learned in his youth in Texas, his richest vein of song was topical compositions such as "The Death of Floyd Collins," "The John T. Scopes Trial" (about the Dayton, Tennessee, court case over the teaching of evolution), "Little Marian Parker," "Farm Relief Song," and other pieces inspired by news stories of the day. Although Dalhart is regarded by most scholars as peripheral to the stylistic development of country music, his recordings undoubtedly circulated widely in the South and disseminated songs that were taken up by both professional and amateur country performers. He is perhaps more important, however, for conveying a flavour of southern song to audiences unaccustomed to it, without the distractions of bucolic humour or impenetrable accent. As the veteran producer Ralph Peer wrote in *Variety* in 1955, "Dalhart had the peculiar ability to adapt hillbilly music to suit the taste of the non-hillbilly population… He was a professional substitute for a real hillbilly." In this respect Dalhart may be seen as a kind of role model for the highly popular folksong collector and singer Bradley Kincaid as well as for more obviously dependent and lesser-known figures such as Frank Luther. Dalhart's recording career virtually ended with the Depression—after 1933 there was just one final session for Bluebird in 1939—and by 1942 he was reduced to working as a factory night-watchman. For a few years he offered his services as a voice teacher, though the thousands of recordings that could have furnished his credentials had long passed out of circulation, and the musical idiom to which he had made so singular a contribution had left him far behind.

– Tony Russell, Adapted from the Country Music Hall of Fame and Museum's *Encyclopedia of Country Music (*Oxford University Press)

HANK PENNY. Herbert Clayton Penny (1918--1992) was an

accomplished banjo player and practitioner of western swing. He worked as a comedian best known for his backwoods character "That Plain Ol' Country Boy" on TV with Spade Cooley. He first entered the studio under the guidance of Uncle Art to record numbers like "When I Take My Sugar to Tea" and Penny's own "Flamin' Mamie". After the Radio Cowboys joined the cast of the Atlanta-based programme *Crossroad Follies*, Forsmark left the group, to be replaced by Noel Boggs; at the same time, they also welcomed a new fiddle player by the name of Boudleaux Bryant. After turning down offers to take over vocal chores for both Pee Wee King's Golden West Cowboys and the Light Crust Doughboys, Penny moved the group to Nashville in 1939, where they again recorded with Satherley. Shortly after, Boggs left the group to join Jimmy Wakely and was replaced by Eddie Duncan. After recording songs like "Tobacco State Swing" and "Peach Tree Shuffle" in Chicago in mid-1940, the band was forced to dissolve after most of its members were drafted. Penny was married to country singer Sue Thompson from 1953 to 63. Penny had three hits on the Billboard Country Singles chart, all of which made it to Number Four: "Steel Guitar Stomp" (1946), an instrumental featuring both Noel Boggs on steel guitar and guitarist Merle Travis, "Get Yourself a Red Head" (1946), and his own composition "Bloodshot Eyes" (1950). He was a lifelong fan of jazz.

BOB WILLS AND THE TEXAS PLAYBOYS. Jim Rob Wills, inducted into the Hall of Fame in1968, became known as the king of western swing. (born 6 March 1905, near Kosse, Texas, U.S.–died 13 May 1975, Fort Worth, Texas) as a country music fiddler, singer, and songwriter. Wills learned fiddle from his father. In Tulsa, Okla., in 1934 he formed the Texas Playboys; their radio performances made him a star in the Southwest, and in 1942, the group moved to California, performing in dance halls and films. They pioneered the "western swing" genre, which blended traditional hoedown fiddling with big-band swing and blues. Wills' best-known compositions include "San Antonio Rose" and "Panhandle Rag". The whole story is told in the book by Charles R. Townsend. *San Antonio Rose* (University of Illinois Press). There's more in Verse Four.)

ROY ACUFF. Roy Claxton Acuff (15 September 1903–23 November 1992) was inducted into the Country Music Hall Of Fame 1962. He was known around the world as the "King of Country Music". He was born in Maynardville, Tennessee, to Ida Carr and Simon E. Neil Acuff as the third of five children. He played semi-professional baseball but a sunstroke in 1929 and a nervous breakdown in 1930 ended his aspirations to play for the New York Yankees. He then turned his attention to his father's fiddle and began playing in a travelling medicine show, often performing in blackface. He toured the Southern United States and eventually formed a band called The Crazy Tennesseans. In 1936, he recorded his two most enduring songs, the traditional "The Great Speckled Bird" and "The Wabash Cannonball". He debuted at the *Grand Old Opry* two years later. He was booked as a fiddler, and he should have played the "Turkey Buzzard" for a square-dancing segment, but he decided to try and sing "The Great Speckled Bird". His decision was not well received; however, Acuff became a regular on the Opry, forming a backing band called the Smoky Mountain Boys, led by friend and dobro player Bashful Brother Oswald. By 1940, Acuff was the star of the show. His recording of The" House of the Rising Sun" on 3 November 1938 is the first known commercial recording of the song. He released several singles in the 1940s such as "The Wreck on the Highway", "Beneath That Lonely Mound of Clay", and "The Precious Jewel". During the 1940s, he also appeared in eight movies. In 1942, a man of many talents, he formed a music publishing venture with Chicago songwriter Fred Rose. Acuff-Rose Music became a country-music phenomenon, owning huge numbers of copyrights including those by Marty Robbins, Felice and Boudleaux Bryant, and all of the songs of Hank Williams. (More in following verses).

BILL MONROE. (191–1996) Known as the Father of Bluegrass, Monroe was inducted into the Country Music Hall of Fame in 1970. William Smith Monroe was the youngest of eight children born to of James Buchanan "Buck" Monroe, a prosperous farmer who also ran timber and mining operations, and Malissa Monroe, who kept house and helped pass along dance steps and British-American folksongs to her children. Other musical influences of Bill's youth include the old-time fiddling of his uncle Pendleton "Uncle Pen" Vandiver and the bluesy guitar playing of Arnold Shultz, a black musician with whom Bill and Uncle Pen sometimes worked local dances. By the time Bill was sixteen years old, both his parents had died, so he followed some of his brothers to Chicago to get work, but all the time playing and singing as a family trio or duo. After a move to Charlotte, North Carolina, things really got going for the by then duo, they were on the radio with the powerful 50,000-watt transmitter at WBT. Their popularity soon equalled that of any of the era's many duos, and they distinguished themselves by their hard-driving tempos, piercing harmony, and Bill's lightning-fast mandolin solos. In 1936, RCA producer Eli Oberstein recorded them for the first time. However, the headstrong Monroes feuded as brothers will, and the act broke up in 1938. Bill would record two more sessions for RCA with his new band, the Blue Grass Boys, named for Kentucky, the Bluegrass State. Monroe headed for Nashville to audition for the *Grand Old Opry.* WSM's George D. Hay, Harry Stone and David Stone, impressed with Monroe's talent and star power, hired him in October 1939 on the strength of his performance of his trademark "Mule Skinner Blues", formerly a hit for the legendary Jimmie Rodgers. WSM's 50,000-watt transmitter and guest spots on the Opry's NBC network portion quickly made Monroe's name a household word. By 1943 he was grossing some $200,000 a year from show dates, many of them staged as part of his own Opry tent show, which combined music and comedy in delighting rural and small-town audiences throughout the South. Still not called "Bluegrass" (this would not come until the mid-1950s), many of the music's basic elements were already present, including its pulsing drive and the intensity of Monroe's high-pitched vocals. During World War II, he added the banjo, first played by Stringbean (Dave Akeman), and experimented briefly with the accordion and harmonica, which complemented the basic mandolin-guitar-fiddle-bass combination he would always retain. (Where guitar was concerned, Monroe himself was a formidable instrumentalist and set high benchmarks for his band members through the years.) In 1945, he added the revolutionary three-finger banjo picking of Earl Scruggs, which provided bluegrass with its final building block.

Monroe's late-1940s recordings for Columbia under Uncle Art's supervision, made with Scruggs and Lester Flatt, his singer-guitarist at the time, were about to set new standards, and Bluegrass was getting closer to a genre. Scruggs and Flatt left in 1948 and formed the Foggy Mountain Boys. Until his death, Monroe continued to propagate the gospel of Bluegrass to worldwide audiences, appearing in all fifty states and Canada as well as on tours of Japan, England, Ireland, Holland, Switzerland, and Israel. His venues ranged from rural festivals to urban performing arts centers and the White House. He kept recording as well, and his career total topped more than 500 selections, most of them made for MCA (formerly Decca). Monroe also won recognition for his accomplishments. In 1982, the National Endowment for the Arts gave him its prestigious Heritage Award, and in 1988 he won a Grammy for his album "Southern Flavor" – the first bluegrass Grammy ever bestowed. A 1991 inductee into the International Bluegrass Music Association Hall of Honor, Monroe was also 1993 recipient of the Lifetime Achievement Award from the National Academy of Recording Arts and Sciences (NARAS), an honour that placed him in the company of Louis Armstrong, Chet Atkins, Ray Charles, Paul McCartney, and other such legends. Although Bluegrass constitutes only a small part of country music's annual sales, such honours testify to the enormous influence Monroe's music continues to exert among musicians in many fields.

– John Rumble. Adapted from the Country Music Hall of Fame and Museum's *Encyclopedia of Country Music* (Oxford University Press)..

GENE AUTRY. See Verse Four.

VERSE 4

COUNTRY GOES WESTERN

Art's answer to why so many musicians were recorded was, "*I wanted to give as many people as possible a chance.*"

Art was well known as the well-dressed, well-spoken, friendly English gentleman. He would give all of his contacts a portrait studio picture of himself with his name and how he could be contacted on the back, or some times even as an autograph on the front – maybe like a relative you hadn't seen for a while or a well-meaning benefactor, someone you might like to contact for help, like an "uncle".

In all of the research, both written and oral, there were only a couple of references to Art being a flash, Jack-the-Lad salesman type, and that was back in Grafton at the pressing plant from one of the German employees. Bill Moeser, youngest son of Otto, recollected that, "Art was a flashy man with gold bracelets." (taken from an article by Alex van der Tuuk, and used with permission). For the most part Art was seen as sincere and charming. The likeable Uncle Art image was something that he would encourage and be good as his word, helping as many as he could and fighting in the corner of the ordinary, "real" American.

* * * * *

Some of the names on Art's recording logs were about to become stars. One was a guy from Texas named Orvon Grover Autry, born on 29 September 1907, the first child of Eleanor (Nora) and Delbert Autry. Delbert, a part-time farm worker and wandering horse-trader wasn't around much during the pregnancy – somewhat of a trademark for the never-at-home-much Delbert. When he was home, he would work his piece of land that belonged to his father. He found the corn he grew made good liquor and was profitable, but he sampled it far too much, to excess, apparently. On many an occasion his mule would return home without him.

By 1913, Orvon had two sisters, Veda and Wilma. By the time he was five years old, Orvon was singing in the church choir because they were short of a soprano! Eventually, Nora upped sticks and moved across the Red River to Johnson County Oklahoma where her brother lived. Delbert was around enough to father another son, Dudley Don, in 1919.

Throughout his school years, Orvon would sing for anyone at the drop of a hat, accompanying himself on a Jews harp, too poor to afford a guitar.

In his teens he performed in a medicine show, and by the time he was sixteen, he had a guitar and took it everywhere with him. Orvon learned Morse code to get a job as a telegrapher and joined the Frisco Railroad at eighteen as an extra operator. He would play guitar and sing in between customers at the telegraph office. He also found time to join a Freemasons' lodge (some family members introduced him) rising to the thirty-two-degree status. After a move to the Sapulpa office, Orvon met fellow employee Jimmy Long, who was also a musician. Together they formed the Autry-Long Duo in1928, entertaining around town. The full story is told by Holly George-Warren in *Public Cowboy No 1: The Life and Times of Gene Autry* (Oxford University Press, 2007).

* * * * *

Like flood gates opening, singers, writers and players were beginning to pour in from everywhere, as radio and seventy-eights opened up the possibilities to everyone, plus the payment of a hundred dollars to entertainers, musicians, or poor farmers whose songs were recorded, enticing them into town, Art Satherley and Victor's Ralph Peer were already out there doing it. Orvon moved to New York to make his fortune, still on the railroads' payroll and taking time off. It was during this time that Orvon Autry became Gene Autry.

He was introduced to Frankie and Johnny Marvin – they worked in vaudeville and already had recorded for various labels.

The big name of the day was Jimmie Rodgers with his yodelling, having a string of hits for Victor and producer Ralph Peer. He was known as America's Blue Yodeller and every record label wanted to copy the style. Frankie Marvin covered a Jimmie Rodgers hit "T for Texas"; this was Gene's introduction to Jimmie Rodgers' way of singing.

Gene had to return to the Frisco Railroad after his leave ran out. However, he was determined to return to New York. Working in the telegraph office, taking guitar lessons, and working on his performance took up a lot of his time, but he also got an unpaid job singing on KVOO radio station in Tulsa. The experience taught him well. Singing and yodelling into a microphone was where he always said his radio career started. The Frisco Railroad Company was very supportive of its singing telegrapher, featuring him in several employees' magazines.

With more time off, Gene returned to New York. Gene's chance to become a recording yodelling cowboy coincided with the Wall Street crash, but he was off and running. By 1930, Gene was becoming well known, playing theatres and tent shows, but an introduction by Johnny Marvin was about to change Gene's life forever.

* * * * *

Art had been given the task of putting a country catalogue together for the American Recording Corporation (ARC) by the owner Mr Herbert Yates but had not signed anyone in that category yet. Gene Autry was introduced to Uncle Art by Johnny Marvin.

Art said, "Well I'd like to hear you."

So, a date for a meeting was fixed. For the audition Gene did some general country songs. Art liked what he saw and heard and booked Gene for a recording session – that was November 1930. Gene was still recording for Victor as well as ARC, both were getting more interested in his potential, Victor because of the yodelling, (they already had Jimmie Rodgers) and Art because he could see a different potential in him.

In the latter part of 1931, Gene brought Jimmy Long to a recording session with Uncle Art (also on guitars were Roy Smeck and Johnny Marvin). One of the songs recorded that day was "That Silver Haired Daddy of Mine" – in Art's words "a winner". The song had been written by Jimmy Long but appeared on song sheets as Autry/Long. Uncle Art was beginning to move closer to getting Gene to sign for ARC, and the same by Eli Oberstein for Victor, but Gene was hanging on to get the best deal.

Gene was unaware that Uncle Art had been working behind the scenes to find a unique way to promote his discovery. He had been talking with Jeff Shay of Sears Roebuck and sent a test pressing of "Silver Haired Daddy" to him. Jeff agreed on the commerciality of the track and suggested that radio station WLS as the next move, (Sears owned 51 of WLS.)

Jeff wrote to Art: "We would like to have Gene on our half-hour morning program, every weekday morning! But we can't pay him; if you could find a way of keeping him there, he'll be big for all of us"'

Uncle Art put it to Gene this way: "Gene, we don't have a lot of money, but if you could spend a couple of months in Chicago, we'll give you thirty dollars a week out of the petty cash. A room is a dollar a night at the YMCA, and the rest you can spend on wine, women and song! Will you do it? I can guarantee you'll be earning up to two thousand dollars a week within the first year."

With the deal clinched at thirty-five dollars a week, Gene started on WLS 1 December 1931. Gene at this time still couldn't decide on whether to sign to ARC. Uncle Art and Jeff Shay decided the best promotion would be the cowboy approach, Art asking Gene to sing only cowboy tunes. Gene was not totally convinced on the image, but trusted Uncle Art.

"Silver Haired Daddy of Mine" was a massive hit, selling thirty thousand copies in the first month and five hundred thousand overall! ARC decided to celebrate the hit by presenting a gold record to Gene, thus another first for Uncle Art, presenting gold records for high sales, then five hundred thousand (eventually reaching a million). No mean feat in the Depression!

All the listeners loved Gene on the radio – a promotional success! Gene was in demand all over the Midwest for personal appearance and gigs.

Sue Roberts and Anne Williams were presenters on WLS and took the young man under their wings. They would introduce Gene on the morning show and say things like, "He's been mendin' fences on the way in folks, and he's just come in on his horse, lookin' fine in his boots and Stetson, oh my", even though he'd just probably rolled out of bed.

Uncle Art said, "Those ladies really did help Gene with his early success."

Well, with all this attention Gene bought all new western clothes, boots, and a white Stetson. He ordered a new guitar from C.F. Martin with his name on the fret board inlayed with mother of pearl, but on thirty-five dollars a week it was hard to afford. To make some extra money he would do the six a.m. slot on WJJD. Program director Dave Knapp gave him the early bird slot.

Gene Autry eventually signed a two-year deal exclusively to ARC, and his first session as an exclusive ARC artist was 20 June 1933.

A major change had taken place one month before. Victor's mega star Jimmie Rodgers had died of a lung haemorrhage on 26 May 1933, two days after his last recording session. He had been suffering with tuberculosis for a considerable time. He was thirty-five years old. Art had been about to sign Rodgers.

There were several bad tribute songs that followed Jimmie Rodgers's death. Gene also recorded "When Jimmie Rodgers Said Good-bye" and a song Gene wrote called "Good Luck Old Pal (Till We Meet Bye and Bye").

Gene's move to the big screen was on the horizon. This was part of the potential Uncle Art had seen, and he had already started an advertising campaign with ARC's public relations man, Leonard Snyder, calling Gene "The Idol of All America". Art was very good at catch phrases, such as " The King of" or "The Idol of". Herbert Yates, head of ARC and Republic Pictures, could not miss the stirrings going on. In Art's own words from the interview with Douglas B. Green (27 June 1974):

> **Art:** So Herbert Yates said to me one day,
>
> **YATES:** Who is this cowboy guy you've got selling records?
>
> **Art:** I said Gene Autry. He said,
>
> **YATES:** Let me hear this fellow's records.
>
> **Art:** Mr Yates used to be a salesman for the American Tobacco Company but later went into the development of films in Fort Lee, New Jersey. Then, he got amalgamated I think with someone by the name of Nat Lavine on the West Coast here, who was associated in the development of films. So, I took some records up to his fabulous office. He played them, and the next day he called me back to his office. I won't use the words he used. He looked at me and he said,
>
> **YATES:** Is this what you're talking about?
>
> **ART:** I says, Yeah, don't you like it? He says,
>
> **YATES:** What is it?
>
> **ART:** I said, That's America – country America. That's what we are selling. I said, This man's a star; this man is going into pictures!
>
> **YATES:** How do you know he's going into pictures?
>
> **ART:** Because they'll all be after him very shortly. He has the

looks. He has everything, I said. Therefore, you have your own picture company called Republic Studios. I know that's in the offing. He said,

YATES: Who told you that?

ART: I said, I'm one of your vice presidents. I should know it. Then he said,

YATES: Well, I can't use that stuff.

ART: And I said, Well, if you can't, let me have him. I'll remain with you if you like, but I could sell him tomorrow to another picture company that's already established!

YATES: Well, how can you do that?

ART: I said, You just turned the guy down! So I said, Think it over! I walked out!"

Two days later, after thinking about, it Mr Yates called Art back into the Office saying,

YATES: This guy's fabulous. I don't know what in the hell he's singing about, but there it is. Where is he?

Art told him he was in Chicago on WLS every day and that money couldn't buy the publicity Sears Roebuck was giving him – all for thirty five dollars a week. Mr Yates arranged a meeting with Nat Lavine at the Blackstone Hotel Chicago with Gene, telling Art,

YATES: Make sure he cleans himself up a little bit, and get him to sing "Silver Haired Daddy".

Nat Lavine signed Gene Autry for the usual contract. A hundred seventy-five dollars a week was the going rate back then. So Gene prepared himself for the Hollywood experience.

Popular belief would have us think that the Frisco Railroad fired Orvon (as he was still listed on the payroll) for the sometimes extended time off, but it seems he was still on very good terms with them, thanking them in letters for the employment. And Frisco reciprocated, rather proud of their now famous ex-employee.

Gene rushed home to tell his wife, Ina Mae, about the meeting and started to make arrangements to move out west. Whilst planning the move Smiley Burnette dropped by. Gene had hired Smiley to play accordion with him on WLS, and they had become good friends. Gene and Ina invited him to join them on the trip.

Gene would find movie work hard work; he wasn't at all natural. In fact, he would say of himself "it looks like all my joints need oiling"; whereas Smiley took to it like a duck to water. Gene's confidence was knocked back; he even said to Ina that perhaps the movies weren't for him after all and that he should return to what he knew best – singing.

Nat Lavine persevered, getting acting coaching and special stunt riding lessons and giving him bit parts to rebuild his confidence.

Ken Maynard, one of the first singing cowboys, had an established career in the movies but that was about to change for the worst. His hard living and drinking finally forced Nat Lavine to drop him, leaving a gap for a leading man in a new film serial, and Gene was offered the job. Ken Maynard's financial situation worsened. He was only able to affording a mobile home to live in. Gene got on well with Ken and would help support him by sending money every month. This was besides agreed percentages out of royalties he was paying Uncle Art and Jeff Shay.

There is no doubt that Art's experience with the mail-order business, particularly with Sears Roebuck, was the major factor in Gene Autry's success, and at this point Art created a new genre of music by adding western to country so the term "country and western" was born.

Through the thirties, there was an incredible growth in entertainment, not only for Gene Autry but music generally. That old hillbilly music and blues, which had caused so much derision with the big-city music folk not many years before, was now making an indelible money-making imprint. Uncle Art would defend the music with a great deal of passion. A journalist who called it corny was told in no uncertain terms that this was music from the heart of real America. It was all too easy for a songwriter to churn out stereotypical sameness from a cosy office some where in Tin Pan Ally!

Uncle Art was at the forefront of this growth. His intuition was becoming a yardstick for the industry. Other record chiefs kept a close eye on what he was releasing, and this certainly influenced the shape of the music.

The Hoosier Hot Shots, the Prairie Ramblers, and Roy Acuff were joining Art's growing catalogue at this time. Bob Wills and his Texas Playboys had already been signed by Art in 1936; Western swing was about to make an appearance.

Don Law had been working as a bookkeeper for the Brunswick label in Texas, when Brunswick amalgamated with ARC in1931, It meant that Arthur and Don were working for the same company, and Law was paired with Art to share the large territory that Art covered.

* * * * *

The following background material is taken from Daniel Coopers entry, "Don Law" in *The Encyclopaedia of Country Music (*edited by Paul Kingsbury, Oxford University Press, 1998), 290-91; and Eric Olsen, "Don Law" in *The Encyclopaedia of Record Producers* (Billboard Books, 1999), 444-46.

DON LAW

(Born 24 February 1902, London, England – Died 20 December 1982, Tamaqua, Texas)

As the head of Columbia Records' country music division through most of the 1950s and 1960s, Don Law was one of the most important and successful producers, not only in the annals of country music, but of popular music in general. Among the top- selling artists he worked with at Columbia were Lefty Frizzell, Ray Price, Marty Robbins, Johnny Horton, and Johnny Cash to name but a few. He also produced his share of rockabilly and rock 'n' roll (the Collins Kids, Ronnie Self, Billy Brown, Billy "Crash" Craddock, and Carl Perkins during his Columbia tenure).

Born in England, Law developed an early fascination for the USA and emigrated there in 1924, eventually landing in Dallas, Texas. He found a job at Brunswick Records, first as a bookkeeper but gradually moving into A&R. When ARC (the American Record Corporation) bought Brunswick in 1931, he began working for a fellow Englishman similarly predisposed toward American roots music, Uncle Art Satherley, who would become his mentor. Ernie Ortles, ARC's talent scout in the mid-South, introduced Law to Robert Johnson, arguably the single most important figure in blues history. Law recorded Johnson's entire twenty-nine-song body of work direct to disc in a San Antonio hotel room in November 1936 and in a Dallas warehouse in June 1937. Fourteen months later, Johnson would be dead.

For Don Law, the blues and country and western were two sides of the same American coin. In 1938 (the year that ARC was acquired by CBS), he recorded "San Antonio Rose" with Bob Wills for Columbia. In 1942, he went to New York to record children's music. Then in 1945, Law returned to country music when he and Uncle Art divided the nation at El Paso, with Law responsible for the Columbia sessions east of El Paso.

After Uncle Art left Columbia in 1952, Law was the sole head of Columbia's country division. By then, he had brought important artists like Little Jimmy Dickens, Carl Smith, and Lefty Frizzell to the label. Frizzell was found through the Jim Beck studio in Dallas, where Law would usually record. It was only after Beck died in 1956 that Law focused his attention on Nashville and moved there. He was one of the first producers to work at Owen Bradley's Quonset hut (the first studio built on Music Row) and also helped found the Country Music Association. In 1962, Law convinced Columbia to buy the Quonset hut turning it into Columbia Studio B. In the 1950s and early 1960s Law recorded some of the greatest country music ever, both artistically and commercially. Lefty Frizzell; Marty Robbins; Carl Smith; Ray Price; Johnny Horton; Stonewall Jackson; Johnny Cash; Jimmy Dean; Flatt & Scruggs; Billy Walker; and Claude King all topped the country charts and "The Battle Of New Orleans" (Johnny Horton, 1959); "El Paso" (Marty Robbins, early 1960) and "Big Bad John" (Jimmy Dean, 1961) were also Number One pop hits, bringing country music to a new audience.

Along with Chet Atkins at RCA, Ken Nelson at Capitol, and Owen Bradley at Decca, Law was instrumental in re-establishing country's commercial viability during the so-called Nashville Sound era (circa 1957–1972). But unlike Atkins and Bradley, Law and his frequent co-producer Frank Jones did not rely so much on the strings and smooth vocals commonly associated with the Nashville Sound.

As successful as he was, Law nevertheless fell victim to the changes sweeping through American music in the late 1960s. In 1967, he was forced to take mandatory retirement from Columbia. Law's place at the helm of the Nashville office was taken by Bob Johnston, who had produced Bob Dylan's "Blonde On Blonde" sessions in Music City the year before.

Don Law and Arthur

Don Law

At Don law's House

Used with permission Judith Keigley and CMHF

Art with the first fish he caught in the USA

Some of the Columbia artists, notably Ray Price, were allowed to continue working with Law as an independent producer. But by the 1970s, Law's role in the business was rapidly diminishing, and by the end of the decade he was fully retired. He died in 1982 in a suburb of Galveston, Texas, at the age of 80. In 2001 he was finally inducted into the Country Music Hall of Fame. Amazingly, he has never been the subject of a book-length biography.

* * * * *

As can be seen, not that much has been written about the working partnership of Art and Don, except passing remarks like "Art was Don's mentor" or "they worked together until Art's retirement".

In the interview with Art and Don Law by Diana Johnson (DJ) on the 18 October 1974 for the Country Music Museum Hall of Fame question, "When did it go electric?" was asked about using portable recording equipment, and Art and Don agreed it was 1929–30 and that the turntable was turned by weights well into the introduction of electricity because the current in the supply was not steady and the speed would fluctuate.

Don also said, "*Things would have been so much easier back then if we'd had tape.*"

Apparently, Art had had a razor-blade machine to shave a new surface on the master disc, which was about two inches thick, so they could reuse it for another take. The power source for the microphone was from the standard electrical outlets, never batteries.

Art added" The equipment was shipped down to where we needed it"

DJ "How about the remote locations?"

Don replied, "Arthur went to the remote locations, but that was before my time. When I started to work with Arthur, we set up – well, we recorded in the Baxter Hotel in Fort Worth and recorded at the Burros Mills Fort Worth. We recorded at the Governor in San Antonio, and then I finally built a studio"'

It's estimated that Art travelled one million miles over his time recording music – three hundred thousand of them with Don Law – mostly in an old Ford. They would work together until Art retired; then, Don would take on Art's role.

Travelling three hundred thousand miles together must have formed a pretty strong personal and working relationship. Don, it would seem, did the driving or maybe even Harriet Melka (Art's girlfriend as she was known then) seeing that Art never drove. Art would use his considerable travel experience to organize recordings – take for instance, the Robert Johnson sessions attributed to Don Law. Art arranged the sessions in an executive role, and Don was producer.

Harriet Melka Art's girlfriend taken about the time they met. Harriet had several hit country songs as writer
Used with permission Judith Keigley and CMHF

Western swing was all the rage. It got people dancing and kept them dancing. Don Law suggested that Art take a look at Bob Wills and his Texas Playboys. Uncle Art wanted to make sure the dancers would get what they wanted, so he often checked the feel and tempo of the music by dancing around the studio. It wasn't unusual for him to be in the "live" room – he had often helped the recording vocalist with the lyric by whispering a word or a line if they were having problems, either because of poor sight (as in Blind Lemon Jefferson's case), or not reading too well.

Art also said that when he was recording the Hoosiers, "I would hit hell out of the drums; I was not adverse to joining in."

Bob Wills could be a bit of

a prickly customer, not suffering fools gladly. Art found this out at his first recording session with the boys. Bob was a fine musician, playing fiddle since a boy with his father's band. Between the time of Art signing Wills and his band and getting them in the studio, Bob had experimented with the line up. He had added a front line of horns to the fiddles – creating more of a big band line up with thirteen band members in all.

Art was a bit surprised and said to Bob, "If I had wanted a big band I would have signed a big band."

Bob replied, "You signed Bob Wills, and this is what I am" adding, "We've been doin' pretty well before you fellas, so we'll just pack up and go back home."

Art was stunned by Bob but agreed to record the band adding, "It won't sell."

But the records cut in 1935 did sell; they sold so well that Art booked more sessions, this time in Chicago and Dallas. Art had hired upstairs rooms in the Buick Building in Dallas, and soundproofed them by hanging material on the walls. The Dallas heat was so great, however, that the masters melted. Barrels of ice were brought and large fans were set up to blow across the ice to help the problem.

Another aspect Art had to deal with was Bob hollering loud "Ah-Ha!"s" and talking to the band over the music.

When Art objected, once again Bob pointed out, "This is what I do. C'mon boys, pack up. We'll go home."

Art's responded, "No! no! no! Let's just get the balance right."

Art and Bob's relationship did not get off to a great start; but Art was beginning to see that here was something very original about Bob. In fact, in later sessions if Bob didn't holler, Art would say, "Where is your Ah-Ha, Bob?"

It took a little while for the working relationship to develop, but Art said, "I wanted to understand what Bob and his music was about. He could be difficult, and so could I. Eventually, we would let each other do our respective jobs,"

The mixture of fiddle music, Negro music, and New Orleans Jazz that Bob had heard since a small boy didn't fit in any category but made a new one; suffice to say the next twelve years with Uncle Art at the recording helm would shape the music.

The sessions in Chicago created another problem for Uncle Art and his engineers: the groove laid down by the rhythm section – the pounding of Al Strickland's piano and Smokey Dracus's drums – had them moving sections of the band around in the studio. Rugs were used to quiet the piano – a stack of rugs to be exact, a good six inches off the ground. Uncle Art's experience told him that rather than asking the boys to hold it down, he, Don Law, and his engineers would sort it. The drums still "too loud man" were moved into the toilet at the back of the room for some parts of the sessions. Eventually, the boys could go for it with the spontaneity to capture the energy in the music.

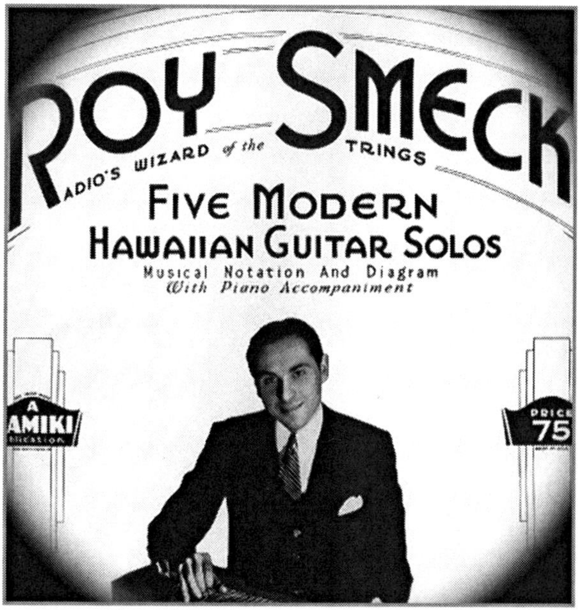

Bob had wanted to record "Steel Guitar Rag" in the first sessions but Uncle Art held off saying, "We already have a steel player, Roy Smeck!" But this time Bob insisted. The track was recorded and became a hit along with "Trouble In Mind" from the same session. Because of that success, more sessions were booked in a makeshift studio back in Dallas. Art recalled "!t was so hot and humid I had to get tubs of ice in with beer in and fans blowing over them to try and keep cool, but they still had to strip down to just underpants."

Let's make a mental image of that – perhaps not! Unfortunately, there aren't any pictures, or should that be fortunately?

The mid thirties were a busy and exiting time for Uncle Art. In a 1938 session Bob was asked to include more fiddle tunes. One of the instrumental tunes Art liked and asked Bob the title. Bob hadn't named the tune so Art suggested "San Antonio Rose", which is now a classic.

Uncle Art Satherley and Johnny Bond taken during a Columbia recording session at CBS studios in Hollywood.

Time: about 1945 or 46
Song: "Baby You Gotta Quit That Noise"

"Uncle Art taught me to write songs and make records." jb

Used with permission CMHF

Johnny Bond; the Hoosiers; the Sons of the Pioneers; the Prairie Ramblers; Patsy Montana (the first solo female million seller with "I Wanna Be a Cowboys's Sweetheart."); Gene Autry; and Bob Wills were all hitting highs, with more to come, much more.

VERSE FIVE

ACUFF ROSE

In an interview with Ken Kingsbury in 1979 for a book that didn't materialize, Art said, "For years I recorded every record Roy Acuff ever made. He was the easiest man I ever recorded and one of the most authentic. I'd say, 'Roy, learn these songs while I'm away.' I'd come back ten weeks later and find he had been rehearsing the entire time. He was an absolute perfectionist, fanatical in his attention to detail".

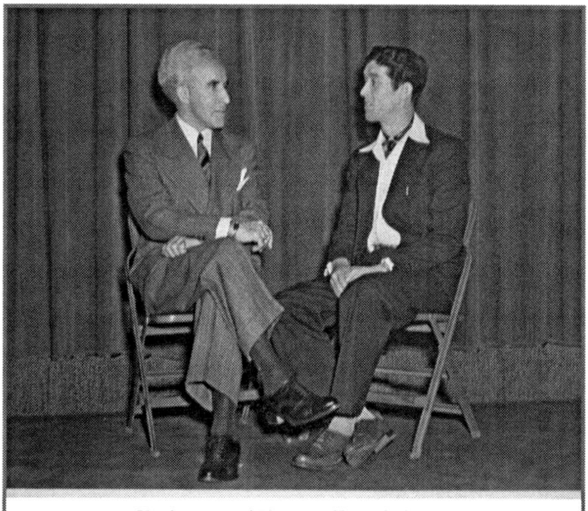
Uncle Art And Roy Acuff. Nashvlle 1942
Used with permission CMHF

Art also gives an insight into a recording session with Roy and his Crazy Tennesseans.

"I would ship my equipment from one town to another, which was a job in itself. The setting up to record was another job. One time, I had Roy in a Memphis hotel room which wasn't big enough to accommodate all the equipment, so I got permission to cut a hole through the wall of the bathroom and put the speakers in there. After I had set up everything, there was no place for Roy to stand except in the bathtub".

Whilst researching this information on Roy Acuff I noted that, even in the Hall of Fame's biography, there was reference to the songs that made a difference to his career but not who ran and produced the recording sessions. For instance "Great Speckled Bird" and "Wabash Cannon Ball" are mentioned as the songs that put Roy as a headliner and W R Calaway as ARC producer, but as Art said "For years I recorded every record Roy Acuff ever made."

Art's recording list says: "Matrix number c-1589 WABASH CANNON BALL date made 10/26/36." And "Matrix number c-1581 GREAT SPECKLED BIRD date made 10/26/36."

It's a tad confusing, but as I found later on, it wasn't the only confusion. Roy was having success on Radio WROL and WNOX Knoxville, and decided to audition for *The Grand Old Opry* Nashville. Opry's G. D. Hay refused his services several times, but promoter J. L. Frank intervened on Acuff's behalf. A 1937 guest appearance produced no results, but on 5 February 1938, another guest appearance, Acuff's performance of the classic "The Great Speckled Bird" generated sacks of fan mail that did the trick.

J. L. Frank suggested a new band name, the Smoky Mountain Boys, and Opry executives, Harry and David Stone immediately put the singer at the center of a budding star system, heavily promoting Acuff's trademark song "Wabash Cannon Ball'.

* * * * *

Art was on the road all the time, and he would often come across situations such as what happened at the recording event in the Memphis Hotel, where he cut a hole in the wall. It wasn't always with the kindness of heart, however, that things got done. Art said that he would carry several thousand dollars with him in a suitcase at all times to help with any difficulties that might arise and so he could deal with the problem – whatever it was – immediately. He told the story of being on a train that had a fire, and every one had to evacuate the train, leaving all personal belongings behind.

Art said, "There was no way I was leaving that suitcase behind, so I went back onto the burning train and retrieved it!"

* * * * *

The lack of recognition in Roy Acuff's biographies of Uncle Art probably had something to do with the forming of Acuff Rose publishing in 1942, when some deals between Freddie Rose and Art were not understood, particularly by Freddie's son Wesley. I explored stories surrounding this situation in a attempt to unravel complex issues.

Judging from the biographical sketch of Freddie Rose in Verse Three, it's clear that he was a prolific songwriter who able to churn out quality songs at the drop of a hat, as it were. Freddie, who had moved to California, started writing songs for the film cowboys. This brought him in contact with Art, who was always looking for a good song. He obviously got to know Freddie well, which is illustrated by a story about buying a car that Art related to Douglas B. Green in the interview for the Country Music Hall of Fame on 27 June 1974:

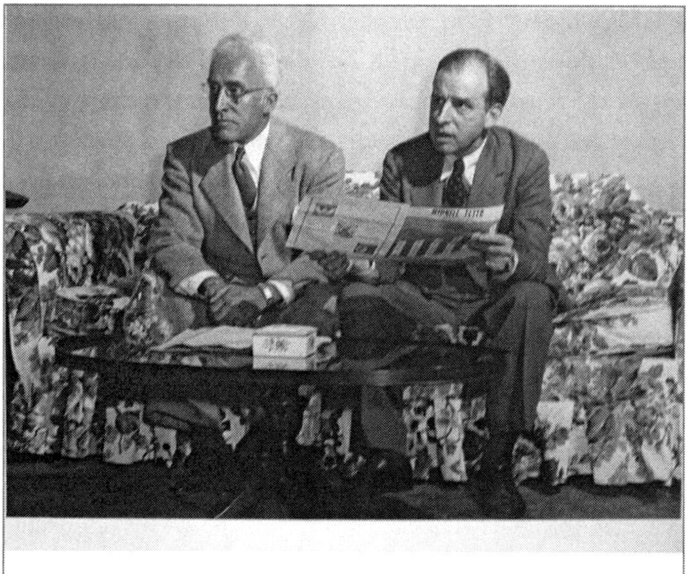

Uncle Art and Fred Rose

Used with permission CMHF

So I said, "Wait a minute Freddie, come here. You don't need that old car anymore - let's get this one here, this station wagon." He said, " Arthur, how in the devil am I going to get that car?" I said "Well,

> take a look at It." Well, we went and looked at it and it looked like a kid with a dirty nose from staring in the window at candy!
> I said, "Freddie, you're going home with that car," so I put up the money then and there and got the car for Freddie. My check [cheque] was good -- I wrote the cheque then and there.
> "Well," he said, "how am I going to take her home to my wife? She'll kill me"! I said, "Well, you've got to drive something, because I got to get back!" So he drove it home, and somehow I never heard the argument about it, but he did take the car and that was it! No paper passed, nothing passed. Our word was good—that's what I thought of Freddie, and I presume that's what Freddie thought of me, because I put him on his feet.
> Now the royalties begin to roll in—and he paid me back the $2,000 in cash, and I put it back in the bank, now, if you call that taking money from people, mister, I think I was somewhat of a philanthropist. I've done it for him, and I've done it for many others in this business. And who came out on the short end? Art Satherley! Art Satherley is here living, smiling, and thanking God for everything that he has allowed me to do in this life, for the pleasure of working with the country boys and girls, irrespective. I came from what I came from, and I tell you I'm very proud of all of them. But this is only the beginning of a long story, Doug, and that was one about Freddie Rose".

From this story it can be seen that more and more money was being created by the industry. Art, being fully aware whispers, allegations, and counter allegations, and of course egos, causing jealousy and greed to rear their ugly heads, the truth almost incidental. Unspoken nods, winks, and "bungs".

A "bung" is a term used in the U K for making an extra payment off-the-record to someone, or a sweetener to make sure a decision goes your way known as "payola" in the US. The music business is particularly prone to these deals. A good many years ago I witnessed such a deal. It's an individual viewpoint whether its good business practice or not. As we have already seen, Uncle Art was receiving agreed percentage royalties from Gene Autry and others, as you might expect with the customary system of management and agency fees.

It is also common practice among songwriters to include names in addition to their own on the writers' credits so the royalties would be split, even if there was very little or no input by the others named. All of this OK if mutually agreed; the morality of these kind of deals another issue. Issues also arise with what some would see as bias between people who, for instance, are members of organisations acting as what is now known as networking. I am not implying dishonesty, but maybe it's just not business as usual anymore. At the time of writing, it can be seen that meltdown is occurring within the financial and banking systems across the world, maybe the winds of change are blowing a little harder, time will tell.

* * * * *

The set- up of Acuff Rose publishing from Uncle Art's perspective as told to Douglas B. Green, sheds some light on what happened to Art and Freddie's relationship.

Art continued:," All of a sudden I found out that he [Freddie] had a son".

It's worth pointing out here that because of Fred's drinking problem, his son Wesley had little or no contact with his father because of the way his father treated his mother when he was drinking. By 1935, Fred had joined the First Church of Christ Scientist or Christian Science, and he reformed his life, stopped drinking, and lived by the churches doctrine.

Art continued, "He didn't tell me he had a son! And we were about to go into a secret business, where I would get a third or some part of his royalties, or else Harriet would, I don't know."

Here is the first mention of Art's long-term partner, Harriet Melka, and this is where Harriet's songs come into focus. Art was reluctant to talk about aspects of his personal life, particularly his first wife Gladys who he had married in Wisconsin in 1918. (There is no sign of annulment or divorce up to and including 1940.) Harriet was also reluctant to speak about how and when she and Art got together. Harriet was born in St Louis in 1907 and was allegedly crowned Miss St Louis 1924 in a Miss America competition, but her father would not let her pursue the title. By the time Art and Harriet got together, she already had a daughter, Judy.

As Art said, he was on the road constantly; this was recalled by granddaughter Judith Keigley: "So that Harriet could join him, Mom was enrolled in a boarding school. She would tell of Harriet and Art visiting her at the school and that she would feel very proud seeing them pull up in a big new Cadillac. Art even bought an English bull terrier puppy to keep her company".

Harriet travelled with Art, with Don Law at the wheel, and attended recording sessions where she would write up the recording logs. This is where Harriet's songs come into focus. Harriet Melka's name later turned up as songwriter on various albums (1940 to 1951) for Big Bill Broonzy, "Double Trouble", "When I Get To Thinking", and "I Feel So Good" in later years; and Ernest Tubb's 1956 "You're Breaking My Heart".

It's not clear if Harriet was the writer (maybe this is how she met Art) or if the songs were knowingly put in her name as part of a deal, like a Freddie Rose, and they were actually composed by someone else. Ralph Peer's publishing company, Peer International, published the songs. The facts are that Harriet and her daughter were now on the scene, and Uncle Art Satherley was already a recording industry legend. In years to come, the family background would be papered over and never spoke of; Art raised Harriet's daughter as his own and was very fond of her. She would appear in a few Hollywood productions as an actress and singer, under the name of Judy Johns, she was featured in *Davy Crocket* with Fess Parker for Disney.

What of Gladys? Well, with no divorce we must assume they were still legally married. However, there is a story – a rumour – that Art had bought a plantation or put money into a land deal in Georgia, but apparently losing a lot of money. The rumour had it that Gladys had "run off" with the guy managing the plantation, which is hardly surprising if Art was never with her. But it was just a rumour.

To make sure it didn't happen again, Art and Harriet decided to be together whatever, until death them did part, and that's what happened, sweeping all skeletons into the cupboard and never speaking of them.

Interestingly, Art did have a mailing address that he called home, when he wasn't flying or driving across America, in Georgia, at the Plantation Inn, Highway 17, six miles south of Savannah. It was a thriving "motor court" hotel in the forties (before they were called motels) as can be seen in the post card image.

RESTAURANTS
Plantation Inn and Motor Court
6 1-2 MILES SOUTH OF Savannah, Ga., on Highway 17

The address came from a newspaper article in the Sheboygan, Wisconsin *Journal* in 1941 (courtesy of author Tony Russell). The article was headed "Talent Scout Visits His Friends At Port." Art was visiting Port Washington after a ten-year absence. The article reads: "Any songs ambitious tunesters want published or recorded can be sent to Art and he will consider every one. He said so himself."

This property, The Plantation Inn, could be the reason Art lost money, not because of plantation growing cotton, but because of the changing fortunes of this motor court. The Plantation Inn was on Highway 17, which was also known as the Coastal Highway, just south of Savannah. When the Interstate Highways Act came into being in the 1950s, the building of I-95 made

Highway 17 a backwater as was true of a lot of the early trans-America roads, like the musically famous Route 66, for instance. Passing trade would have disappeared almost over night, which was not very good for turnover. And, of course, there's Gladys. Her social security number was generated in Georgia. The plot thickens! More on this in a later verse.

* * * * *

Art continued his recollection of the beginning of Acuff Rose Publishing. Art and Harriet would stay at Freddie's house and combine social and business activities. "And I was giving Freddie plenty of numbers, and we were making sure everybody else got his numbers, and I'm getting a few checks [cheques], maybe for a few hundred dollars, I don't know – not enough to even talk about. And all of a sudden, the deal I had made with Freddie was off."

There had probably been nothing in writing, since Art thought his word was good enough. Art had received a letter, saying that any deal made with Freddie was cancelled and that Wesley was now working for his father, The letter was signed by Freddie Rose. Art said "[It was] Signed by Freddie, but I knew who wrote it. I didn't reply to the thing – forget it! Who cares? That was the beginning of the fabulous Acuff Rose".

"Arthur, I'm in the publishing business now," Freddie said, telling Art that Roy Acuff had put the money up by opening five separate accounts in different banks for $5000 dollars in each.

Art was not impressed with how he'd been treated saying, "I didn't care for that kind of deal, rather dirty, considering. I didn't tell. Wesley Rose doesn't know what I did for his father!"

Although Art did say that he got pleasure from doing things that no one knew anything of.

Wesley contacted Art and said that Freddie was broken hearted because their friendship wasn't what it used to be.

Art said, "Maybe there's a reason for it".

Wesley said, "We want to make amends somehow, Art,"

"What amends can you make?

You can't make all the amends necessary now that you're associated. Why, all I want to do is good work for the people that's paying me my salary, and let it go like that."

Freddie and Art did see each other after that, but the friendship was never the same. Art was asked to be a pallbearer at Freddie's funeral in 1954. Who knows what would have been if the deal with Art had been honoured: Acuff Rose & Satherley? Maybe. Perhaps pride got in the way; perhaps Art should have set the record straight – what do you think?

Uncle Art presenting Roy Acuff with a gold record 1945
looking on WSM's Harry Stone used with permission CMHF

* * * * *

Through the thirties and into the forties, the records that Art produced created many hits for his artists, both established and new. Art's recording logs were impressive. Uncle Art Satherley put the following list together on the 1 October 1982 for the commemorative album, *Uncle Art Satherley American Originals* (Columbia CK 46237 1991) eleven of the tracks were finally used.

(This was one of the items that I viewed in Forrest White's office in 1998 now donated to the Hall Of Fame Museum):

Gene Autry from 1931 'That Silver Haired Daddy Of Mine'.

Elton Britt in 1933 with 'Swiss Yodel' and 1934 'Chime Bells'.

The Original Carter Family 1935 'Will The Circle Be Unbroken' and 'Wildwood Flower'.

Tex Ritter 1933 'Rye Whiskey' and 'Ridin' Old Paint'.

Red Foley 1934 'I Got The Freight Train Blues', 1935 'Old Shep'.

Eddie Dean 1935 'Red Sails In The Sunset' and 'Roll Along Prairie Moon'.

Patsy Montana 1935 'I Want To Be A Cowboy's Sweetheart' and 'Ridin' Old Paint'.

Sons Of The Pioneers, (Leonard Slye, who formed the band would change his name to Roy Rogers) 1937 'Let's Pretend' and 'Love song Of The Waterfall'.

Roy Rogers 1937 'Power In The Blood' and 'Cowboy Night Herd Song'.

Roy Acuff 1936 'Wabash Cannon Ball' and 'Great Speckled Bird'

Bob Wills And His Texas Playboys 1936 'Steel Guitar Rag' and 1938 'San Antonia Rose'.

Gene Autry 1939 'South Of The Border' and 'Back In The Saddle Again'.

Ted Daffan (and his Texans)' "Born to Lose' and 'No Letter Today' both recorded in 1942 and released in '43.

Tex Williams (with the Spade Cooley Band) 'Shame, Shame On You' recorded in 1944 and released in '45, and 'You Can't Break My Heart' recorded and released in '46.

Bill Monroe & His Blue Grass Boys 'Kentucky Waltz' recorded 1945, released '46, 'Blue moon of Kentucky' recorded 1946 released '47.

Johnny Bond 'Cimarron' and 'Oklahoma Waltz' both recorded 1947 released '48.

Little Jimmy Dickens 'Take An Old Cold 'Tater And Wait', ' Sleepin' At The Foot Of The Bed' recorded and released in 1949.

George Morgan 'Candy Kisses' and 'Room Full Off Roses' recorded and released in 1949.

Stuart Hamblen 'It Is No Secret (What God Can Do)' and 'He Bought My Soul At Calvary' recorded and released 1950.

Lefty Frizzell 'If You've Got The Money I've Got The Time' 1950.

* * * * *

In 1938, Gene Autry walked out on his movie deal because of a dispute over money; the studio was left looking for a replacement. Leonard Slye had been appearing in westerns for three years, also alongside Gene. The studio offered the role to Leonard, who accepted, and Roy Rogers was born. After Gene had sorted out his contract, Roy Rogers successfully became his main competition.

But two events were about to change things yet again: World War II and the AFM strike.

America joined the Second World War on the 8 December 1941.The effect on the record industry was dramatic. Shellac was imported, and so it went on short supply, which restricted the pressing of records. Art complained that he had to impose a quota of how many artists could be recorded. One of these artists was Eddy Arnold who had talked to Art on several occasions, but Art couldn't sign him because it would have put Eddy on the shelf as it were – he was too good! So Art took Eddy to see his friend Steve Sholes at RCA, who signed him. Eddy was always very grateful for that introduction, and he went on to become a big country star.

Eddy Arnold Uncle Art

courtesy CMHF

The musicians' strike of America started on the 1 August 1942. There had been some discontent between Musicians' Union president, James Petrillo, and record companies over royalty payments or rather the lack of them.

Interestingly, vocalists were not seen as musicians. I guess that's where the band joke came from: How do you know when a singer is at the door? It's easy; they never know when to come in!

Anyway, there were several anomalies in the strike conditions. Harmonica players, that meant Larry Adler, were allowed to record – why? –and drums. (Here's another band joke: What's the difference between a drummer and a drum machine? You only have to punch the numbers in once on a drum machine!)

Okay enough – well, seeing I am a guitar player: How do you make a guitar player play quietly? Put music up in front of him! That really is it now.

Surprisingly, Art had some really big hits during the war. Was that because Mr Petrillo wouldn't allow country-music players in the union at the time? Eventually, artists such as Roy Acuff earned so much money for his label that the union capitulated. Or was it that Art was able somehow to sneak them under the radar?

Speaking of radar, television was about to start, but development was delayed because of the war. The link was that TV sets and radar used similar components, such as cathode ray tubes, and of course TVs used them exclusively until the introduction of LCDs and Plasma screens.

* * * * *

The V Disc

In 1941, the American government went into the record business, using various record companies – Columbia being one of them – supplying records on vinyl, not the shellac mix, free to servicemen abroad between 1942 and 1949. The idea was to keep morale up: a propaganda tool with entertainment.

The Musicians Union allowed its members to record for the V Disc label as long as the product did not become available to the public. After the war all copies were destroyed, except government copies. Anyone found in possession of unauthorised copies faced a fine and or imprisonment. There are compilations of these tracks stored at the Library of Congress available on CD.

* * * * *

In Verse Three there's is a small biography piece on Al Dexter. Here is more to the story, showing how Uncle Art worked with his artistes. As I have already stated, the war years enforced changes on the record industry but Art was still travelling, recording songs. In March of '42 he had booked a suite at the Adolphus Hotel Dallas to set up his recording gear. One of the sessions was to be used to record local guy, Albert Poindexter, from Troup. He turned up fully turned out in Stetson, chaps, and cowboy boots, bringing his six-piece band and thirty-five songs he had written, mostly about lost love and the departure of friends to the after life. Art chose twelve songs to record, a love song called "Rosalita", and a steady driving' song about a Pistol Packin' Mama who finds out that her husband had been rather too friendly with a lady in a bar, and was threatening to shoot his lights out.

One year later, "Rosalita" was released with "Pistol Packin' Mama" as the B side. In an interview with Maurice Zolotow for the *Dallas Evening Post,* 12 February 1944, Art said, "To be honest about it, I never dreamed it would be the hit it turned out. We only released it because we needed a contrast to put on the other side of Rosalita." By the middle of 1943, Al Dexter had a hit on his hands. The jukebox record suppliers preferred the song to all others. By December 1943, it had become one of the biggest selling records in the history of American recording, selling 1.6 million. Because of the war shortages, orders for a further half million could not be met.

Al Dexter Uncle Art Gene Autry
(Pistol Packin Mama) Courtesy CMHF

The song never appeared in the hit parade at the time because of the opening line of the song. It went, "Drinkin' beer in a cabaret" – that was enough for the radio stations to ban the playing on air, so the publishers went to court. The outcome was a small change of the lyric to "singing songs in a cabaret" and the song then showed as Number One in the hit parade.

Zolotow wrote "Uncle Art was wearing his pince-nez spectacles, a scholarly and dignified man who speaks with a British accent and looks somewhat like an Oxford professor of Greek history, would gloat a little over the success of his artistes Elton Britt and Ted Daffan also selling over a million each."

In this interview Art would point out that the thing that really counted was the emotion in the voice of the performer – the heartfelt delivery of the song – that's what he would look for. Art tells the story of a mountaineer that he chanced upon in Hattiesburg many years before. He sang railroad songs fairly well so Art recorded a couple of his songs, paid him fifty dollars, a bottle of bourbon whiskey, and a straw hat. On the next visit, Art found out that the man and his wife had argued over the fifty dollars and he had shot her dead and was now on Death Row. He had written a new song, "The Hangman Blues", so Art recorded the song in the cell on Death Row.

"He put his heart and soul into it," Art said, "It was one of the most sincere songs I ever recorded!" (This could be the song attributed to, and recorded by Blind Lemon Jefferson, 1928).

Asked if he had any more stories, Art related the tale of recording preachers giving a sermon. It was in Augusta, Georgia. He had passed the word that he was looking for a good preacher with songs.

An immaculately dressed man of African descent in a reversed collar appeared carrying a nickeled guitar saying, " I'se a man of God and I hears you is lookin' for a sermon. I brung my flock with me"

It was the most moving sermon Art had heard, and he paid the man a hundred dollars. The following day, the congregation came back asking for payment.

When Art told them he had paid the pastor, they said "He ain't our paster. He runs all our dens of 'nicquity and 'bonimation round here. He ain't no churchgoin' man. He's blacker'n the devil hissel!

Art did more than one of these kinds of recordings – could this one be the Rev. Chambers on the unknown list? It's just a guess.

* * * * *

With Bob Wills and the Texas Playboys swinging through the forties, it brought about a plethora of performers and bands. The Spade Cooley story was one of them, showing that fame and fortune was not enough to stop him going to jail after bizarrely killing his wife!

* * * * *

Forrest White did an interview with Harriet in preparation for his book on

Art. It was after Art's death; it would seem she could be a bit feisty. Forrest asked general questions about the artists and how the working relationships were. Harriet had good recall about some of them (remember she was at the recording sessions writing up the studio logs). She said that Gene Autry got real jealous because Art was sharing songs between his artists and that Gene thought he should have all the best ones. He hated the fact that Art had Spade Cooley.

She went on to say, *"And Bill Monroe was all me, me, me."*

Others got it in the neck as well. Stuart Hamblen's sudden move to God she considered fake! Of course this was only Harriet's viewpoint. When it came to questions about getting together with Art, recall seemed to be harder – questions like what year did you and Art get together? And what year were you married?

Answer: "Well... I think it was... 1942; no... maybe 1940... er... um."

Forrest would then say, "We'll leave that for now."

I wonder how Forrest was going to write up the personal aspects? I couldn't find anything in his notes about Gladys, for instance.

* * * * *

Come 1944, the AFM strike was over. The two largest companies, Victor and Columbia, had held out but then settled on Armistice Day, 11 November 1944. They agreed to pay into a trust fund set up by the AFM on every record sold.

VERSE SIX

AMERICA'S BOOM YEARS

With the musician's strike over and World War II coming to an end, there was a rekindling of prosperity in the air. The years after the war were to become known as America's boom years. The war had seen another technological leap forward, particularly in electronics. FM radio and television picked up from where they had left off before the war, preparing to go on air. Recording techniques were to take on broader dynamics, or high fidelity (hi-fi). This would mean a standardization of playing equipment to play new formats, such as the long-playing record at 33-1/3 rpm, and later forty fives.

Radios would have to have the VHF band to receive FM. During World War II, the US government issued the V disc label, using vinyl microgroove records for their product. This was an invention of a Hungarian engineer, Peter Carl Goldmark. He worked for Columbia and also was responsible for the first colour TV experiments for CBS. But his system used a spinning wheel, as did that of Scottish inventor, John Logie Baird. It was the completely electronic system that would win out, using the cathode-ray tube.

Sound recording was already changing with experiments using electromagnetism – first with wire recorders, then thin plastic with a coating of ferrous oxide (iron) dust, commonly called tape. The German company AEG had built such a machine in 1935 called the Magnetophon K1. Two of these machines were captured during the war and found their way to Jack Mullin who served in the US Army Signal Corps. He was assigned to investigate German radio and electronics experiments.

He brought them back to the US, where he worked for a small company making generators and motors called Ampex of Santa Carlos, California. He modified the design and demonstrated his tape recorder to the movie studios for recording sound. At the same time, singer Bing Crosby was trying to find a way of recording his radio show to escape the tight time schedules of going live, but NBC wouldn't hear of it They didn't want to broadcast the show from disc, so Bing pulled out of the show.

One year later, he saw Jack Mullins' demonstration and was so impressed with the quality and the fact you could edit and re-record, that he commissioned Mullins to record a demo radio show. The success of the recording prompted Bing to invest $50,000 in Ampex to develop the tape machine.

Jack Mullins, by then chief engineer at Ampex, produced the model 200. Bing gave one of the first machines to his guitar-playing friend Les Paul, who modified the machine by adding more recording and playback heads and multi-tracking was born.

The first tape-recorded radio programme, "the Bing Crosby Show" was aired by ABC in 1948, and again radio was ahead of the recording studios.

* * * * *

Uncle Art in the studio late 40's
Used with permission CMHF

Uncle Art now in his late fifties, with the restrictions of the war over, showed no signs of slowing down his commitment to country music. Gene Autry's career had picked up from where it left off. Autry served in the United States Army Air Forces as a pilot, with the rank of flight officer. After a court case over his contract with Republic Studios, Autry formed his own movie production company, and he was just as prolific with his record albums and singles.

Bill Monroe was also enjoying success in 1945. Lester Flatt on guitar and Earl Scruggs on banjo had joined Bill and his Bluegrass Boys; in the three years that they were with Bill, the Bluegrass sound they made became the template for what we know as Bluegrass Music. Those definitive tracks recorded by Uncle Art at that time included "Blue Moon of Kentucky". Flatt and Scruggs formed the Foggy Mountain Boys in 1948.

Johnny Bond's career got going again after stalling during the war. Nineteen forty five saw Tex Williams fronting Spade Cooley's Band with "Shame on You." The song was Number One for nine weeks on the *Billboard* charts and became the band's signature song. The "B" side reached Number Eight as well, showing that Uncle Art could pick the hits.

Bob Wills and his Texas Playboys never really hit the previous peaks they had enjoyed before the war. Wills had enlisted in the Army but was discharged for health reasons in 1943. Wills moved on from Columbia and Uncle Art in

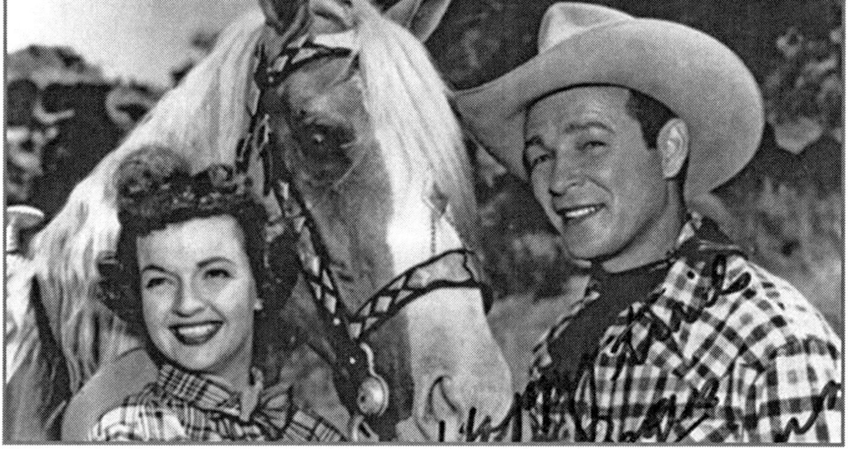

1947 to MGM, something that he later regretted saying, *"It was the worst decision of my career"*

Although Gene Autry's movie career was up and running again, others surfaced as celluloid cowboys. Roy Rogers had become Autry's main competition. I remember as a boy attending the Saturday morning cinema club in the late fifties at the Odeon Kingswood, Bristol, and watching Roy Rogers, Dale Evans, Trigger the horse, and Bullet the dog. Gene was still recording hit songs, along with a few novelty Christmas tunes. It was such a tune that he recorded on 27 June 1949. Gene was not crazy about the song but did it anyway – it was "Rudolph the Red Nose Reindeer".

The writer, Johnny Marks, had been suggesting that Gene cut the song for a piece of the publishing action, something that Art took up. On one of the *Billboard* Top Twenty charts for Christmas 1949 the writers were listed as J Marks and A E Satherley. The song sold two-million copies and many more in subsequent years.

Stuart Hamblen appeared in many cowboy movies along with his radio show, song writing, performing, and racehorse training. He was very well known. He was also known as a womaniser and "Jack the Lad", so it was quite a surprise when his lifestyle changed direction.

Evangelist Billy Graham was building his congregation around this time with his crusade revivals. He appeared on Stuart's radio show, promoting a local gathering, Stuart also attended the meeting. It was obviously an "on the road to Damascus" event – he was "converted". This presented a problem for Art. Stuart's current single produced by Art, on Columbia, "I Won't Go Hunting with You, Jake, but I'll Go Chasing Woman" was a hit, but Stuart wanted it withdrawn. It didn't fit with his new image

Uncle Art pictured here with evangelist Billy Graham

As Art said, "It took a bit of doing, but they finally agreed to pull the song at head office. I told them I had something even better to replace it. Stuart wrote "It Is No Secret What God Can Do", after I had said you have got to give me something to replace it with". That song went on to be recorded by Elvis and Johnny Cash.

It wasn't long before Stuart's radio show was cancelled, and he moved into fulltime religion and started "The Cowboy Church of the Air". He went on to write "This Old House", which was a big hit for Rosemary Clooney. Not everyone though, was convinced his conversion was authentic.

Spade Cooley ("The King of Western Swing") was another movie cowboy both as Roy Rogers' stand-in and in his own right. He was a classically trained violinist as a boy and part of the western swing dance craze with his large dance band. He became very popular, rivalling Bob Wills and the Texas Playboys. He also had a life-changing experience but of a very different sort. He was found guilty of murdering his wife in a rage of jealousy in front of his fourteen-year-old daughter. Cooley was convinced she was having an affair with Roy Rogers – this of course, strenuously denied by Roy. Spade died in prison of a heart attack after performing for the prison governor. At the time, he was apparently an ideal inmate heading for parole.

The singing cowboys still had a while left with the western format but things were changing. John Wayne was coming to dominate the scene –his impact is well known in movie history. Tex Ritter, who Art had signed in1933, was still to have great success with the background theme song in the movie "High Noon".

VERSE SEVEN

MUSIC CITY

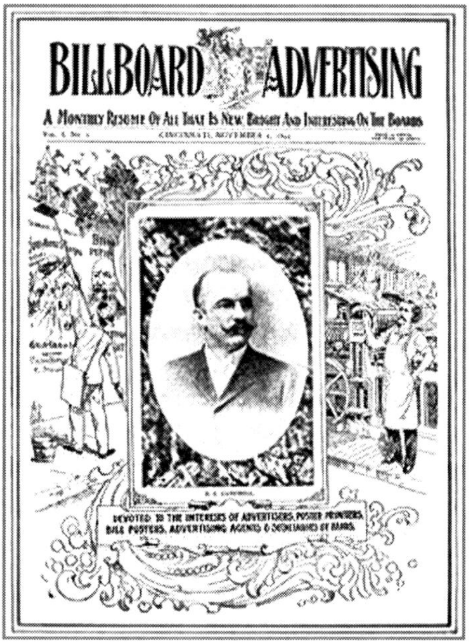

Billboard magazine was becoming the oracle of all things musical in the U S. This from Wikipedia.

> **Billboard** is a weekly American magazine devoted to the music industry. It is often considered to be one of the "holy grails" of the entertainment industry, and the official trade publication of the music industry; it is typically regarded as one of the most relevant and unbiased sources of information on the music industry, as opposed to others that can have a significant bias. It maintains several internationally recognized music charts that track the most popular songs and albums in various categories on a weekly basis.

Among the two most important charts, the Billboard Hot 100 ranks the top 100 songs regardless of genre and is frequently used as the standard measure for ranking songs in the United States based on physical sales, digital sales, and radio airplay, while the Billboard 200 survey is the corresponding chart for album sales.

When founded in Cincinnati in 1894, *Billboard Advertising* magazine was a trade paper for the bill posting industry, hence the magazine's name. Within a few years of its founding, it began to carry news of outdoor amusements, a major consumer of billboard space. Eventually, *Billboard* became the paper of record for circuses, carnivals, amusement parks, fairs, vaudeville, minstrels, whale shows and other live entertainment. The magazine began coverage of motion pictures in 1909 and of radio in the 1920s.

On January 4, 1936, *The Billboard* published its first music hit parade, and on July 20, 1940 the first Music Popularity Chart was calculated. Since 1958, the Hot 100 has been published, combining single sales and radio airplay.

Billboard currently puts out over 100 charts each week, the most popular ones being Hot 100, Billboard 200, and Hot 100 Airplay.

With the "Uncle Art" image already established as a record man of legend, Art was now playing more of an executive role with Don Law becoming the man in the studio. Although the territory had been split between the two, El Paso being the dividing line (Art everything to the West, Don everything to the East) the two still worked closely together. Don drew on the vast experience of Arthur (Don always referred to him as Arthur – never Art or Uncle Art). Art signed the new artists to the label.

Nashville was to become a centre for recording but, Dallas, New York, and Hollywood, at this time were still preferred locations. Law had lived and worked in Dallas for some years and Art regularly recording there, but of course, Art had recorded in New York for a long time as well as in Chicago and Hollywood, with his major success coming with Gene Autry's and Roy Rogers' entry into films.

In 1948, Martha White's Biscuits and Flour Company sponsored the first part of the nationwide *Grand Old Opry* show, sponsorship of programs becoming one of the most popular and effective streams of revenue for radio and television stations. The sponsors were guaranteed their voice would be heard about their product or services. The Martha White sponsorship is one of the longest continuous sponsorships known on radio, and they still are sponsors today.

Whilst visiting a radio station in Saginaw Michigan, Roy Acuff saw "Jimmy the Kid" performing, liked it, and suggested to Art he should take a look at him. Art signed the youngster who became Little Jimmy Dickens; he has had a sixty-year continuity on the Opry show. 1950, Jimmy Dickens was on the touring Opry show at KPHO television in Phoenix, Arizona, where he saw Marty Robbins, who had his own show, and linked Marty with Art. Art signed him, and put Don Law as Marty's producer.

It was a similar story for Lefty Frizzell. Lefty recorded demos at Jim Beck's studio in Texas, and we know that Art and Don used that studio. The story goes that Jim Beck took the demos to Nashville, where Don Law listened to them, and then Art signed Lefty. Jim Beck died an accidental untimely death from inhaling *carbon* tetrachloride fumes, a cleaning solvent/degreaser used for cleaning electrical and electronic switch contacts in his studio.

Art's list of artists shows that in fact he signed Lefty as the executive, and Don would produce. This pretty much holds up after the telephone conversation I had with Ray Price. He confirmed that Art would visit Don in the studio in his executive role and run songs past Ray that he thought might suit him.

"It was Don that looked after my recording career," Ray said.

The music that came from studio sessions eventually turned into a sound known as "the Ray Price beat", a 4/4 shuffle rhythm and walking bass, a style still very much used today.

Ray also confirmed that he recorded at Jim Beck's studio in Dallas, Castle Studios in Nashville, and at Owen Bradley's in Nashville.

As the 1950's arrived, popular music was about to be transform again. Columbia's folk and country division under the guidance of Uncle Art Satherley was still a major force. George Morgan had a huge hit "Candy Kisses" in late 1949. Carl Smith and his song "Let's Live a Little" was a big hit in 1951 and signed about the same time as Ray Price. Billy Walker also was becoming a big country star. Marty Robbins was about to begin his Columbia recording career.

Nashville had just one studio run by three engineers who worked for WSM radio at that time. Aaron Shelton, Carl Jenkins, and George Reynolds used equipment the station had bought to record a live Eddy Arnold show. The studio was at WSM to begin with, and then moved to the Tulane Hotel on the corner of Church Street and Eighth Avenue.

They named it "Castle Studios" after a nickname and logo of WSM "Air Castle of the South".

It was quite basic, the board (mixing desk) was a small one with no extras, such as echo, and cut straight to disc. Castle Studios inspired two brothers, Harold and Owen Bradley, to open a studio but they didn't want to step on the toes of their friends at Castle, so they would only record people who didn't want to record at Castle in the beginning. The brothers saw the popularity of television as creating a growing need for more studios, so they experimented with video. They tried several locations before buying a house on 16th Avenue South. This was the first move that would eventually turn 16th and 17th Avenues South into "Music Row".

* * * * *

I remember driving to Music Row in the late nineties for a song-writing appointment with Gary Cotton, a staff writer for Island Bound Music at the time, feeling a bit overwhelmed. I know it's said that there were around 3,000 songwriters at any one time trying to get listened to in Nashville, and any one of them would give their eye teeth to be doing what I was doing that day. I felt honoured.

Another similar experience was a meeting with Jack (Cowboy) Clements at his studio in Nashville. I was invited to record an instrumental that I had written called "Open Reel" by a guy I knew as Stax, a very good musician and recording/mastering engineer. Stax played on and produced the track; he used one of Lee Roy Parnell's band members on fiddle. (Sorry can't remember his name, great player though) Anyway, Stax took me round to Cowboy's studio to play him the track.

He liked it and said, "Bring me more."

I was going to do more with Stax but lost touch with him after he left town. It was a most enjoyable experience. Again the honour was all mine.

* * * * *

The house at 804 Sixteenth Avenue South proved to be too small, so a Quonset hut was erected as a bigger studio out back, (a Quonset hut is known as a Nissan hut in the UK – a galvanised roof, semicircular shed). This was to become "Studio B" of Columbia Nashville, after the Bradley's sold to the major label.

Ray Price told me, "It was my idea that they buy Owen's studio, it had such a good sound in there, so they did"

Columbia had introduced the 33-1/3 rpm long playing record (LP) on vinyl in 1948. Then, RCA Victor brought in the single at forty-five rpm in 1949. *Billboard Magazine* had much more to contend with. The success of Acuff Rose publishing was a very large factor in Nashville becoming Music City. They signed Hank Williams whose hits helped to propel the publisher worldwide.

To learn more, a book by Michael Kosser, *How Nashville Became Music City: 50 Years of Music Row* (published by Hal Leonard Corporation) tells the story.

VERSE EIGHT

A BOLT OUT OF THE BLUE

As the fifties started a-rock'n and a-roll'n, Arthur Satherley's life underwent a massive change, second only to the steamship ride from Bristol forty years earlier. He had been a vice president in the music industry for half of that time – forging ahead making blues and hillbilly music respectable, available, and profitable. He was still searching out and recording new talent through 1950 and 1951.

Then, Billboard carried this column on 7 June 1952:

SATHERLEY QUITS COLUMBIA JOB. New York May 31$^{st.}$, Goddard Lieberson, executive Vice-President of Columbia Records, this week announced the resignation of Arthur Satherley and the appointment of Don Law as director of Folk Music Artist and Repertoire. Law has assisted Satherley for more than five years.

Lieberson noted that "Uncle Arthur" launched the recording careers of many leading artists and developed such outstanding stars as Gene Autry and Roy Acuff.

Lieberson said in part: " It is with profound appreciation for his distinguished service, and with warmest regards, that his associates at Columbia Records accept Arthur Satherley's retirement from the company.

This was followed by a paragraph on Art's achievements..

Well, from the outside, this seemed like a bolt from the blue, but was it? Retiring eighteen months before his sixty-fifth birthday, without a pension? Compulsory retirement at sixty five was the rule at Columbia. Even if he was unhappy or even very unhappy about someone or something, it's almost unbelievable that this man would cut his nose off to spite his face. He was apparently in good health with everything going for him!

These days we often hear stories from politicians saying, "I'm leaving to spend more time with the family" or "taking gardening leave." The cynics amongst us say "Yea right".

This kind of spin is not just being used but over-used, and the statement from Columbia sounds just like spin of the highest order to me. What did really happen? We're in the speculation zone here, but are there any clues? Maybe, did Columbia let Art go? That is, suggest he leave? The conversation would go something like: "Art, you take early retirement and nothing will be said about 'It', but you lose your pension."

A bit draconian? And what could "It" have been?

The speculation: It could be seen that, over the years, Art had made arrangements with artists and songwriters that he be paid an ongoing commission, as you might with management/agency, and/or promotional fees. Back then, record producers didn't automatically get a one-point royalty as they do today (or sometimes even more).. The payments were individual agreements because Art did not have a separate company for handling such deals. Rumours had it that Art's percentage was on the high side – as I say rumours – agent's fees always being on the gross earnings not net earnings. The question was, did Art's Columbia contract allow for these kind of actions? Was this a contributing factor to the letting go, or was it a fundamental change in direction? It would appear not – after all, Don Law was continuing where Art left off, and Art had been his mentor! What if Art was setting up his own company for him to pursue at retirement? Well, it's a possibility.

Here's another column from *Billboard*, 6 September 1952:

Art Satherley To PM; Hollywood Plans Own Song Firm Hollywood Aug 30. – Art Satherley who resigned as Country and Western a. & r. chief of Columbia Records early in July, has gone into personal management and intends by late fall to announce either a pubbery [music bar and eatery] connection or formation of his own song firm.

> Satherley, who recently returned from Northern Mexico, where he scouted south of the border warblers, has inked Polly Possum and Joe Wolverton, country duo currently in North Western Nighteries, and the Callahan Brothers, comedy-song duo currently in Texas, all of whom are with Columbia Records.
>
> Satherley starts next week on a junket of the South, New York and Chicago, returning to the coast via British Columbia. He is seeking talent for recording and publishing.

And again in *Billboard,* 24 Oct 1953:"Art Satherley Publications claiming to be only national pubbery with head offices in Dallas and expects others to set up in the Texas City."

The official line was, as the press statement had said, and I guess we will never really know. I wonder if Forrest White knew? I saw no evidence that he was going to refer to Art being removed, but if pushed, my hunch would be, that even after all Uncle Art had done for the music and Columbia records, sadly, he was let go. Corporate cut-throatedness showing itself?

So one thing is clear: Art was starting, or had already started a personal management firm as well as song publishing called Art Satherley Publications, This, of course, is what Art was known for in the business anyway, operating as a quasi-freelancer but always with a salary as part of a larger organisation. Then there is the reference to a chain of Pubbery's with the headquarters in Dallas. I could find no other reference to café, bar, or restaurants, singular or plural, being set up in Dallas. In fact, I ran it past Ray Price who still lives in Dallas during my interview with him. He said he had never seen or heard of anything like that.

It could be argued that fellow pioneer, Ralph Peer, had done the very same thing. Arthur and Ralph had worked closely together over the years. The difference was that, by the fifties, Ralph had set up a very large international publishing house standing alone with many subsidiaries. But Ralph came at it from the business direction. I believe I am right in saying that Ralph didn't particularly like country music, but recognized the potential for the music industry. Later in life, he switched his attention to horticulture, becoming an expert in the growth of camellias. Ralph's son took over the publishing in the mid-fifties. Ralph Peer died in 1960 and was posthumously inducted into The Country Music Hall of Fame in 1984.

* * * * *

As I have already stated, Art's thinking came from historical roots: the migration of settlers with their music, particularly those from the British Isles. This was the driving force behind his move to America. His intention was to map the movement of the English West Country dialect across the states of the US. This was even before the "call it fate if you will" move into the newly emerging record industry. It was his passion, and then a factor in his philanthropic attitude. Maybe this attitude suited the discovery and recording of all of those artists and their songs more than the business side of things and the huge corporateness it turned into. I don't know, but something went seriously out of tune with Columbia Records and Art at this time.

With all the industry connections that Art had built up over the years, he must have felt that continuing with the scouting, recording, and song-publishing would be more than adequate to keep him going financially even without a pension from Columbia. Presumably the royalty income would have been substantial from the publishing he had acquired. Things must have been OK, because Art and Harriet took a flight from Idlewild Airport New York to Bermuda for a vacation in 1954 with Harriet travelling as Harriet H. Melka, this probably not being a budget holiday, if you get my drift.

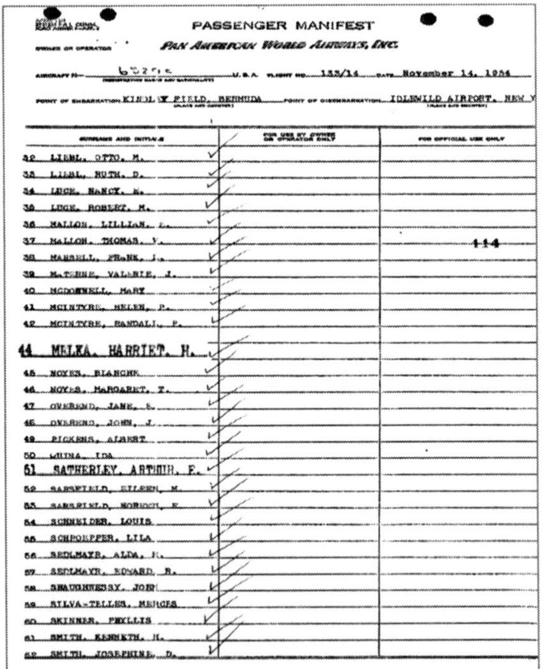
PASSENGER MANIFEST

PAN AMERICAN WORLD AIRWAYS, INC.

FLIGHT NO. 133/14 DATE November 14, 1954

POINT OF EMBARKATION KINDLEY FIELD, BERMUDA POINT OF DISEMBARKATION IDLEWILD AIRPORT, NEW Y

SURNAME AND INITIALS	FOR USE BY OWNER OR OPERATOR ONLY	FOR OFFICIAL USE ONLY
32 LIEBL, OTTO, M.		
33 LIEBL, RUTH, D.		
34 LUCE, NANCY, E.		
35 LUCE, ROBERT, M.		
36 MALLON, LILLIAN, [illegible]		
37 MALLON, THOMAS, [illegible]		114
38 MANSELL, FRANK, J.		
39 MATERNE, VALERIE, J.		
40 MCDONNELL, MARY		
41 MCINTYRE, HELEN, P.		
42 MCINTYRE, RANDALL, P.		
44 MELKA, HARRIET, H.		
45 NOYES, BLANCHE		
46 NOYES, MARGARET, T.		
47 OVEREND, JANE, [illegible]		
48 OVEREND, JOHN, J.		
49 PICKENS, ALBERT		
50 [illegible], IDA		
51 SATHERLEY, ARTHUR, E.		
52 SARSFIELD, EILEEN, M.		
53 SARSFIELD, [illegible], E.		
54 SCHNEIDER, LOUIS		
55 SCHROEPFER, LILA		
56 SEDLMAYR, ALDA, [illegible]		
57 SEDLMAYR, EDWARD, R.		
58 SHAUGHNESSY, JOHN		
59 SILVA-TELLES, MERCES		
60 SKINNER, PHYLLIS		
61 SMITH, KENNETH, H.		
62 SMITH, JOSEPHINE, D.		

PREPARED BY M. Dickens PAGE 2 OF 3 PAGES

Perhaps nothing had changed as far as Art's thinking was concerned with talent scouting, production, and personal management still a requirement, but what had changed was the very business he had help create, a very large industry with big teeth, and shareholders to please. These days, the internet and reality TV have changed everything again – where *Pop Idols, Got Talent, Ballroom Dancing on Ice,* and *X Factor,* have people, with none of the aforementioned, chosen to be ridiculed by a panel of drudges, sorry judges, deliberately included in the show to create sparks and rudeness. It helps if the victim has a member of their close family die or dying, or at least tragic circumstances, to wind up sympathy and the string section even more. For those that make it through and win, and are successful in a difficult business, congratulations and fair play to them I say. (That's my little rant over with)

Back to the fifties.

With the music industry now being enveloped with what some called "the Music of the Devil", Rock and Roll was here to stay. But it was just another progression with music moving on, just as it had done from the start of the popular recording scene. The blending of music, blues, twelve bar, and folk songs being picked up by the kids and adding the passion and energy that only the young can do. In conversations with Chet Atkins, he told me that he had been assigned by Steve Sholes at RCA to produce a young man from Memphis called Elvis Presley; Chet had just been put in charge of the studio in 1525 McGavock street Nashville, where he played on and produced many of Elvis's tracks.

RCA studio McGavock St 1954-2006 (Authors collection)

Chet said he remembers ringing his wife Leona after the first session and saying, "I think we have us a star." Chet also added, "I couldn't carry on producing Elvis; too many fans would turn up. So, I had to hand over to someone else who could do the night shift in secret. I was playing guitar and running the studio. That's why I couldn't do nights". He added, "Elvis was a quiet, respectful, and talented country boy".

Chet Atkins and Owen Bradley created what became known as the Nashville Sound, by introducing slicker recording techniques and using songs that would cross over to "pop." This was the cause of dislike to people who thought the music should stay pure, but as Chet said to me "Head office wanted more record sales, more of the market, so to keep our jobs we obliged".

But with wider vision, perhaps it can be seen that this increase in popularity of country-crossover material also brought many to country, bluegrass, and roots music that perhaps would not have experienced it otherwise, especially outside of the US. The production techniques in Nashville today have become second-to-none and have earned the title "Music City", a term first used by radio DJ David Cob in the early fifties and used by some satirically, as "Cashville".

During the fifties that Sun Records in Memphis, started by Sam Phillips, recorded all of those tracks by names that became synonymous with country, rockabilly, and rock and roll. The story of Sun Studios is well documented but it's worth re-looking at part of the Elvis story. When "Colonel" Tom Parker became Elvis's manager, he and Sam Phillips negotiated the deal with RCA Victor Nashville for an unprecedented amount, $40,000, that included $5,000 back royalties from Sun Records.

Here is what The Elvis encyclopedia. By Adam victor. Stanley and Coffey 1997, had to say; To boost earnings for himself and Presley, Parker also cut a deal with Hill & Range Publishing Company to create two separate entities—"Elvis Presley Music, Inc" and "Gladys Music"—to handle all of Presley's songs and accrued royalties. The owners of Hill & Range, Julian and Jean Aberbach, agreed to split the publishing and royalties rights of each song equally with Presley. Hill & Range, Presley, or Colonel Parker's partners then had to convince unsecured songwriters that it was worthwhile for them to give up one third of their due royalties in exchange for Presley recording their compositions. One result of these dealings was the appearance of Presley's name as co-writer of some songs he recorded, even though Presley never had any hand in the songwriting process.

The point of this reference is to show that deals like this were (and still are) commonplace in the music industry, so Art's deals could be considered normal practice.

VERSE NINE

THE PLANTATION INN (AND OUT)

As the 'fifties continued, Art followed his tried and trusted work ethic, with an office in Hollywood, scouting trips and artiste promotions. His Plantation Inn project just outside of Savannah, Georgia, was costing a lot of money to convert into a retreat for people in the country music business to use. He was perhaps ahead of his time again; this was Art once again spotting an opportunity. Now, we are used to seeing and visiting or living in gated communities around a golf course, and coastal resorts again featuring golf.

Art, wanting to keep his private life private left only a small amount of clues, such as the previous references to a mailing address at the Plantation Inn, and those small columns in Bill Board Magazine. It's interesting that Gladys, Art's wife's, social security number was raised in Georgia, and not in Wisconsin or New York. My question is, did Art and Gladys own the Plantation Inn? Art might have been trying to assist Gladys because of his admission, *"I would make an awful married man, never being home, always on the road"* and maybe through illness Gladys could no longer run the Inn. She died in February 1965, 69 years of age.

I finally got to the bottom of the Plantation Inn after a land title search. It revealed that Art was the executor of the will of Rufus Yaw, owner of the Plantation Inn, and that Rufus bequeathed the property in that will to Gladys

J Satherley and Arthur E Satherley equally in the will. It was part of the Silk Hope Plantation known as Silk Hope Farms; the Plantation Inn was referred to as; The Plantation inn, all fixtures, fittings and equipment, in the bequeathment. The address was 5008 Ogeechee Road, Chatham County, Georgia.

The Satherleys owned the property for fifteen years from 1949 to 1963, when it was sold to G B Mckenzie on the 22nd of May 1963. Art's dream of turning the property into that retreat not realised.

The Plantation Inn and Motor Court became The Plantation Estates Mobile Home Park, with 65 mobile home spaces.

I spoke with the current owner, Patsy Hall, to find out if any stories remain about those times back then. She told me that Gene Autry was thought to have kept his horses there-this would fit perfectly with Art and Gene's close working relationship for all those years.

* * * * *

As the sixties progressed, there was less PR surrounding Art's music management and publishing company with more behind the scenes consultancy maybe, or did he have to sell his publishing catalogue to raise money? The country-music scene was being stretched in different directions, as we have seen, being profit-driven by the large record labels. The smoother Nashville Sound was becoming more "pop", even producing TV titles like *Pop Goes The Country* in the seventies. The thirty-minute show on ABC was on air for eight years

The record industry got more sophisticated. The National Academy of Recording Arts & Sciences, known as the Recording Academy or NARAS, was established in 1957 in Los Angeles. It is a US organization of musicians, producers, recording engineers, and other recording professionals dedicated to improving the quality of life and cultural conditions for music and its makers. The Recording Academy is famous for its Grammy Awards.

The first trade association was formed in 1958 to promote a music genre. The Country Music Association was born in rather austere conditions: one desk, a borrowed typewriter, and one full-time employee, Jo Walker, someone who eventually would make a big difference in leading the expansion of country music worldwide. The organization's mission statement reads:

> CMA is dedicated to bringing the poetry and emotion of country music to the world.
>
> We will continue the tradition of leadership and professionalism, promoting the music, and recognizing excellence in all its forms.
>
> While fostering a spirit of community and sharing, we will respect and encourage creativity and the unique contributions of all.
>
> CMA will be a place to have fun and celebrate success. We will take risks, embrace change, and always exceed the expectations of those we serve.

The early sixties saw the CMA grow into the organisation we know today, with Jo Walker executive director, a post she held until her retirement in 1991. Nineteen sixty one saw the founding of the Country Hall of Fame by the

CMA. It was originally housed at the top of Music Row, but now resides downtown in a purpose-built development (2001).

This picture of the new building demonstrates the symbology in the architecture. The shape of the building is that of a bass clef, the windows are representative of a piano keyboard, the tower depicts different size discs (records and CDs) and the tower is a representation of the WSM transmission tower.

The association in 1967 started what was to become one of the biggest annual events, the CMA Awards. The show was not televised the first year, but has been every year thereafter. In 1972 Fan Fair was started in Nashville by the CMA, a four-day festival where fans of the music could come and meet and greet their favourite performers. It's now called the CMA Music Festival.

In 1967, Jo Walker had some personal tragedy, when her husband Charles "Smokey" Walker was fatally injured in a motorbike accident, leaving Jo with their young daughter Michelle. Jo remarried in 1981 to businessman Bob Meador, and became step-mother to Karen and Rob, keeping her Walker name, now known as Jo Walker-Meador.

Jo's Biography

A native of Orlinda Tennessee, Josephine Denning Walker-Meador joined the Country Music Association in 1958 as office manager. After only a short time in that position, she was named the trade association's executive director. Owing her almost thirty years at CMA, Jo helped a struggling organization grow to a membership of more than 7,000, governed by a Board of Directors comprised of dozens of international music industry leaders.

During her distinguished career, Jo was instrumental in establishing several groundbreaking projects and activities, such as the Country Music Hall of Fame, the annual CMA Awards Show, Fan Fair (now CMA Music Fest), and other events designed to enhance the image of country music throughout the world.

Jo has been recognized for her myriad contributions to the country music industry numerous times. In 1970, the city of Nashville presented her with the Metronome Award, given each year to the person who has done the most to further Nashville as an entertainment centre. In 1981, she was named Lady Executive of the Year by the Nashville Chapter of the National Women Executives. Other honours bestowed upon her include SESAC's Ambassador of country music and BMI's Commendation of Excellence.

The Academy of Country Music honoured her in 1983 with its Jim Reeves Memorial Award in recognition of her role in establishing CMA's London Office and her twenty-five years of distinguished dedication to country music. During the 1991 CMA Awards Show, she received the prestigious Irving Waugh Award of Excellence.

In one of the crowning achievements in an illustrious career, in 1995, Jo was inducted into the prestigious country music Hall of Fame.

Jo has also been active in community activities, including the American Cancer Society, the Metropolitan Tourist Commission, the Board of the National Music Council, Travellers' Aid, and is also active in many other charitable and civic organizations. In 1977, she became the second woman ever elected by the membership of the Nashville Area Chamber of Commerce to serve a three-year term on its Board of Governors. In addition, she is the first woman elected to the board of Big Brothers and in 1989 became the first woman elected as the organization's president.

She currently serves on the Minnie Pearl Cancer Foundation, as a SCORE (Service Core of Retired Executives) counselor, and as an advisor to several internationals involved in country music. In 2003, Jo was inducted into the Academy of Women of Achievement In 2008; Big Brothers honoured her with its first Big Tribute Award.

> In the same year, her name was installed in Nashville's Walk of Fame.

Jo is featured in more verses, not just because she knew Art after he retired, but for her help to me during the writing of this book. I asked her who the founders of the CMA were. Who better to ask? She was there! Here's the reply. (Used with permission)

> The main ones were Wesley Rose, Acuff-Rose Music Publishing; Connie B. Gay, a man who began his career as a country music DJ, but in late 50's owned several radio stations and he also promoted country music concerts, managed Jimmy Dean; Hubert Long, a talent manager and booker, a music publisher (came to Nashville from Corpus Christi, TX; W. D. (Dee) Kilpatrick, manager of the Grand Ole Opry. All of these gentlemen are now deceased. Dee Kilpatrick just passed away in 2008 during CMA's 50th year.
>
> The idea for founding CMA was born in a hotel room in Miami, Florida. These above named gentlemen returned to Nashville--that is 3 of them (Connie lived in the Washington, D. C. area.) And they formed what they called the Steering Committee. Others such as Jack Stapp, former Grand Old Opry Manager and founder of Tree Publishing, and Jim Denny, also a former Grand Old Opry Manager and founder of Cedarwood Publishing Company, Jim Denny Artists Bureau, joined the original four in holding meetings and making plans throughout the summer and fall of 1958.
>
> The first organizational meet took place in November during what was then called WSM'S Disc Jockey Convention and the first members were signed. I came to work December, the first employee of CMA."

Nineteen sixty four saw the start of another association, this time in California, when two country music performers Eddie Miller and Tommy Wiggins, teamed up with club owners Mickey and Chris Christensen to establish the Country and Western Music Academy. Their vision was to promote country music in the thirteen western states supported by artists based on the West Coast. They called it "The Country And Western Music Academy". The name was changed in the early seventies to the current name "The Academy of Country Music". The Academy introduced a pioneer award in 1968. It was awarded to Art. Apparently, he also had the first membership card.

Johnny Bond Art Satherley Tex Ritter
ACM awards Courtesy CMHF

Academy of Country & Western Music

HONORS

Arthur Edward Satherly

In 1925, Art Satherly began searching the backwoods of this nation for authentic folk talent, representing the musical art of Rural America. His quest produced some of the world's greatest country and western performers. Thus contributing to one of the great art forms, the Academy of Country and Western Music honors him as a

Country Music Pioneer

April 25, 1968
Hollywood, Calif

Johnny Bond

Nineteen seventy one was a very important year for Art. He was about to be recognized for his part in the development of country music. The CMA was about to bring Uncle Art's name permanently to the annals of country music history, with a plaque of his likeness and a statement of his career, to be displayed amongst many of the stars that Art was responsible for in the Hall of Fame, and many more to come that were signed, produced, and promoted by the record man.

Tom Smothers Art Satherley Glen Campbell ACM awards. Courtesy CMHF

Jo Walker-Meador remembers (used with permission):

> In 1971, CMA nominated Art Satherley for the Hall of Fame in the Non-Performer category, and he was elected by a panel of more than 200 industry people that same year. (Some people have been nominated year after year and been in the five finalists for a period of time before being elected. It is quite rare that one is elected the first time his or her name appears on the ballot.) He was very pleased to have been elected. He asked me to be his escort the evening of his induction, which was officially done on the annual CMA Awards Show on CBS-TV. I agreed and we sat together during the show, and I was privileged to escort him on the stage.

COUNTRY MUSIC
HALL OF FAME
ELECTED 1971
ARTHUR EDWARD SATHERLEY
OCTOBER 19, 1889
FEBRUARY 10, 1986
BORN IN BRISTOL, ENGLAND, "UNCLE ART" WAS STEEPED IN THE TRADITIONS OF ANGLO - CELTIC FOLK ART. HIS EARLY WORK WITH THOMAS A. EDISON QUALIFIED HIM AS AN EXPERT IN THE FLEDGLING AMERICAN RECORDING INDUSTRY. AS A TALENT SCOUT, HE PRODUCED SUCH GREATS AS GENE AUTRY, BOB WILLS, ROY ACUFF AND MOLLY O'DAY. RETIRED SINCE 1953, SATHERLEY WAS A PIONEER RECORD MAN CONTRIBUTING GREATLY TO THE WORLD-WIDE GROWTH OF COUNTRY MUSIC.
COUNTRY MUSIC ASSOCIATION

country music foundation

COUNTRY MUSIC FOUNDATION LIBRARY & MEDIA CENTER · COUNTRY MUSIC HALL OF FAME & MUSEUM
700 SIXTEENTH AVENUE SOUTH · NASHVILLE, TENNESSEE 37203 · 615/256-7008

April 18, 1972

Mr. Arthur Satherley
8841 Longden Avenue
Temple, California 91780

Dear Mr. Satherley,

It gives us great pleasure to inform you that you have been selected as one of the Pioneers of Country Music. The Country Music Hall of Fame and Museum is now preparing a display honoring these individuals. The Pioneers are a group of non-performers who influenced the development of the Country Music tradition in its earliest years. The men to be honored in this exhibit are: Edwin Craig, J. L. Frank, Dave Kapp, Jack Kapp, Eli Oberstein, Ralph Peer, Fred Rose, Art Satherley, and Frank Walker.

The Pioneers were selected by a committee of the Country Music Foundation Board of Trustees after exhaustive historical research into the roots of Country Music. Each of the people mentioned here made a distinctive contribution to the development of the Country Music field in its early years. Although the Pioneers rarely received the acclaim awarded performers, their contributions to Country Music influenced the direction of a major segment of American music. Your inclusion in this group is a distinct honor.

The attached news release detailing the contribution of each Pioneer will be made available to the Press.

Sincerely yours,

Frank Jones, Chairman of the Board
Country Music Foundation Board of Trustees

Brad McCuen, President
Country Music Foundation Board of Trustees

FJ BM/ta
Enclosure

Picture with Jo Walker – Meador, Faron Young, Roy Acuff and Uncle Art. (Courtesy of Jo Walker-Meador)

At last, a behind-the-scenes mentor gaining recognition Uncle Art Satherley inducted into the country music Hall of Fame.

You might have thought news like that would have filtered back to Art's home town, Bristol, but nothing. Mind you, in fairness the UK has never had a radio station just playing country music, Scotland and Ireland faring better with a more vibrant scene. This wasn't because the music wasn't popular; it was, and always had been, and continues to be, getting maybe an hour or so show a week. No one apparently knew how to promote the music, not even the record companies, but even so, a very large percentage of people liked what they were hearing, so calling it "country" didn't matter.

In fact, sometimes the response was negative – that "ole yee ha, straw in the mouth" image taken completely out of context by the media. It was as if the music wasn't good enough or not hip, cool, and trendy. British DJ and music historian Paul Gambaccini hosted a radio program pointing out that a large percentage of "pop" hits started out as country songs. Now, the Internet is forcing another change. Whatever your preference in music, it's available worldwide. The iPod is revolutionizing the way we can buy music, which is a bit of a learning curve maybe, but just plug in your iPod to your PC, Notebook, or whatever, even your latest phone gizmo, and there you go. And the cost? Music is now more available than ever for less money, without any import taxes, *Hallelujah!*

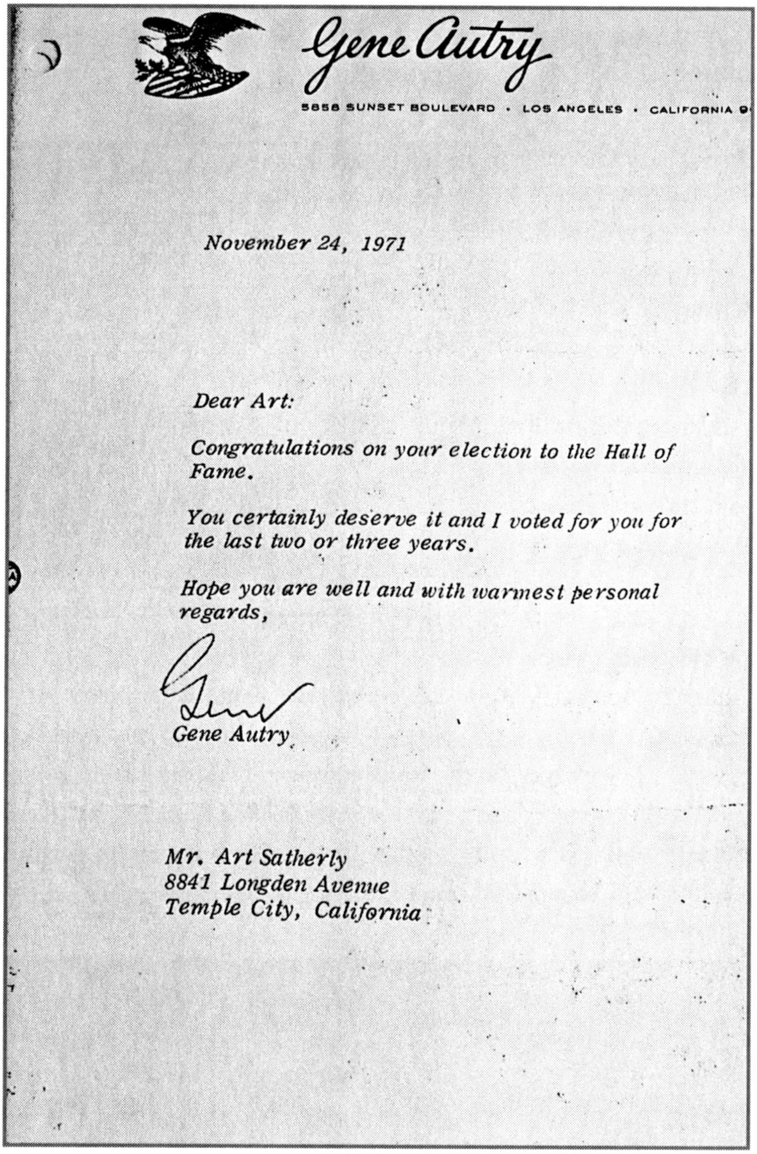

Gene Autry

5858 SUNSET BOULEVARD • LOS ANGELES • CALIFORNIA 9

November 24, 1971

Dear Art:

Congratulations on your election to the Hall of Fame.

You certainly deserve it and I voted for you for the last two or three years.

Hope you are well and with warmest personal regards,

Gene

Gene Autry

Mr. Art Satherly
8841 Longden Avenue
Temple City, California

Of course, some may not approve of the new technology, or be positively "agin it" (didn't I write something like this earlier about electricity?) but the fact is, it's here, and people will decide what they want to hear and by whom and when! "Hello," record companies, people want choice, just as Uncle Art Satherley proved so many years ago. I bet he'd have loved an instant audience worldwide!

* * * * *

Johnny Cash Uncle Art Tennessee Ernie Ford. Courtesy CMHF

At a gathering celebrating Uncle Art, Johnny Cash stood on stage and said; "Uncle Art, we owe you everything. If it wasn't for Uncle Art Satherley I doubt whether any of us would be on this stage tonight! He is the Daddy of us all, and what he has done, we're all thankful for". From the interview for the country music Hall of Fame by Douglas B Green 1974.Johnny voiced the opinion of so many in the music business.

It is amazing to think still none of this was picked up in the music press in England, and Art saying in the same interview "Even my parents could now be proud of their renegade son now, country music's founding father, me".

He was fleetingly referring to that deep ravine between his family back home in England, caused by Art not following his mother's and father's wishes

"Reunion '80"
"Reunion '80"
ACADEMY OF COUNTRY MUSIC
"Reunion '80"....A Tribute To Art Satherly
ACADEMY OF COUNTRY MUSIC
1964
BEVERAGE
BEVERAGE
FRIDAY, MAY 23, 1980 — 6:30 p.m. til Midnight
MAGIC MOUNTAIN VALENCIA, CA.
GOLDEN CIRCLE PARTY & SEATING
$25.00
"Reunion '80"
Six Flags
Magic Mountain
MAY 23, 1980
ADMISSION
084

to become a minister of the church, the reason for his education, and then Art becoming a travelling salesman. He must have been working for the Devil himself! Family feuds. eh!

All of this celebrating of Art's achievements was in sharp contrast to Art's finances. NARAS had arranged the trip from California to Nashville for the award show. Art's granddaughter, Judith, pointed out that her grandpa had taken a book-keeping job with Abbott Labs, a pharmaceutical company in California, to help pay the bills. He was injured in a fire at the Labs, needed hospital care, and money was tight.

VERSE TEN

A FRIEND IN NEED AND A FRIEND INDEED

Forrest White had known Art since their fortuitous meeting in the old Andrew Jackson in Nashville in 1971. They discovered that they had many things in common; they lived in the same area of California; and knew many of the same people in the music business. They became good friends.

At the time, Art was retired from Columbia but, as we have seen, he was still involved in the promotion and publishing of music, eventually being inducted into the Hall of Fame in the early seventies. Things from the outside were looking good.

As Art's age slowed him down, his friendship with Forrest grew stronger. Forrest would take Art out on trips and reminisce in conversation, as you do; Art trusted Forrest to look after his business affairs, which he did, realizing at the same time that Art's and Harriet's financial situation was not good. Forrest felt that the industry in which Art had played such a role could and should help out. Because of Art's pride, he would have to be very careful how he approached the subject.

So, Forrest and Art hatched a plan. Forrest approached Columbia Nashville about releasing an album to celebrate Art's work; the idea was met favourably.

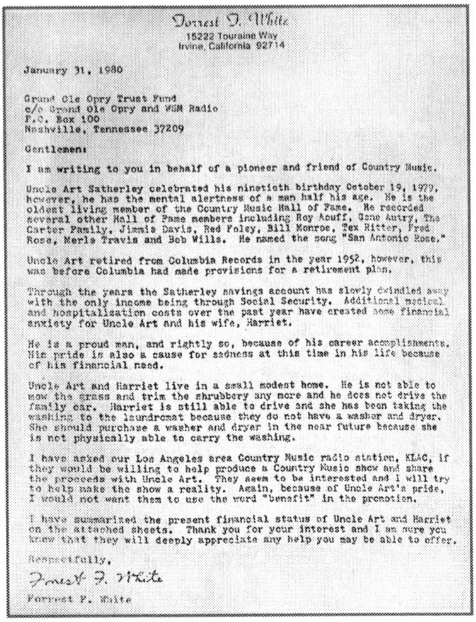

Forrest F. White
15222 Touraine Way
Irvine, California 92714

January 31, 1980

Grand Ole Opry Trust Fund
c/o Grand Ole Opry and WSM Radio
P.O. Box 100
Nashville, Tennessee 37209

Gentlemen:

I am writing to you in behalf of a pioneer and friend of Country Music.

Uncle Art Satherley celebrated his ninetieth birthday October 19, 1979, however, he has the mental alertness of a man half his age. He is the oldest living member of the Country Music Hall of Fame. He recorded several other Hall of Fame members including Roy Acuff, Gene Autry, The Carter Family, Jimmie Davis, Red Foley, Bill Monroe, Tex Ritter, Fred Rose, Merle Travis and Bob Wills. He named the song "San Antonio Rose."

Uncle Art retired from Columbia Records in the year 1952, however, this was before Columbia had made provisions for a retirement plan.

Through the years the Satherley savings account has slowly dwindled away with the only income being through Social Security. Additional medical and hospitalization costs over the past year have created some financial anxiety for Uncle Art and his wife, Harriet.

He is a proud man, and rightly so, because of his career accomplishments. His pride is also a cause for sadness at this time in his life because of his financial need.

Uncle Art and Harriet live in a small modest home. He is not able to mow the grass and trim the shrubbery any more and he does not drive the family car. Harriet is still able to drive and she has been taking the washing to the laundromat because they do not have a washer and dryer. She should purchase a washer and dryer in the near future because she is not physically able to carry the washing.

I have asked our Los Angeles area Country Music radio station, KLAC, if they would be willing to help produce a Country Music show and share the proceeds with Uncle Art. They seem to be interested and I will try to help make the show a reality. Again, because of Uncle Art's pride, I would not want them to use the word "benefit" in the promotion.

I have summarized the present financial status of Uncle Art and Harriet on the attached sheets. Thank you for your interest and I am sure you know that they will deeply appreciate any help you may be able to offer.

Respectfully,

Forrest F. White

Forrest F. White

OPRY TRUST FUND, INC.
WSM
NASHVILLE, TENNESSEE

606

1 · 24 19 80

87-4
640

PAY TO THE ORDER OF ART SATHERLY $ 5,000.00

Five thousand and no/100 DOLLARS

THIRD NATIONAL BANK
IN NASHVILLE
NASHVILLE, TENNESSEE

OPRY TRUST FUND, INC.

TREASURER

FOR Contribution

⑈0640⑈0004⑆ 604 344 5⑈

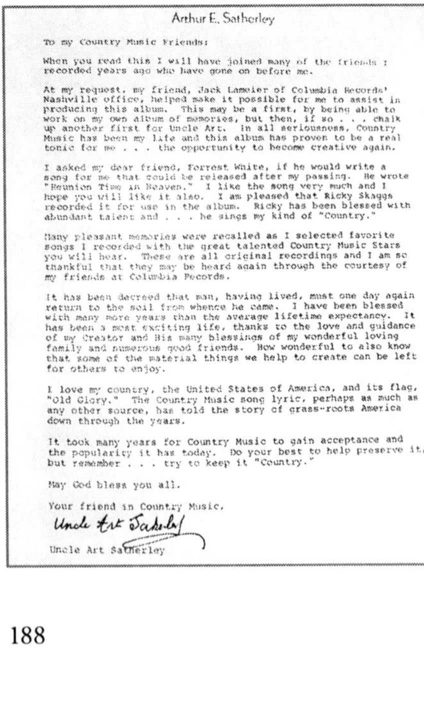

Arthur E. Satherley

To my Country Music Friends:

When you read this I will have joined many of the friends I recorded years ago who have gone on before me.

At my request, my friend, Jack Lameier of Columbia Records' Nashville office, helped make it possible for me to assist in producing this album. This may be a first, by being able to work on my own album of memories, but then, if so . . . chalk up another first for Uncle Art. In all seriousness, Country Music has been my life and this album has proven to be a real tonic for me . . . the opportunity to become creative again.

I asked my dear friend, Forrest White, if he would write a song for me that could be released after my passing. He wrote "Reunion Time in Heaven." I like the song very much and I hope you will like it also. I am pleased that Ricky Skaggs recorded it for use in the album. Ricky has been blessed with abundant talent and . . . he sings my kind of "Country."

Many pleasant memories were recalled as I selected favorite songs I recorded with the great talented Country Music Stars you will hear. These are all original recordings and I am so thankful that they may be heard again through the courtesy of my friends at Columbia Records.

It has been decreed that man, having lived, must one day again return to the soil from whence he came. I have been blessed with many more years than the average lifetime expectancy. It has been a most exciting life, thanks to the love and guidance of my Creator and His many blessings of my wonderful loving family and numerous good friends. How wonderful to also know that some of the material things we help to create can be left for others to enjoy.

I love my country, the United States of America, and its flag, "Old Glory." The Country Music song lyric, perhaps as much as any other source, has told the story of grass-roots America down through the years.

It took many years for Country Music to gain acceptance and the popularity it has today. Do your best to help preserve it, but remember . . . try to keep it "Country."

May God bless you all.

Your friend in Country Music,

Uncle Art Satherley

Uncle Art Satherley

With Art now in his late eighties, Forrest decided to record Art introducing the tracks and narrating the album to be called *American Originals*. To do this, they would record Art's words on a portable recorder on trips out over a period of time. They wanted to keep it from Harriet, knowing that she would be upset at the thought it would be for release after Art had passed on. And so Art's last recordings were made as he started, in the field, this time in a car in a park in California. This would also generate some money for the moment with Art being paid as producer. The correspondence is reprinted with permission of the Country Music Foundation and Judith Keigly.

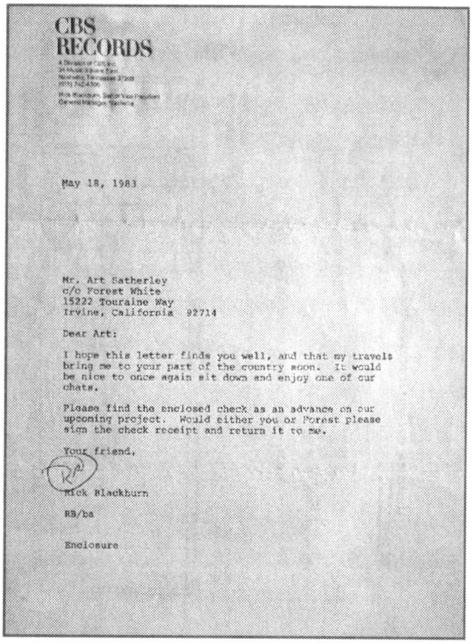
CBS RECORDS

May 18, 1983

Mr. Art Satherley
c/o Forest White
15222 Touraine Way
Irvine, California 92714

Dear Art:

I hope this letter finds you well, and that my travels bring me to your part of the country soon. It would be nice to once again sit down and enjoy one of our chats.

Please find the enclosed check as an advance on our upcoming project. Would either you or Forest please sign the check receipt and return it to me.

Your friend,

Rick Blackburn

RB/ba

Enclosure

Forrest worked hard to make the music industry aware of Mr Country Music, as he called Art, and it responded with donations and tributes.
The California radio station KCLA did a tribute concert, plus there were various radio interviews on other stations. Forrest had to find a way to convince Art to accept the help, because Art's pride sometimes got in the way.

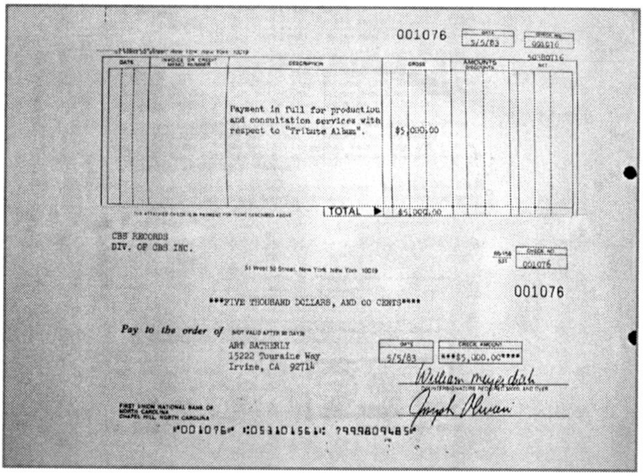
001076 5/5/83

Payment in full for production and consultation services with respect to "Tribute Album". $5,000.00

TOTAL ▶ $5,000.00

CBS RECORDS
DIV. OF CBS INC.

51 West 52 Street, New York New York 10019

001076

001076

FIVE THOUSAND DOLLARS, AND 00 CENTS*

Pay to the order of
ART SATHERLY
15222 Touraine Way
Irvine, CA 92714

5/5/83 ***$5,000.00****

FIRST UNION NATIONAL BANK OF NORTH CAROLINA
CHAPEL HILL, NORTH CAROLINA

It's true to say that because of Forrest's persistence people in the music business were able to help out in those times of need. Gene Autry and Art had not spoken to each other in fifteen years after a disagreement, but again Forrest reconnected them. Curtis White, Forrest's son, remembered;

> I only know that they had not spoken in many years for reasons that I infer involved a very unfortunate breakdown in communications – quite an irony, considering Mr. Autry owned a number of radio and TV stations. I remember seeing a picture of

Uncle Art and Mr. Autry, both smiling broadly, that was taken inside Mr. Autry's private box at Anaheim Stadium where the Angels, the baseball team he owned, were – and are still – headquartered.

Mr Autry was persuaded to help out with donations by people in high places, convincing him what a good idea it would be. Jo Walker-Meador was one of them. This is how she remembered it:

> Uncle Art and I were talking about some financial matters in the early 80s at which time he told me that he was arranging his financial matters and that if he only had $5,000 more, he would be fine. I asked him at that time "Why don't you ask Gene Autry for it?" He said, "Oh, no. You see we had a disagreement about a matter, and I don't think he would do it." I saw Gene in the Madison Hotel in Washington, D. C., in 1983. We were both there for CMA's 25th Anniversary Television Special on the CBS network. (Gene was President of CMA in 1963, and I knew him quite well.) I asked Gene if he would consider giving Art $5,000. He was a bit reluctant, but did give Art the money.

There was movement elsewhere to remind people of the importance that Uncle Art Satherley had been to the history of the recording industry.

In 1985, Ricky Skaggs was honoured with a star in the walkway at the Country Music Hall of Fame, when it was situated at the top of Music Row Nashville. Ricky was at the height of his commercial country-music career, with many hits under his belt. He had grown up in East Kentucky amongst the rural music of America.

By the age of sixteen he was more than proficient on mandolin, fiddle, banjo, and guitar, playing with the Stanley brothers. Being around those legendary names must have been like attending a university course. There was one name cropping up over and over, Uncle Art Satherley.

And so began Ricky's association with getting Uncle Art's name linked to how the music came to be what it is today.

In the paperwork from Forrest White's office were two letters, one from Ricky dated 27 February 1986 to Gene Autry, asking for support for a star in the walkway

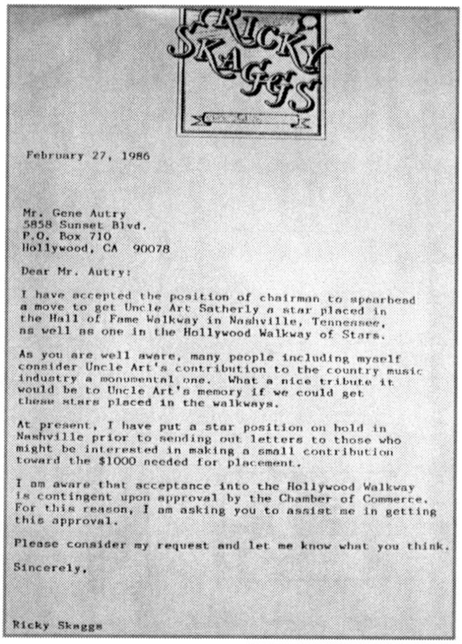

February 27, 1986

Mr. Gene Autry
5858 Sunset Blvd.
P.O. Box 710
Hollywood, CA 90078

Dear Mr. Autry:

I have accepted the position of chairman to spearhead a move to get Uncle Art Satherly a star placed in the Hall of Fame Walkway in Nashville, Tennessee, as well as one in the Hollywood Walkway of Stars.

As you are well aware, many people including myself consider Uncle Art's contribution to the country music industry a monumental one. What a nice tribute it would be to Uncle Art's memory if we could get these stars placed in the walkways.

At present, I have put a star position on hold in Nashville prior to sending out letters to those who might be interested in making a small contribution toward the $1000 needed for placement.

I am aware that acceptance into the Hollywood Walkway is contingent upon approval by the Chamber of Commerce. For this reason, I am asking you to assist me in getting this approval.

Please consider my request and let me know what you think.

Sincerely,

Ricky Skaggs

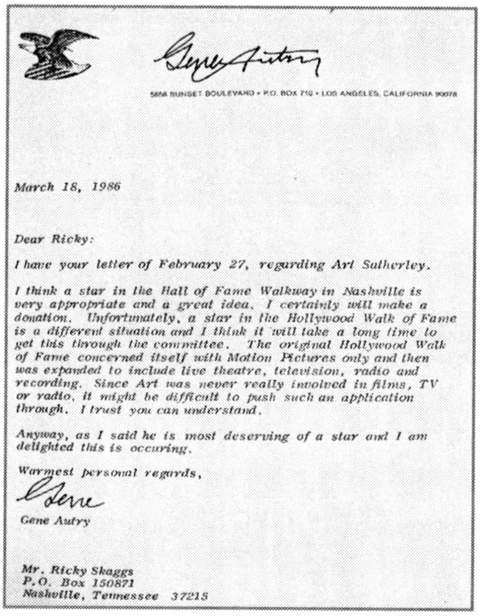

5858 SUNSET BOULEVARD • P.O. BOX 710 • LOS ANGELES, CALIFORNIA 90078

March 18, 1986

Dear Ricky:

I have your letter of February 27, regarding Art Satherley.

I think a star in the Hall of Fame Walkway in Nashville is very appropriate and a great idea. I certainly will make a donation. Unfortunately, a star in the Hollywood Walk of Fame is a different situation and I think it will take a long time to get this through the committee. The original Hollywood Walk of Fame concerned itself with Motion Pictures only and then was expanded to include live theatre, television, radio and recording. Since Art was never really involved in films, TV or radio, it might be difficult to push such an application through. I trust you can understand.

Anyway, as I said he is most deserving of a star and I am delighted this is occuring.

Warmest personal regards,

Gene Autry

Mr. Ricky Skaggs
P.O. Box 150871
Nashville, Tennessee 37215

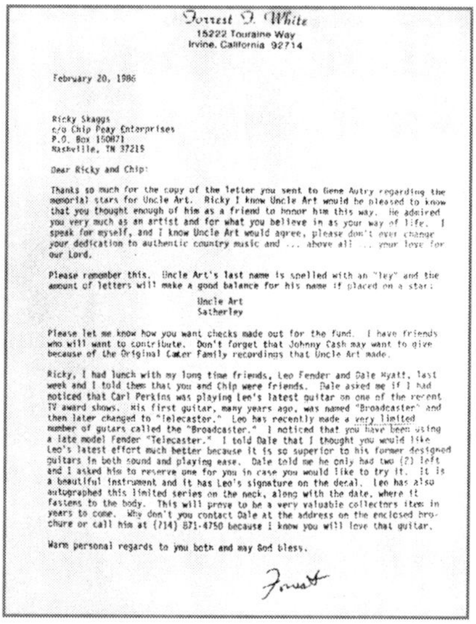

Forrest F. White
15222 Touraine Way
Irvine, California 92714

February 20, 1986

Ricky Skaggs
c/o Chip Peay Enterprises
P.O. Box 150871
Nashville, TN 37215

Dear Ricky and Chip:

Thanks so much for the copy of the letter you sent to Gene Autry regarding the memorial stars for Uncle Art. Ricky I know Uncle Art would be pleased to know that you thought enough of him as a friend to honor him this way. He admired you very much as an artist and for what you believe in as your way of life. I speak for myself, and I know Uncle Art would agree, please don't ever change your dedication to authentic country music and ... above all ... your love for our Lord.

Please remember this. Uncle Art's last name is spelled with an "ley" and the amount of letters will make a good balance for his name if placed on a star:

Uncle Art
Satherley

Please let me know how you want checks made out for the fund. I have friends who will want to contribute. Don't forget that Johnny Cash may want to give because of the Original Carter Family recordings that Uncle Art made.

Ricky, I had lunch with my long time friends, Leo Fender and Dale Hyatt, last week and I told them that you and Chip were friends. Dale asked me if I had noticed that Carl Perkins was playing Leo's latest guitar on one of the recent TV award shows. His first guitar, many years ago, was named "Broadcaster" and then later changed to "Telecaster." Leo has recently made a very limited number of gutars called the "Broadcaster." I noticed that you have been using a late model Fender "Telecaster." I told Dale that I thought you would like Leo's latest effort much better because it is so superior to his former designed guitars in both sound and playing ease. Dale told me he only had two (2) left and I asked him to reserve one for you in case you would like to try it. It is a beautiful instrument and it has Leo's signature on the decal. Leo has also autographed this limited series on the neck, along with the date, where it fastens to the body. This will prove to be a very valuable collectors item in years to come. Why don't you contact Dale at the address on the enclosed brochure or call him at (714) 871-4750 because I know you will love that guitar.

Warm personal regards to you both and may God bless.

Forrest

in Nashville and Hollywood for Uncle Art, and a reply from Gene saying what a good idea it was. Here are the letters.

The stars in the walkway didn't happen. Wondering why, I contacted Skaggs Family Records to ask for an interview with Ricky. Eventually, when the timing was good I spoke to Ricky about it.

Apparently, there was not just one thing that stopped it from happening; several things cost it momentum.

"Probably there was something about a new development taking place, moving the Hall of Fame causing a lack of interest" Ricky recalled. It did motivate a visit to Uncle Art by Ricky in California at a nursing home where Art was being looked after:

"He talked about his hands on, and early days, and then said to me, out of all the new artists I was the only one he would sign! I was really flattered".

There's a quote from Chet Atkins that thanked Ricky for "saving country music". Well, I guess you must be doing something right with that sort of quote!

Ricky was in conversation with Art and some photographs were taken. Ricky kindly supplied the one used here; his quote reflects the respect for Uncle Art's achievements.

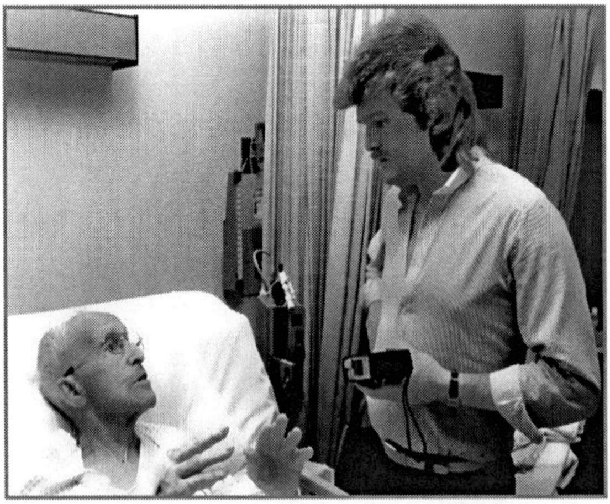

"The master and student. Uncle Art's mind was still sharp as ever"

I asked Ricky if there were any stories he had heard about, concerning Uncle Art. He recalled being told that Art was flying from New York to Bristol, Tennessee, and a rumour had gone ahead, mistakenly saying the President Harry S. Truman was on board the flight. Of course, when the aircraft landed, Art disembarked, dressed as dapper as usual with locks of grey hair and wearing his "bling." People at the airfield assumed it was the president, something that Art himself didn't deny or confirm – he just jumped into a car and drove off, much to the embarrassment of the good ole country boys in the car who had come to collect him! As we have seen before, Art was not adverse to creating a bit of attention.

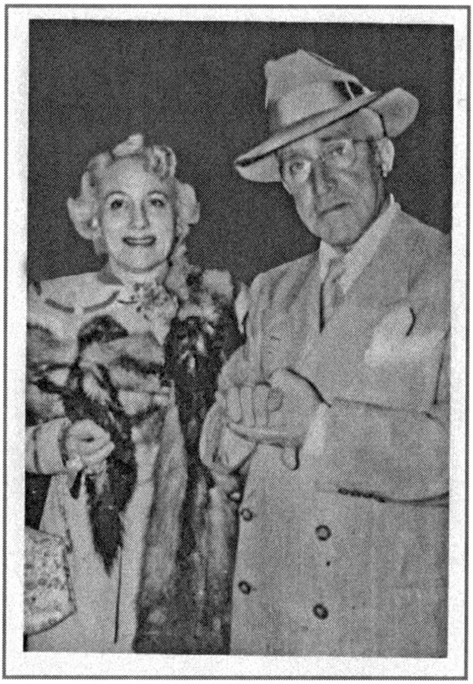

Ricky is passionate about the heritage of the music and has a deep and knowledgeable interest in the music of the past. He talks of hearing the history in the melodies and the instrumentation, the melancholy vocal sound added to the Celtic and old English songs that came with the settlers, the sound of knowing they were never going back to the homeland and that they had to survive those difficult early times in the new land. This understanding shows in his own music, with authentic interpretation. Even when he was in the chart-topping phase of his career, the shape and sound said it all. This was something that Art had recognized throughout his life as "the record man".

* * * * *

We are now at a time that some find it difficult to deal with shuffling off our mortal coil, passing over, and going to meet our Maker. These are just some of the euphemisms used to describe the end of physical existence, something we are all on, the long and winding road toward that destination. Whatever our beliefs, teachings, and culture, we arrive there. Tuesday, 10 June 1986 was the day that Art's earthly "session" ended. He was ninety-six years old.

The term "celebrate the life of" is used at gatherings and wakes. I think you will agree the life of Arthur Edward Satherley was extraordinary and well worth telling for posterity.

BRIDGE

CODES WITHIN MUSIC

(Old records and notes for thought)

History is the study of the past, particularly the written record of the human race, but more generally including scientific and archaeological discoveries about the past. Recently, there has been an increased interest in oral history, passed down from generation to generation. New technology, such as photography, sound recording, and motion pictures, now complement the written word in the historical record. (Wikipedia)

This is what shapes us, the past, experiences, upbringing etc, and that's the same for music. I have looked at the movement of people to the Americas, mostly from the British Isles and Europe taking music and instruments with them, "Country music originated from the folk music brought by the British settlers into the southern backcountry of America." (*Grove Dictionary of Music*) If we look even farther back, what do we find? Musically speaking that is, we find a thread that connects all peoples, a shape in their music, folk tales, and mythologies.

I am going to spool backwards and look at some interesting and thought-provoking material. Everything we take for granted didn't appear overnight; it came into existence somehow, music is no exception.

This old Chinese saying might be relevant

"The mind is like a parachute, it works best when open" .

When we look back at the distant past we are told that stone circles, pyramids, and the like go back approximately 5,000 years or so. I say "or so" because I get the feeling they could be much older – not that I'm an expert – it's just a feeling. Anyway, if we look at the land that was once called Mesopotamia meaning "land between two rivers", an area that is now Iraq and Iran, it was peopled by the Sumerians. They appeared quite quickly and were an advanced race, having a good infrastructure such as buildings, roads, farming, and libraries. They invented a form of writing called cuneiform. The libraries included information on how the civilization started. The following is an extract from an article by Walter Baucum that refers to works written by Zecharia Sitchin, author of *The 12th Planet* and later by Lloyd Pye author of *Everything You Know Is Wrong.* It is used with permission.

The Sumerian "Epic of Creation" has obvious parallels to the Hebrew Scriptures' Book of Genesis. Called Enuma Elish, it is an allegory that relates a complex, thrilling tale of battles raging between fearsome "gods" in heaven.

What can we make of this? Both Pye and Sitchin seem to believe in things [and gods] taken pointblank from the Sumerian writings, and who take them quite more literally than most people have done. Without going into more detail about these translations, Sitchin basically believes in another planet in our solar system, so far not discovered by modern science, that comes around only once in every 3,600 years. Their inhabitants came to earth and, by gene-splicing and genetic manipulation of themselves with Neanderthals [or Homo erectus], created modern man for the purpose of slave labor.

Some of the information appears to have been ever so slightly airbrushed out of general history, or if not airbrushed out overlooked because it might not fit main-street teaching. As a matter of interest at the start of the war in Iraq, when coalition forces invaded, it wasn't the oilfields or the WMDs they went for, it was the libraries and museums.

Here's some more from the article.

"There is evidence that as these Sumerians spread out to different parts of the world, perhaps even to every continent on earth. They mapped it and used what today we call the zodiac as a direction finder. The first so-called zodiacs were direction maps that radiated out from Sumer and which used the star configurations as compass points".

Here is my point, what if these people as they migrated took the stories and folklore of who they were to the four corners of the earth? Then, in those cultures certain aspects of their beliefs would have formed the bedrock of their society, in storytelling and song, as Lloyd Pye says: "They produced poetry, songs, and dances, through which, the Greek scholar Philo claimed, they sought to gain 'worldwide harmony and unison' ".

Is there any evidence for these claims? For me there is; it's in the shape of the music.

What do I mean by the shape? I mean – put simply – a code. These codes have been understood by some of the great classical composers and used in their work. Across the world different cultures developed, but some things remained embedded, in stories, myth, and of course music. Here's what Sitchen had to say.

What is striking about such music and songs is not only the conclusion that Sumer was the source of Western music in structure and harmonic composition. (As in the diatonic scale.) No less significant is the fact that as we hear the music and read the poems, they do not sound strange or alien at all, even in their depth of feeling and their sentiments. Indeed, as we contemplate the great Sumerian civilization, we find that not only are our morals and our sense of justice, our laws and architecture and arts and technology rooted in Sumer, but the Sumerian institutions are so familiar, so close. At heart, it would seem, we are all Sumerians.

So, did this music become the indigenous folk music of the planet? And does it show itself through the music of the people who are now known as the Celts? That may be a big leap but maybe the instruments give it away, for instance the pipes, whistles, and strung instruments such as the Sumerian Lyre (Harp) forerunner to the guitar, etc.

Let's take a look at the pipes. Across the world the wind instrument is used. It's constructed of a tube that's blown down or bellows pumped to fill a bag of air. The bag of air is then squeezed to release the air down the pipe, past reeds, with fingering holes to form the notes, but has one interesting thing, a drone note is produced. (To be musically correct, the drone note usually consists of notes of the tonic of the piece, especially the root and the fifth. Sometimes they are even played together. However, it is quite often to merely use *any* notes for drones from one or more pipes depending on the size of the instrument.) The history of the pipes can be traced all the way back to Sumer.

The thing about all of this is, that using drone tuning shapes the music, and this shaping becomes very recognizable in construction, simple harmony, and melody, the lack of the use of thirds, which doesn't pin the piece of music to major or minor keys, and frequent use of sevenths in the diatonic scale, plus very energetic dance rhythms, is fully demonstrated for instance in River Dance, and is still there in Bluegrass and modern country music, no matter how you dress it up – it's there. Incidentally, Chinese and Japanese music use drone tunings; the sound of the music is a cultural difference.

It's worth mentioning here the reference to ancient symbology in Nashville. Known as "Athens of the South" until the current nickname "Music City" came along; there is a copy of the Greek Parthenon building complete with a 41ft 10inch statue of Athena (12.8mtrs) and a 2,200ft rod that cost millions of dollars to build, as Nashville's William Henry says; "Nashville is, unquestionably, a city whose talismanic symbols place it in the Hermetic big leagues along with Washington DC and Paris. Perhaps it is time for Nashville's secrets to ring". Read much more on www.williamhenry.net
Modern Architecture has symbolism as well; the CMHF building is a musical symbolic construction, as can be seen in Verse Nine.

Etta D. Jackson is a best-selling author and friend (www.arvestacommunications.com). Her books contain many references to ancient symbolism and the journey of human consciousness. What follows is a summary of a conversation she and I had.

For those who are able to decipher symbolisms, it becomes very clear the linkages in of all our cities to one master plan that connects all cities, all races, and all cultures. And that in the beginning we were one people who went out from Sumer as the prodigal son went out from his home into the far country. It is clear to my mind that those records existed in Iraq. Mankind is at the end of his long journey into forgetfulness and is remembering his connection to his brothers and sisters in all this lands. He is now using the codes and the symbols, which were embedded in our music and dance, to identify all the peoples of the Earth as members of his Earth Family. Nothing can stop or hinder this reunion of mankind.

This takes nothing away from any other type of music; take the black Blues and Jazz, and the fusion with traditional folk and hillbilly that produced Rock and Roll. You know you can't get away from it by mentioning the black race. Why? Because on the North West Coast of Africa live the Dogon, people who say their ancestors came from a big bright star called Sirius, or, as it's also known the Dog Star!

Whatever we make of the Sumerians' library writings, that we are hybrids, that our ancestors come from the stars, and carried universal galactic building codes, one thing is fact: music touches the human in very deep places, heart and soul, even at DNA level. Two percent of DNA is understood; now then, the other ninety-eight percent must be "junk" biologists said. I'm glad that's sorted that out!

Moods can be induced and changed with music, knowingly and unknowingly. Everything is frequency; we are frequency. I like to imagine an infinite piano keyboard, starting at the low end, .5 – 60 Hz is the brainwave range, then the normal audio range of a piano 27.50 - 4186.00.Hz, then continuing along and up in frequency until we go out of the human audio range at 20,000 Hz where dogs and some other animals can still hear, onward and upward eventually reaching light and colours having gone through radio frequency, still moving up into gamma, that's about it as far as normal science was concerned. Science has entered a new zone of late with quantum physics, a quote from the *New Scientists* magazine (July 2004): "Rule 1. Nothing exists until it is measured, Nils Bohr 1930. Rule 2. Ignore rule 1, The Quantum Rebellion. Maybe we are getting a little closer to remembering, or perhaps coming out of our amnesia – a consciousness shift.

When we say we "resonate" with someone or something, what do we mean? It probably means we feel comfortable, or we are "in tune". To explain resonance would take another book, so to simplify, if everything is frequency, if an understanding of that intuitively, or mathematically could be gained, the world we think we live in would be a very different place. It would seem our ancestors might have understood a lot more than we thought. The musical scales of nature, demonstrated by the Fibonacci scale and the golden mean or ratio, are formulas that every thing in nature responds to, from a flower to a mountain and the great Pyramids to sacred symbols and the human form. In other words, they are codes. See a book by John Reid called *Egyptian Sonics*.

He is doing remarkable work on frequencies and resonance within the great Pyramid if this subject interests you.

CHAKRA	COLOR	MUSIC NOTE
Crown	**VIOLET**	**B**
Third Eye	**INDIGO**	**A**
Throat	**BLUE**	**G**
Heart	**GREEN**	**F**
High Heart	**Turquoise**	**F#**
Solar Plexus	**YELLOW**	**E**
Navel, Sacral	**ORANGE**	**D**
Base, Root	**RED**	**C**

Musicians are well aware of a squealing howling microphone when the PA's too loud, and a guitar string apparently vibrating on it's own, but in reality the string is responding sympathetically to it's frequency with something close by. It's all resonance. Undertones and overtones called harmonics play a very important role in the health of the planet and us. If it's out of tune it causes dis-ease, in tune = harmony. The human body has energy centres we know as coloured chakras, colour = frequency = musical notes

Our senses are apparently separate – eyes, ears, nose etc. – but in reality it's all one band of frequency, and our brain deals with it that way, although our receptors are separate. One thing is for sure, nothing is like it seems. Some people say that they can see music in colour! I happen to be one of them. This could make an interesting conversation in a redneck bar don't ya think? No? Oh well, make mine a large one, please, bartender.

Art was driven to seek out the old music that reminded him of home the British Isles, was it just that? Or is it that some people have a remembering, some kind of genetic recall that underpins our actions? Maybe it's worth considering – same again bartender, and a packet of crisps. All of this is food for thought, but remember, creation made it all.

ART'S LIST FOR FURTHER RESEARCH

MRS JIMMY ALLEN
THE ANDREWS BROTHERS
THE BACK YARD FOLLIES
GEORGIE BARNS
THE BLACK CATS AND THE KITTENS
THE BOAS CABIN BOYS
JOHN BOYD
BOB McGIMZIE
THE REV. BENNIE CAMPBELL-MEETING HOUSE IN DIXIE
CHARLIE CAMPBELL AND HIS RED PEPPERS
CARGILL AND KEENAN
LEROY CARTER AND HER MILK- BULL
THE CAULEY FAMILY
THE REV. CHAMBERS AND CONG
LOU CHILDRY
CROWDER BROTHERS
PETER CHAPMAN

EMERSON JUNIOR
THE FARMER SISTERS
EDDY HAWL
THE FOUR SALTY DOGS
THE FRIEND BROTHERS
GEORGIA BROWNS
GROUSE AND CAMPBELL
RAJA EVANS
THE DIAMOND FOUR
THE DEVIL'S DADDY IN LAW
BIG BOY EDWARDS
AUNT IDA HARPER AND THE COON CREEK GIRLS (Lilley May Ledford)
AMBROS HAILEY AND HIS OZARK RAMBLERS
ARTIE HALL AND HIS RADIO RUBES WITH RUFF DAVIS
GRACE AND SCOTTY MACLEAN
LESTER HEARN WITH BLACK BOY SHINE
HENDERSON'S WANDERING COWBOYS
FISHER HANDLEY AND HIS ARISTOCRATIC PIGS
THE HIGH – FLYERS
THE HIGH NEIGHBOR BOYS
THE HILL BROTHERS
ALFONCE HARRIS
GRACE AND CURLY GRAY
KITTY GRAY AND HER WAMPUS CATS
THE HAPPY VALLEY FAMILY
JOHN AND JOE GILBERT
HANK AND SLIM – THE NEWMAN BROTHERS
COYBOY ED CRANE
DUSKY DAILY
JOE AND ALMA THE KENTUCKY GIRLS
BANJO IKE AND IVORY CHITISON
DENNIS CRUMPTON
THE JOHNSON SISTERS TRIO,
JOHNSON AND LEE
HANK KEEN AND HIS RODEO STARS,
JACK KELLY KID

STORMY WERTHER
BILLY STAR
YELLOW JACKETS
BILLY BROWN
SADDLE TRAMPS
JOHNNY HICKS
BETTY JOHNSON
LITTLE MAE KISLEMON
THE JOLLY THREE
LEROY JENKINS
EUGENE JONES
DUSTY WALKER
RALPH WALDO

OUTRO

For me this has been a labour of love, love for music, or as Shakespeare put it:
The man that hath no music in himself,
Nor is not mov'd with concord of sweet sounds,
Is fit for treasons, stratagems, and spoils;
The motions of his spirit are dull as night,
And his affections dark as Erebus:
Let no man be trusted. Mark the music.
-William Shakespeare
Merchant of Venice
Act V-Scene 1

This has been the story of a man who was swept along with recording history in a new form. He was able to steer this new industry to include any human that could express themselves in lyric and melody. Uncle Art Satherley, as we have seen, took that primitive early recording equipment to the people and recorded forever their voice. Something that previously had been done by word of mouth, myth, legend, and folk song. It was Guido of Arezzo (and the Chinese before him) in medieval times who started writing notes down to teach and recall music. What I am referring to is what is termed "ordinary people" their feelings and experiences that are sung and

played from the heart. That whatever suffering and pain, love and ecstasy, this expression just cannot be suppressed. The power and creativity of every individual has no boundaries, only the ones we impose on ourselves.
Just as Arthur's pain at being rejected by his parents for not becoming a minister of the church as planned and being labelled wayward and ungrateful, he displayed an endeavour to move on, and thankfully he did, as Johnny Cash pointed out in his earlier quote.

If I can take you back to chapter one and the chat I had with the development office at QEH school, you may recall the mention of another old boy who is at the time of writing Managing Director of Sony music's Columbia records UK.

His name, Mike Smith.

Because of the QEH-Columbia connection I was keen to talk to Mike to see if he was aware of this, what could be seen as "interesting synchronicity." In the first of two phone interviews Mike was surprised to hear that recording pioneer Uncle Art Satherley was a QEH old boy (1899-1905). He was aware of Art as a famed Columbia historic producer. In the second call, Mike talked of his musical inspiration that included blues artists Bessie Smith, Ma Rainey, and Robert Johnson the very ones that Art had recorded almost a century ago!

He then talked of joining the Columbia label: "I wanted to be part of that rich heritage of the oldest continuous record label in the world." He continued

"It isn't just about money, although the company has to be profitable, it's about the heart felt expression of creating music, and getting it out there, and not losing sight of tradition."

A&R or M.D. it's what's in the heart that counts, and it would appear there's more than one similarity between the Columbia men.

Arthur Satherley had all the usual human attributes, not wanting to discuss areas of his life that appeared negative, his early family life, his wife Gladys, and his departure from Columbia Records. Speaking of leaving Columbia, I don't think we will ever really know what happened, so it remains speculation. Maybe he did think, "*after all I did for them*", having no pension, and feeling ashamed of not having his own company, he apparently had thoughts of returning to England and selling country music.

Art and his partner Harriet were together for forty years. I couldn't find records for their marriage or any annulment regarding Gladys. This can be corrected if documents come to light, but does it matter?

I got to know Art well through all the research, particularly his work ethic and respect for and helping so many around him. This was confirmed by people who knew Art: Jo Walker-Meador, Ray Price, Ricky Skaggs, and Forrest White, all of which I've had the pleasure to talk with.

The purpose of this book has been to share a story that in my opinion needed greater attention; it's importance in the history of music, particularly in the fact that Art was English, and Bristol? I think it's about time some rightful recognition was given to one of its sons, Arthur Edward Satherley, Uncle Art. country music's Founding Father.

Some Satherley family photos, Art's grandchildren and their mother (Judy Rieck)

Darin Rieck. Judy Keigley. (Mom) Judi Rieck. Tony Rieck.

Art. Harriet. Leroy Reick

Judy's daughter
Arts great granddaughter,
Rachel Keigley.

Photographs courtesy Judith Keigley

The record "Our Silver Haired Daddy", was made as a special presentation
The wording on the bottom of the plaque
"Presented to Arthur E Satherley in recognition of his invaluable contribution to recorded music in America for the past 37 years, during which time he supervised more than 27,000 recordings and was responsible for the sale of millions of records.
Columbia Records Inc"

Lightning Source UK Ltd.
Milton Keynes UK
16 March 2011

169341UK00001B/6/P

9 781452 083889